Corporate Governance Adrift

WITHDRAWN FROM STOCK

The Saint-Gobain Centre for Economic Studies series

Series Editor: **Robert M. Solow**, *Institute Professor Emeritus, Massachusetts Institute of Technology, USA*

This innovative new series – edited by Nobel Laureate Robert Solow – is an important forum for debating major issues in European economic policy. Drawing on the latest theoretical and empirical research, it will make an authoritative contribution to economic debates.

Showcasing cutting-edge research by world-renowned economists, the books in this series will be essential reading for both scholars and policymakers concerned with the economic challenges facing Europe in the twenty-first century.

Corporate Governance Adrift

A Critique of Shareholder Value

Michel Aglietta

Professor of Economics, University of Paris-X; Scientific Advisor, CEPII; and Member, Institut Universitaire de France

Antoine Rebérioux

Associate Professor of Economics, University of Paris-X, France

THE SAINT-GOBAIN CENTRE FOR ECONOMIC STUDIES SERIES

Edward Elgar
Cheltenham, UK • Northampton, MA, USA

Published by
Edward Elgar Publishing Limited
Glensanda House
Montpellier Parade
Cheltenham
Glos GL50 1UA
UK

Edward Elgar Publishing, Inc.
136 West Street
Suite 202
Northampton
Massachusetts 01060
USA

This book has been printed on demand to keep the title in print.

A catalogue record for this book
is available from the British Library

Library of Congress Cataloguing in Publication Data

Aglietta, Michel.
    Corporate governance adrift: a critique of shareholder value / Michel Aglietta,
Antoine Rebérioux.
        p.   cm. —   (The Saint-Gobain Centre for Economic Studies series)
    Includes bibliographical references and index.
    1. Corporate governance. 2. Corporations—Valuation.   I. Rebérioux,
Antoine, 1975-   II. Title.   III. Series.
    HD2741

                                                                                    2004062630

ISBN 1 84542 137 X (cased)
ISBN 1 84542 138 8 (paperback)

(

Contents

Figures

Tables

Boxes

Acknowledgements

The English edition of this book saw the light of day thanks to the expertise of Therrese Goodlett. Many thanks for her hard work and her eye for critical detail. Special thanks also go to Eoin Coleman, Richard Crabtree and Timothy Slind for translating the book.

Vincent Bignon, Régis Breton, Laurence Scialom and Yamina Tadjeddine read over the manuscript. The pertinence of their critiques was invaluable. Yuri Biondi, Olivier Brossard, Edouard Challe, Philippe Crouzet, Ariane Ghirardello, Guillemette de Larquier, Nicolas Meisel, Sabine Montagne, Héloïse Petit, Pascal Petit and Xavier Ragot, as well as the members of the MINI-FORUM seminar, also contributed to improvements in this work through their attentive reading. Hélène Baudchon helped us in collecting statistics. Sophie Dessalé formatted the manuscript, which was no small task. They all have our warmest thanks.

Lastly, we thank the Saint-Gobain Centre for Economic Studies for providing us with the resources for writing, promoting and distributing this book. We are particularly grateful to Jean-Louis Beffa, who founded this Centre to encourage a renewal of economic thinking, and to Jean-Philippe Touffut, its indefatigable Director. Their encouragement and high standards were powerful stimulants.

It thus goes without saying that any errors that may remain are entirely our responsibility.

Foreword

The book that the reader is about to discover is the fruit of several years' pre-occupation. Its origin goes back to a project of collective research launched in 1999, on behalf of the *Commissariat Général du Plan*. One of the authors coordinated this research; the other gave it major impetus. Four research centres participated in the project: the FORUM in Nanterre, the IDEFI in Nice, the INSEAD in Fontainebleau and the CPDR of the Catholic University of Louvain. This research culminated in a report published in September 2001 and entitled: *Régimes de gouvernements d'entreprise: différences nationales et stratégies d'entreprise* ('Corporate Governance Regimes: National Differences and Corporate Strategies').

From this period on, we became mistrustful of the dominant ideology – a skilful mixture of legal and economic theory – championed by Anglo-American consulting firms, the larger investment banks and certain academic circles. In the euphoric atmosphere of large-scale stock market speculation and the golden age that the 'new economy' was expected to bring, the shareholder was king. Creation of shareholder value established itself as the pillar of a new form of governance, guaranteeing uninterrupted prosperity for the economy as a whole, including workers. There was no doubt, according to the enthusiastic promoters of this doctrine, that the whole world would convert to it. Globalization of the economy, by exerting its influence on the firm itself, would penetrate deeper strata than the level of the capital markets alone.

In the report cited above, we expressed doubts about this unilateral, indiscriminate interpretation of the transformations that were indeed shaking up the corporate world. We did not consider stock market overbidding provoked by the stimulus of shareholder value as a sustainable process. We did not see, in the frenzy of mergers and acquisitions, a restructuring process of self-evident economic efficiency. We did not observe the whole world being converted to this new religion. Because our study extended beyond the field of finance, exploring the interlacing of relations between the different partners of firms, we were contemplating a diversity of forms of governance that had no reason to disappear.

The Enron affair broke just one month after the publication of our report. It was to be followed by many other scandals. During this period, finance displayed an instability that could only be controlled through sustained intervention, of exceptional duration and on an unequalled scale, by the Federal Reserve Board. The events that have occurred in business, in finance and in the global economy have prompted us to deepen considerably the scope of the analysis of which the 2001 report was the first milestone. It is the properties of finance-led capitalism that must be examined. To do so, we must study in detail the developments in contemporary finance, the logic of its functioning and its sources of fragility. We need to explore the nature of the modern firm, of the powers it contains and of the objectives actually pursued by its executives, without letting ourselves be blinded by the ideology of shareholder sovereignty, which persists despite the profound crisis provoked by its application. Above all, we need to analyse the close links between the expansion of market finance and the strategies adopted by firms, to highlight the perversity of a model of capitalism in which stock markets play a dominant role.

The approach adopted in this book is therefore above all analytic and positive (empirical). It is essential to deconstruct the predominant ideological discourse in order to demonstrate the deficiencies in its theoretical foundations, both legal and economic. Nevertheless, we could not avoid completely a normative point of view, which is encountered on every page written by the advocates of a form of governance oriented exclusively towards comforting the well-being of the shareholders. Essentially, our normative propositions, leading us to set one principle of governance against another, are presented in the last chapter.

At an analytic level, we therefore begin by examining the conception of finance-led capitalism which currently prevails in academic and political circles, and which can be summed up in two propositions:

- The strengthening of the finance-led model results in better risk-sharing and greater economic efficiency in the allocation of capital;
- Shareholder primacy puts an end to the usurpation of power that characterized 'managerial capitalism'. It (re-)establishes the respect of private property – the linchpin of capitalism.

Accepting these propositions leads one to foretell the 'end of history', as capitalism succeeds in imposing an efficient form of regulation throughout the world. The joint difficulties encountered by finance and corporate governance in the wake of Enron have failed to dent this apologetic vision within the dominant intellectual current. The two phenomena have been treated separately in recent literature; their interactions lie at the heart of this book. On the one hand, the stock market crash has been attributed to market exuberance. On the other hand, failures in governance have been explained as a deterioration in managerial ethics, the origins of which are extra-economic.

Our approach, both positive and normative, lies within an institutional tradition which, though interrupted, goes back to the seminal work of Berle and Means. As early as 1932, these authors raised the issue of corporate governance that results from the separation of ownership and control. Our interpretation of this problem is radically opposed to that upheld by the champions of shareholder sovereignty. Those who advocate exclusive control by shareholders as a solution to the dilemma of separation cannot explain the paradox at the heart of the current crisis in governance. This paradox is the following: the greater the number of control mechanisms in the hands of the shareholders, the greater the exploitation of the dependency of firms on the stock markets by corporate executives for their own personal enrichment.

Against the principle of externality of the firm's objectives (maximization of the well-being of shareholders alone, in an agency relationship), we set another: the principle of the political elaboration of the firm's objectives by the board of directors, considered as a body mediating between the executives and the internal and external stakeholders of the firm. This principle raises the problem of the overlapping of market and democracy in contemporary capitalism. To the extent that it is progressing, participative democracy in France tends to be confined to the non-profit sector. The experience of Scandinavian countries in the compatibility between the preservation of social cohesion and the assimilation of innovations leads us to believe that an advance in democracy at the heart of the most essential economic institutions is indispensable to the *regulation* of European capitalism at the beginning of this new century.

OUTLINE OF THE BOOK

We begin our analysis by defining the context in which the doctrine of shareholder value has flourished: the diffusion of information technology and financial globalization. The most relevant characteristics of these two factors in terms of corporate governance are studied in Chapter 1. We then criticize the 'end of history' thesis, in both its normative dimension (optimality of shareholder value) and its positive dimension (system convergence). Chapters 2 and 3 thus aim to 'denaturalize' (deconstruct) current finance-led capitalism, by demonstrating that the ideology it conveys is contingent to the intellectual and institutional watershed experienced by the United States at the beginning of the 1980s.

The two following chapters explore the mediations between finance and firms, namely regimes of governance and accounting standards. The denaturalization of shareholder value leads us to examine both the diversity of forms of control (Chapter 4) and accounting representations of the firm (Chapter 5).

In Chapters 6 and 7, we study the logic of finance-led regimes and their macroeconomic effects. By highlighting the interdependencies connected with risk management, we bring out forms of instability which redistribute the systemic risk of banks towards other institutional sectors and which exert powerful influence on the economic cycle.

Chapter 8 analyses the crises in governance from the firm's point of view. It studies the lessons to be learnt from symbolic financial scandals such as Enron and Parmalat. Using concrete cases, we demonstrate that current explanations of these failures are insufficient and that the very principle of control by external shareholders must be called into question. Consequently, based on these reasoned observations, Chapter 9, after giving a synthetic presentation of the results of the whole book, outlines another conception of corporate governance founded on the idea of economic democracy.

1. Finance-led capitalism: an inventory

The starting point of this book lies in an observation: the rise to power of market finance since the mid-1970s has radically altered the characteristic traits of contemporary capitalism. This process of 'financialization' is driven by two movements. The first is the growth in the liquidity of capital markets, expressing increases in the breakdown and transfer of risks. The second is the upsurge, in these same markets, of investment funds, responsible for the management of continually increasing savings. Far from remaining limited solely to the financial sphere, these changes have profoundly affected listed companies, the main players in the world economy. In this respect, the ideology of 'shareholder value'[1] has played and continues to play an essential role. The concept of 'finance-led capitalism' can be used to describe this new growth regime, in which a decisive role is given to the profitability of stock market assets, in both the creation and distribution of value added. Our aim here is to grasp the principal moving forces behind this 'finance-led capitalism', in other words to understand not only the regularities which maintain its functioning, if not its durability, but also its most widely recognized weaknesses – factors of instability.

To this end, we concentrate on two questions. The first deals with the dynamic induced by the continual expansion of risk transfer in the financial markets. The second explores corporate governance, and the governance of listed companies in particular. The term 'governance' covers all the measures, procedures, institutions and practices that determine the exercise of power in firms during a given period. Our hypothesis is that power relations within the firm, which determine the firm's strategy in different markets (finance, products, labour), have been drastically altered by transformations in the financial sphere. The result is that these relations, formed among the main stakeholders in the firm (shareholders, executives, employees), around the control of the firm, have taken on a new dimension. Whereas the cycles specific to what is generally called 'Fordism' found their source in markets, we demonstrate that cycles are now driven from within large corporations.[2] Today, corporate governance is a central institution, through the detailed study of which we can reach an understanding of the current regime.

1

This book is structured around three questions:

1. What are the consequences, in terms of stability and cyclicity, of the increase in the liquidity of capital markets?
2. What transformations have been induced in corporate governance?
3. How does this governance, in return, influence the dynamic of the growth regime?

The United States constitutes the principal reference in our analysis; it is the country in which the expansion of market finance is most advanced. France and Germany are analysed in counterpoint: the model of capitalism they embody enables us to appreciate fully the transformations currently taking place.

This first chapter gives a stylized presentation of the main facts which will serve as a reference throughout the book. The first section presents a synthesis of transformations that have taken place in the financial sphere. The second section concentrates more succinctly on an essential process in the current dynamic: technical changes connected with the diffusion of information and communication technology (ICT). This presentation is justified by the fact that our analysis will call for numerous detours into ICT issues. The third section underlines the articulation of the two processes, financial and technological.

THE RISE TO POWER OF MARKET FINANCE

From the end of the Second World War through to the 1970s, corporate governance, though assuming a different form on each side of the Atlantic, nevertheless concurred on one point: the weakness of market mechanisms in general, and of capital market mechanisms in particular.

In the United States, the dominant form was 'managerial capitalism', characterized, in the words of Berle and Means (1932), by the *'separation of ownership and control'*. The wide dispersion of share ownership left executives with a very high level of autonomy in their strategic choices. The absence of controlling interests, linked to a fragmentation of financial institutions that had been initiated before the war (Roe, 1994), meant that direct sensibility to the desires of the shareholders on the part of managers remained illusory. Hostile takeovers were hardly more effective in controlling executives, who formed a 'technostructure' at the top of the biggest firms (Galbraith, 1967). The increase in the number of conglomerates, to satiate the power-hungry executives, was without a doubt the most obvious symptom of this particular configuration. The level of dividends remained relatively low during the 30 years following the war.

In continental Europe (notably in France and Germany), on the contrary, it was the tightness of capital markets which protected firms from stock market control. The concentration of ownership and the stability of shareholders made managers insensible to capital market logic: profits were massively reinvested – to the detriment of the distribution of dividends – and hostile takeovers were almost inexistent. The highly institutionalized nature of industrial relations (collective agreements in France, co-determination in Germany) also contributed to the independence of firms in relation to the capital markets. In short, internal control, very often family control, prevailed, while few companies were listed on the markets.

A process of liberalization and integration of capital markets was initiated in the mid-1980s, and was to have decisive consequences. This process was accompanied by substantial rises in interest rates, with the hardening of monetary policy and priority given to the fight against inflation on both sides of the Atlantic. Institutional reforms undertaken with the aim of favouring the tradability of securities and the transfer of risks were thus built up within a context globally favourable to creditors (shareholders and lenders). These transfers were facilitated by the creation of new, ever more sophisticated financial products, traded on the new markets.

On the supply side, as on the demand side of financial securities, the trend was very favourable and accelerated during the 1990s. If we concentrate on the stock markets, a first quantitative evaluation is provided by the evolution of the ratio between national market capitalization and GDP (see Table 1.1) for the three countries under consideration.

Table 1.1 National market capitalization as a percentage of GDP

	United States	France	Germany
1980	50	8	9
1990	56	26	22
1995	95	32	26
1996	112	38	28
1997	133	48	39
1998	149	68	51
1999	181	111	72
2000	153	112	68
2001	152	103	61

Sources: FIBV, *Eurostatistics*, Eurostat (August–September 2001) and Van der Elst (2000).

On the securities supply side, the number of listed companies has risen, as have share issues. France is a characteristic case in point: whereas total share issues in 1980 were worth 7.9 billion euros, they reached the value of 33.7 billion euros in 1990, and then 113.7 billion euros in 2000 (Plihon, 2003, p. 55). This process has been boosted by the series of privatizations carried out since the second half of the 1980s.

For a firm, the primary objective of a call for public savings is the transfer of claims: the tradability of securities enables incumbent shareholders who wish to liquidate their stakes to withdraw from the capital (Lazonick and O'Sullivan, 1999; O'Sullivan, 2001). The financing of investments, on the contrary, is rarely the motive for entry onto stock market listings or for the issuance of new securities. This is the conclusion drawn from all the quantitative studies (see for example Rajan and Zingales, 1998): contrary to one persistent belief, the stock market does not serve primarily to finance new investments. It can be used for this purpose, notably in the sector of new technologies (see below), but this only occurs to a small extent. Table 1.2 gives a good illustration of the minor role the market plays in terms of investment, with firms generally preferring other sources of finance (retained earnings, bank loans and bond issues).

Recently, we have seen the emergence of two new functions of capital markets, in addition to the traditional function of stock market calls (the transfer of claims). The new functions bear witness to more strategic uses of these markets. They are performed by the secondary market, with fundraising on the primary market only constituting a preliminary to the daily evaluation of securities. The first of these functions is external growth. Over the last decade, the stock markets have made it possible to finance takeovers, whether friendly or hostile, by means of share exchange offers. Once again, this has been particularly true in the sector of new technologies (see below). Market quotation therefore provides access to a new currency of exchange (shares), whose buying power increases with the price of the share. Capital markets are consequently at the service of an industrial

Table 1.2   Net percentage of share issues in the total financing of firms for the 1970s and 1980s

USA (1970–89)	Germany (1971–92)	France (1971–92)
−8.8	0.1	4.3

Note: The negative value in the United States is the result of share buy-back programmes carried out during the 1980s, with the principal objective of increasing capital profitability.

Sources: Corbett and Jenkinson (1996), Mullineux (1996), quoted in Burkart (1999).

strategy, the aim of which is to lay hands on the income and/or competence of competitors or trading partners. The second function also concerns the management and retention of key skills, as it involves the introduction of stock options. Today, this mode of payment is indispensable in certain sectors for attracting and keeping employees with the rarest skills. Here again, managers use the capital markets as strategic leverage.

On the whole, although firms in both the United States and Europe have called on public savings to a greater extent over the last 20 years, this has not been to renew their sources of financing so much as to increase their possibilities of external growth and to provide themselves with new competence management tools (stock options).

On the securities demand side, the density of the savings flow has increased with the ageing of the population in Western countries. At the heart of this movement, institutional investors are playing an increasingly important role in capital markets.[3] In the United States, this process is already long established: pension funds, which manage the pensions of employees in both the public and private sectors, began to establish themselves in the capital markets as early as the 1950s. Berle (1963), in a remarkable essay, analysed this phenomenon in the following manner:

> Thus far, these funds are on the way to accumulating 4% or 5% of the total stock outstanding. This percentage is bound to grow as the pension funds themselves grow. They are expected to level out, in twenty years or so, when their total assets have reached $125 billion. [. . .] Forecast that these funds will eventually own about 10% of all American industry (as represented by the value of its stock outstanding) may not be too far out. But it will not be realized for a number of years. (pp. 54–5)

In 1974, the adoption of the Employment Retirement Income Security Act (ERISA), whose aim is to guarantee pensions by ensuring the transfer and security of the rights acquired, boosted the industry far beyond anything Berle could have predicted. Today, the assets managed by pension funds exceed $8000 billion, nearly half of which are in national shares (Jeffers and Plihon, 2002). These funds hold not 10, but 25 per cent of US capitalization. The ageing of the population, and therefore the sustained accumulation of financial saving by households, gives us good reason to believe that this rise to power of pension funds is far from over.

This fantastic growth in pension funds has been overtaken by the development of mutual funds, which saw the value of their assets triple between 1980 and 1987, and then quadruple between 1990 and 1997, to reach a current value of $5000 billion. More than half of this sum is held in the form of shares, representing about 13 per cent of national (US) market capitalization. This growth, which has been greater than that of pension funds over the last 20 years, has greatly benefited from the dynamism of the pension industry, of which more than one-third of the assets are currently managed by mutual funds through delegation.

In 1950, pension funds and mutual funds held less than 3 per cent of national shares between them; by the end of the 1990s they held nearly 40 per cent. During the same period, the proportion of national shares held by insurance companies, banks and households fell from 95 per cent to about 55 per cent. These figures illustrate how much the US stock markets have changed over the last half century by a process of 'institutionalization'. By this term we mean the rise to power of institutional investors – to the benefit of collective savings funds (pension and mutual funds) rather than insurance companies.[4] This process of market institutionalization is also present in continental Europe, as Table 1.3 demonstrates for the 1990s. It takes on a particular appearance in France and Germany: alongside national investors (SICAV and OPCVM in France; insurance companies in Germany) can be felt the growing presence of US and British investors, whose entry is part of an international strategy to enhance the value of their portfolios. Thus in France, in 1998, one-quarter of the national capitalization was held by non-resident investors; in 2000, this share had risen to 36 per cent. In Germany, the penetration rate of big groups reached 40 per cent in 2002 (Gehrke, 2002).

Not surprisingly, these transformations in the financial sphere have had consequences on the control of firms. In the United States, the 1980s saw a large rise in the number of hostile takeovers (takeover bids and exchange offers). These operations exert constant pressure on executives, for whom any fall in their stock prices represents a direct threat. While hostile takeover mergers only represented 8.4 per cent of mergers between 1973 and 1979, this proportion rose to 14.3 per cent over the 1980s. Between 1986 and 1989, at the height of the activity of what can be called the 'market for corporate control', nearly 20 per cent (in value) of takeovers were hostile. This movement has obliged almost every company to restructure in an effort to avoid being absorbed by another company. The takeover movement has been

Table 1.3   *Financial assets held by national institutional investors as a percentage of GDP*

	1992	1993	1994	1995	1996	1997	1998	1999	2000
United States	127.2	136.3	135.9	151.9	162.9	178.4	192.0	207.3	195.2
France	61.9	73.9	71.8	77.7	86.6	97.0	107.3	125.4	133.3
Germany	34.0	38.9	41.3	45.3	50.6	58.7	66.1	76.8	79.7

Source: OECD (2001).

made easier by the growing presence of investment funds in the securities market, because these institutional players have no qualms about selling their shareholdings during hostile operations (Holmström and Kaplan, 2001). The first consequences of this shareholder revival have been a rise in the level of dividends, drastic reductions in the workforce and the dismantling of conglomerates, symbols of the 'managerial delinquency' of the past (Batsch, 2003b).

Nonetheless, it would be wrong to consider executives as the first victims of this return in strength of the stockholders. Their activity certainly became riskier, but it also (and above all?) became more lucrative. The awarding of compensation plans based on share prices became systematic. This system made it possible to align the interests of the executives with those of the shareholders. The result has been a significant increase in executive compensation (see Graph 4 of Söderström, 2003, p. 18) and an extreme deepening of the inequalities within firms: whereas in 1965 the average compensation of Chief Executive Officers in the United States represented 44 times the average pay of workers, this had risen to 419 times the average wage in 1998 (Lazonick and O'Sullivan, 2000a). This process of concentrating wealth in the hands of a small group (Krugman, 2002) is one of the most striking paradoxes of finance-led capitalism. Far from being paradoxical, this drift is deeply embedded within the structures of the new capitalism as we will show. Stock options are also enjoying a favourable dynamic in Europe, but on a significantly less pronounced scale. Disparities of income within firms are consequently much smaller. (see Figure 1.1.)

Takeovers slowed down in the mid-1990s, when most US states, and notably Delaware, where more than half of the big companies are registered, adopted legislation to curb hostile takeovers.[5] Following strong pressure from management lobbies, the use of anti-takeover mechanisms was legalized. These mechanisms include, in descending order of frequency, staggered boards, white knights, legal relocation, poison pills, and so on (Beffa *et al.*, 2003). This was so effective that the proportion of hostile takeovers fell to 4 per cent during the 1990s. In continental Europe, the threat of takeover bids and exchange offers only became credible in the mid-1990s. The bank war in France, which resulted in the takeover merger of Paribas by BNP, the victory of the British operator Vodaphone over the German champion Mannesmann, or the operation launched by Sanofi-Synthélabo to take over its Franco-German competitor Aventis each bears witness to the fact that these operations have become one factor of regulation among others in the European economic zone.

Faced with the legislative obstacles raised at the end of the 1980s, shareholder power has taken an alternative, complementary path, favouring

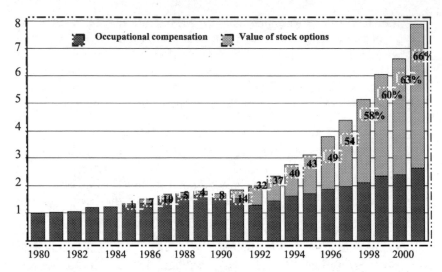

Source: B. Hall, 'Incentive strategy II: executive compensation and ownership structure', Teaching Note N9-902-134, 2002, Harvard Business School.

Figure 1.1   *Median compensation of the CEOs of companies in the United States (in millions of dollars, at 2001 prices, for the period 1980–2000)*

participative influence (voice) rather than the sale of securities (exit). This movement relies on the growing weight of institutional investors. Aware of their strength in the securities market, these investors, and notably the public pension funds, have promoted a new type of 'responsible and active' behaviour. Shareholders are encouraged systematically to use the legal means available to them to control corporate management. First among these means are the voting rights attached to the ownership of securities. The main driver of this 'institutional activism' is the proposals submitted and then voted on in general assemblies within the framework of Securities and Exchange Commission Rule 14–8 of the law on share exchanges. Essentially, these proposals concern procedural aspects of the running of the firm, in particular the composition and functioning of the board of directors. Wider separation between executives and members of the board has been sought, notably through the presence of 'independent' directors. The creation within the board of directors of *ad hoc* committees responsible for controlling executive compensation and the links between internal audits and statutory auditors have also become a central concern. Lastly, the introduction of compensation plans linked to financial performance for executive officers (stock options) has also been encouraged.

The desire to promote internal control mechanisms rather than external ones (takeover bids and exchange offers) is evident. All these principles share the objective of making management more accountable to shareholders. They have been codified in a series of reports – veritable charters of good conduct for firms – the first and most famous of which, *Corporate Governance Principles*, commissioned in 1978 by the American Law Institute, appeared in its definitive version in 1993. This was followed by the Gilson-Kraakman Report (1991) in the United States, the Cadbury Report (1992b) in the UK, the Viénot I (1995), Viénot II (1999) and Bouton (2002) Reports in France, and, on an international level, the *Principles of Corporate Governance* from the OECD (1999, 2004). An initially US idea has thus crossed frontiers, transmitted by the globalization of capital markets and spurred on by institutional investors.

These charters convey a specific conception of the responsibility of the · firm and its executive officers, a conception labelled as 'shareholder value' or 'shareholder sovereignty': a well-managed firm is a firm that is at the service of its shareholders, and the ultimate criterion of success is the increase in the stock market price.

The concept of Economic Value Added (EVA) was invented and copyrighted by the Stern & Stewart consulting firm at the beginning of the 1990s. It is the symbolic indicator of shareholder value, and it fulfils two functions. The first is operational: EVA is set down as the management criterion for executives, who must seek to maximize it in each fiscal period. The second function is informational: EVA is considered the most relevant criterion for the prediction of stock market prices. As such, it constitutes a valuable tool in the choice of portfolios. EVA is therefore an aid both to executives, in their mission to act in the shareholders' interest, and to shareholders, in their investment choices. This dual function endows EVA with dual status, both internal (to the firm) and external. Its construction is therefore based on both accounting data and market values. To understand this latter aspect, we must take a short detour through standard financial theory, the keystone of which is the capital asset pricing model (CAPM) (see Box 1.1).

BOX 1.1　PRICING OF ASSETS IN THE CAPM

The CAPM is a model for evaluating the performance of capital assets, developed in the 1960s (Sharpe, 1964; Lintner, 1965). This model is based on the distinction between the specific risk and the systemic risk (or market risk) of a security. The former is diversifiable; the latter is not. Consequently, only market risk should be taken into account, and only market risk justifies obtaining a risk premium. This risk is defined as the variation in the return on an asset following the variation of a portfolio comprising all the risky assets in the market, the 'market portfolio' (m). For an asset i, we thus measure this risk (denoted β_i) by the covariance of the asset with this portfolio, giving:

$$\beta_i = \mathrm{Cov}(i\,;m)\,/\,V(m) \tag{1.1}$$

The greater the β of an asset, the more sensitive the asset is to market variations and the higher the level of profitability required to hold on to the asset. The fundamental result of the CAPM is thus an equilibrium equation providing a linear relation between return and risk, giving:

$$k_i = k_f + \beta_i(k_m - k_f) \tag{1.2}$$

where k_i is the profitability of the asset i, k_f the profitability of a risk-free asset (a government bond, for example) and k_m the profitability of the market portfolio. Thus the risk premium of an asset ($k_i - k_f$) rises in direct proportion to its β. Within this framework, a firm can calculate its weighted average capital cost (WACC):

$$WACC = k \cdot E/K + r \cdot D/K = k - (k - r)D/K \tag{1.3}$$

where k is the cost (or the profitability) of equity as calculated by the CAPM (see (1.2)), E the book value of equity, D the book value of debts, r their average cost and $K = E + D$ the book value of the economic asset. The second expression brings out the principle of 'financial leverage': when the profitability of equity capital is greater than the average debt cost ($k - r > 0$), a firm can reduce its weighted average capital cost by increasing its debt-to-equity ratio.

The assumption that there are no tax deductions or exceptional results simplifies the calculation, so that the current result merges with the net result. By denoting Re the operating result, R the net result, D the book value of debts and r their average cost, we obtain:

$$R = R_e - rD$$

The simplest expression of EVA, where k is the profitability of equity as calculated by the CPAM and E the book value of equity, is thus:

$$EVA = R - k \cdot E$$

This equation brings out the specificity of EVA: whereas the wealth returned to shareholders is usually measured by the net result (R, that is, the profit after the employees have been paid and the debts serviced), here it is considered that the true wealth created for shareholders corresponds to the surplus gained in relation to the profitability required by the market. In other words, if the effective return on investment is the rate k, which corresponds to the equilibrium market return for this class of risk, then the EVA model considers that no value has been created. Likewise, if the investment is ultimately remunerated at the rate $k - n > 0$, then there is destruction of value: there is some return on investment, but less than the market has a right to expect. The difference is identified as a loss, even if the shareholders are paid for their investment. The equilibrium market return is thus perceived as the minimum justifiable return, on the basis of which one can appreciate the true creation of value. For Lordon (2000), the result of this principle is that shareholders are paid twice: once at the opportunity cost k, and again at the EVA. The 'hijacking' of the concept of capital cost (k) is obvious: this concept originally constituted an equilibrium value, whereas here it is conceived as a minimum value, 'always to be exceeded' (Batsch, 1999, p. 36). EVA thus proceeds from a logic of disequilibrium, encouraging all the players to beat the market. From a macroeconomic point of view, the inconsistency of this commandment is evident.

From the preceding expression, we can obtain the two most widely used expressions of EVA:

$$EVA = (R/E - k)E = (ROE - k)E \tag{1.4}$$

or again:

$$EVA = R + rD - kE - rD$$
$$= R_e - (kE + rD)$$
$$= \left[\frac{R_e}{E+D} - \frac{(kE + rD)}{E+D} \right] \cdot (E + D)$$
$$= (ROA - WACC)K \tag{1.5}$$

where ROE is return on equity and ROA is return on asset and WACC the weighted average capital cost (see Box 7.1). Equations (1.4) and (1.5) demonstrate that the creation of shareholder value entails, in a strictly equivalent manner, either that ROE is maintained at a level higher than the expected return on equity (k) or that ROA is maintained at a level higher than the weighted average capital cost.

Finally, the market value added (MVA) is defined as the discounted total (using the weighted average capital cost) of expected EVA, written:

$$MVA_{t0} = \sum_{t=t0}^{T} \left[\frac{EVA_t}{(1 + WACC_t)^t} \right] \qquad (1.6)$$

Thus, how is shareholder value created? The most obvious, and in the end very classic, means is to increase the profitability of the capital invested. In this respect, using financial leverage, in other words increasing the debt-to-equity ratio (see equation (1.3)), remains the most direct way of increasing capital profitability, as long as economic profitability is higher that the interest rate. Indeed the champions of EVA particularly insist on the need to economize not only equity, but capital in general, whatever its definition (productive capital, equity capital or working capital). The underlying idea is that capital is a scarce resource, of which the opportunity cost (k or $WACC$) must be pointed out most emphatically to its users (the executive officers). In addition, the application of EVA within the firm takes place in a decentralized manner, or at least that is the wish of its advocates. Consequently, the firm must be organized into profit centres, each one being responsible for a local creation of shareholder value. To this end, the capital cost must be calculated for each centre. The difficulty of this operation has led most of the companies which use EVA to adopt a 'holistic' approach to the creation of value, at the most aggregate level possible (Lordon, 2000). Whatever the level of decentralization, the adoption of EVA goes hand in hand with a reduction in capital invested, in the form of a saving in productive capital, a cut in working capital requirements or the buying-back of shares. A complementary means of creating shareholder value, less classic than that of increasing profitability, can be found by examining equation (1.4): the reduction of capital cost (k). Equations (1.1) and (1.2) indicate the path to follow: it involves acting on one's beta (β), in other words the (non-diversifiable) risk component of one's activity (Piluso, 2003). That means minimizing the elasticity of operating results in relation to turnover, so that market movements have the least possible influence on profits. The easiest way to reduce the volatility of operating results is to increase the variability of costs (Colasse, 2001). The higher the variability of costs, the less the firm is affected by a slowdown in activity. Wage bills represent the preferred component of 'variabilization', through the systematic use of atypical contracts.

Although few firms have adopted the canonical form of the EVA/MVA method because of the difficulties in its practical application, this method has nevertheless taken on an essential symbolic dimension. It structures the arguments for the creation of shareholder value by giving them a relatively simple theoretical foundation. In the words of Plihon (2002), it 'constitutes the central reference justifying the validity of the market convention of ROE at 15 per cent' (p. 17, our translation). The speculative effect of this convention, hardly sustainable on a path of balanced growth, is one of the factors behind the stock market corrections that began in the spring of 2000.

A TECHNOLOGICAL REVOLUTION?

Appraisal of the movement of the US economy towards financialization changed substantially between the 1980s and 1990s: the judgements, initially critical, became much more eulogistic as the US economy gradually asserted its domination over the 'global economy'. During the 1980s, the loss of competitiveness of US firms was at the centre of the debate. In the sectors of the car industry, machine tools, and so on, Japanese and German firms enjoyed growing success. Responsibility was most often laid at the door of work organization methods: the hierarchical system of the United States was said to suffer from structural weaknesses compared with the organizational integration specific to Japanese and, to a lesser extent, German firms. In addition to the issue of organization, parallels were also drawn between the financial systems of the three countries and their comparative performances. Certain authors observed that the classic ownership structure of the Japanese and German models, by protecting managers from capital market fluctuations, encouraged long-term investment, favourable to productivity. The system in the United States, on the contrary, by favouring the penetration of firms by stock market logic, drove managers to adopt short-term behaviour, harmful to structural competitiveness. The terms of the debate were altered, however, by the crisis in Japan and Germany and, above all, by the exceptional performance of the US economy in the 1990s. In particular, the progress of the United States in the domain of information and communication technologies (ICT) caused perplexity: many commentators interpreted this dynamism as the result of the domination of the economy by market finance. At the junction of these two sets of themes – market finance and new technologies – arose the concept of the 'New Economy', which was severely deflated by the bursting of the bubble in March 2000. For certain authors, the upheavals connected with these new technologies are much more important than the institutional transformations pushed forward in the financial sphere. That is not the point of view adopted here; nevertheless, it is essential to grasp the main elements of the new economy, which constitutes the backdrop to our exposition.

The singularity of the US cycle in the 1990s is the direct source from whence came the idea that the United States had entered a 'new economy', globally freed from the laws that hitherto had governed the production and distribution of wealth (Boyer, 2004). The statistics are indeed remarkable. Between 1992 and 2000, the economy grew at an average annual rate of 3.7 per cent. This growth is similar to that of other cycles; gains in labour productivity, on the contrary, are totally unique: over the same period, hourly productivity grew at a rate of 2.2 per cent per year in the corporate sector and 4.3 per cent in the manufacturing sector, in other words at a rate much higher than the long-term trends of 1.6 per cent and 2.9 per cent respectively between 1974 and 1999 (Baudchon and Brossard, 2001). Even more surprising, this growth in productivity accelerated at the end of the cycle: in 2002, gains in labour productivity in the manufacturing sector reached 6.8 per cent, then 4.3 per cent in 2003. During the same period (1992–2000), inflation stabilized at an average of 2.6 per cent, while unemployment fell from 7.5 per cent to 4 per cent (in 2000). European performances are not very flattering in comparison.

The United States' renewed economic vigour has been accompanied by the massive diffusion of ICT, in other words the goods produced in the computing, electronics and telecommunications sectors. This expansion is part of a relatively prolonged movement, with the gradual expansion in computing since the 1960s, and the acceleration that occurred in the 1990s with the introduction of computer networks (Bellon *et al.*, 2003).

The easiest way to appreciate the scale of the spread of ICT is to look at the share of ICT expenditure in the total of gross fixed asset formation (excluding buildings): in France this share grew from 12.2 per cent in 1970 to 23.6 per cent in 1998, and in the United States it grew from 16.9 per cent to 36.1 per cent over the same period. Thus, in the United States more than one-third of investments currently concern new technologies. In parallel with this diffusion, the price of new technologies has displayed a clear downward tendency: between 1992 and 1998, the average annual rate of increase in the price of computer equipment was −17 per cent (−1.6 per cent for software). This fall in prices, calculated using the hedonic price method (see Box 1.2), is the result of both an improvement in quality and a drop in production costs. The reduction in production costs is mainly due to a continual increase in demand in sectors with significant fixed costs. Given this fall in prices, the volume of investment in computer equipment grew nine times faster than investment in other equipment in the United States between 1967 and 1997 (Cohen and Debonneuil, 1998). The diffusion has been particularly powerful in the service industries, where the informational content of services provided is generally sizeable. As for the diffusion to households, in 1999, there was an average of 222 personal computers per 1000 inhabitants in France, compared with 511 per 1000 in the United States (Petit, 2003a).

The connection made between the vigour of the US cycle and the increasing weight of ICT derives from the particular nature of these technologies. They are generic, used both in production processes and by consumers. Furthermore, and from a technological point of view, ICTs include two major processes: the digitizing of information and the rise to power of networks. These characteristics (generic nature, technical novelty) have significant consequences. First, ICTs induce changes in the organization of firms because they affect, in particular, the coordination activities. They subsequently influence the structuring of markets in that they modify both inter-firm relations (competition and cooperation) and producer/consumer interfaces. ICT specificity is also of an economic order (Shapiro and Varian, 1999): it is now widely acknowledged that these goods are characterized by particularly strong scale and network effects. On the supply side, scale effects derive from the extreme rapidity of the circulation of information, achieved through digitizing and increasing the density of networks. Goods with high informational content may be costly to create, but they then circulate at a near-zero marginal cost. Returns of scale therefore increase (decreasing average cost), contrary to those of classic economic goods. The telecommunication sector is particularly susceptible to these scale effects: once the networks have been installed, often at very high cost, communications then cost practically nothing. The first consequence of growing returns of scale is a tendency towards concentration: the greater the production, the lower the average cost, giving a competitive advantage to the largest structures. On the demand side, totally original network effects come into play. Informational goods are generally sought, not for strictly individual use, but for their capacity to establish relations, to guarantee the smoothness of communications with others. Users are therefore strongly influenced in their choice by the goods (or technologies) used by others. A typical example is software: the greater the number of other individuals known to use a particular software, the higher the demand for that software will be. Consequently, the establishment of its model or standard becomes decisive in the competition between producers. This is reinforced by the fact that significant learning effects also exist, which are connected to the relative novelty of these technologies, leading to a form of irreversibility in users' choices. All in all, the combination of scale and network effects results in the elaboration of original strategies, or 'business models', which emphasize the necessity of being among the first to enter the market.

The originality of ICT in terms of production and distribution has been widely recognized, but it is insufficient to justify the argument that the dynamism of the US economy is directly related to the spread of these technologies. *A fortiori*, the diagnosis of a third 'technological revolution', at the heart of the 'new economy' concept, is not based solely on this observation. Today, the debate has therefore shifted onto empirical ground, involving an evaluation of the real contribution of ICT to the acceleration in growth and productivity gains that has characterized the US cycle. This brings us to the famous paradox raised by Solow (1987): 'You can see the computer age everywhere but in the productivity statistics'. Since then, studies on the link between ICT and productivity have multiplied (see Box 1.2).

BOX 1.2   ICT AND PRODUCTIVITY: SOLOW'S PARADOX SOLVED?

Growth accounting, pioneered by Solow (1957), is the standard method for measuring the impact of a factor of production on growth or productivity based on macroeconomic data. It uses a macroeconomic production function with substitutable factors and constant returns of scale, which can be written (using a Cobb-Douglas production function and suppressing the time index):

$$Y = F(K_{nontic}; K_{tic}; L) = aK_{nontic}^{\alpha} K_{tic}^{\gamma} L^{1-\alpha-\gamma} \qquad (1.7)$$

where Y is the level of the product, K_{nontic} the quantity of non-ICT capital, K_{tic} the quantity of ICT capital, L the quantity of labour, a a parameter of technical progress (of or the total productivity of factors, TPF) and α, γ, $1 - \alpha - \gamma$ are the production elasticities of non-ICT capital, ICT capital, and labour respectively. As returns are constant, we can express this function in per capita variables:

$$y = ak_{nontic}^{\alpha} k_{tic}^{\gamma} \qquad (1.8)$$

where $y = Y/L$ is labour productivity, $k_{nontic} = K_{nontic}/L$ is per capita non-ICT capital, and $k_{tic} = K_{tic}/L$ is the per capita stock of 'technological' capital. By denoting $\hat{x} = \dot{x}/x$ the growth rate of the variable x, we obtain:

$$\hat{y} = \hat{a} + \alpha \hat{k}_{nontic} + \gamma \hat{k}_{tic} \qquad (1.9)$$

Equation (1.9) simply breaks the labour productivity growth rate down into pure technical progress ($\hat{a}$, the growth of TPF) and capital deepening, linked to ICT investment ($\hat{k}_{tic}$) or non-ICT investment ($\hat{k}_{nontic}$). If we assume that the economy is in a situation of competitive equilibrium, then the coefficient α (γ respectively) represents remuneration of the factor k_{nontic} (k_{tic} respectively) in total income. This remuneration is calculated directly by multiplying the stock of each factor by its gross return. Based on the result of this equation, we consider that there has been a veritable technological revolution if the increase in labour productivity results essentially from pure technical progress (Artus, 2002). If, on the contrary, productivity gains are simply the result of an accumulation of technological capital, we consider the effect to be transient: in this case, the marked rise in ICT investment during the 1990s would ultimately have had the very classic effect of increasing hourly labour efficiency (productivity).

Various subsequent studies have sought to locate the origin of TPF gains on a sectorial basis when such gains have previously been identified.[6] If these gains can only be observed in the ICT-producing sector, then the diagnosis of a technological revolution becomes less apposite. If, on the other hand, the ICT-using sectors are also involved in the acceleration of TPF, then the novelty of the period appears to have a firmer footing: in this case, the technological diffusion is real. The results of the different sectoral studies conducted on this basis (Gordon, 2001; Oliner and Sichel, 2000; Jorgenson and Stiroh, 2000) all converge in identifying a clear influence of ICT on growth and productivity: the new technologies account for somewhere between half and two-thirds of growth – a considerable proportion given their relatively low weight in terms of total capital (the ICT sector represents little more than 8 per cent of US GDP). The authors, however, are far from unanimous on the question of whether these productivity gains should be attributed to a rise in TPF or to the growth of capitalistic intensity. Gordon (2001) defends a 'pessimistic' or sceptical view of the new economy, according to which the rise in TPF is close to zero outside the ICT-producing sectors. This is not the conclusion drawn from either the study by Oliner and Sichel (2000) or that by Jorgenson and Stiroh (2000).

In fact, locating the TPF poses a problem in that it is highly dependent on the method chosen to distinguish between price effects and volume effects in the diffusion of ICT. We have already described the downward movement of constant-quality prices specific to ICT. If this movement is ignored, we run the risk, for example, of underestimating the volume of ICT and therefore overestimating the productivity. US and French accounting systems use the hedonic price method to take into account the quality effect specific to ICT. In this 'quality adjusted price' evaluation method, the value of an investment is determined according to what can be produced with it, and not according to what was required to produce it (the 'cost-based' method). It must be noted that the first method (quality adjusted price), by construction, tends to erase increases in TPF in the ICT-using sectors: investments in ICT are written up positively if they are more efficient. Labour productivity rises, but the TPF does not change (technical progress is incorporated into the technological capital). With the 'cost-based' methodology, on the other hand, if the ICTs still cost as much, despite the increase in their efficiency, the additional labour productivity is directly taken to be an acceleration of the TPF. This discussion illustrates the complexity of a macroeconomic approach to ICT influence on productivity. In particular, it highlights the difficulty inherent to adopting a reasoning which bases its assessment of the importance of ICT solely on distinguishing between the location of TPF in the producing and using sectors. This location, however, is highly sensitive to the method used to separate volume effects from quality effects (Baudchon and Brossard, 2003).

Studies based on individual (company) data have the advantage of being able to distinguish, within the ICT-using sector, which firms have really invested in ICT and to measure directly the impact of these investments in terms of productivity.[7] Compared with macroeconomic data, microeconomic data make it possible to identify precisely the individual factors liable to influence the productive effect of ICT. For example, it is now widely recognized that successful introduction of new technologies requires organizational innovations (see Benghozi and Cohendet, 1999; Askenazy, 2000). Firms which fail to reorganize generally do not derive much benefit from their investments and may even see their productive efficiency fall. At the aggregate level, this can totally hide the beneficial effect of ICT in firms which have succeeded in restructuring their coordination pattern. Almost all the microeconometric studies have concluded that ICT has a positive impact on the productive efficiency of firms (see Stiroh, 2002, for an overall review). The positive impact of reorganization as regards ICT is also a widely shared conclusion. It should be noted, however, that this type of study is subject to biases of endogeneity that are very difficult to control: the positive correlation between ICT and productivity may simply reflect the fact that it is the most efficient firms which are most inclined to invest in ICT. In that case, the causal link is from productivity figures to new technologies, and not the other way around.

In light of these different studies, it appears that ICTs do have a real effect on the productive efficiency of firms, from both a macro- and microeconomic point of view. ICT accounted for one-third of growth in 2003 (Henry and Dalton, 2003), although representing less than 10 per cent of domestic product. We can therefore consider that Solow's paradox has been largely solved, despite measurement difficulties linked to the constant improvements in the quality of these technologies (see Box 1.2). In fact, it would be more accurate to recognize that the measurement difficulties are at the origin of this paradox: ICTs are used massively in the service industries, where the very concept of productivity is problematic, as the difficulties in measurement are so daunting. The growth of the service industries in Western economies may thus explain why the spread of ICT cannot be seen in productivity statistics (Griliches, 1994; Petit, 2003b). It can be observed that the growth in services also contributes to masking the scale of the rent transfers taking place, due to financialization, between the different players (employees, managers and shareholders). In the same way, it also facilitates these transfers, which escape objective evaluation. All in all, ICTs should be considered as an essential factor in the re-composition of modern capitalism – all the more so since they possess specific characteristics in terms of the structuring of markets and production relations – but without adopting the extreme and apologetic view of the once 'new economy'.

MARKET FINANCE AND ICT: CROSS-FERTILIZATION

One of the strong points of finance-led capitalism resides in the cross-fertilization of its two main driving forces: market finance and the diffusion of ICT. Clearly, these two movements are not orthogonal. They have mutually strengthened each other. The financialization of the economy has enabled the spread of new technologies, while dramatic technological changes have catalysed the establishment of the finance-led regime.

It is obvious that funding of the new technology sectors has relied heavily, in the United States, on the financial innovations characteristic of the 1980s and 1990s. The development of venture capital – which accompanies the

firm during the first stage in its cycle of development and up until its flotation on the stock market – has played a key role: the funds thus drained
amounted to $3 billion in 1990, compared with $19 billion in 1998 and
$52 billion in 1999. Afterwards, quotation on the stock market enables these
young firms, which do not have a sufficient flow of income to finance their
own development, to obtain funds. For new economy firms, the role of the
stock markets in the financing of investment is therefore more significant
than it was for the firms of the old economy (see above). Whereas the
Nasdaq, the market specialized in high technology firms, only registered
124 admissions in 1990, this figure rose to 510 in 2000 (Artus, 2002). In addition to financing, these markets have enabled firms in the ICT sector to
attempt to reach a substantial size as fast as possible. We have seen that size
plays a fundamental role in the domain of new technologies, because of
growing returns to scale. Firms have therefore turned to capital markets to
further their growth, through the takeover of competitor and/or complementary firms: rather than using their often insufficient treasury to fund
these operations of external growth, newly quoted firms have used their
own shares as currency of exchange (exchange offers). During the 1990s,
share exchange thus became the main mechanism of mergers and takeovers:
57.8 per cent of these operations were performed entirely by means of share
exchange during the period 1990–98, compared with 32.9 per cent between
1980 and 1989 (Andrade *et al.*, 2001).

In the other direction, the diffusion of ICT has enabled finance to impose
its logic with greater efficiency. Market finance (we shall go into this point in
more detail later) is based above all on a logic of public evaluation (Orléan,
1999): firms, credits, and so on are evaluated daily on public markets by
means of the confrontation of a high volume of supply and demand. The
efficiency of a market therefore depends primarily on its capacity for processing information about the firms themselves and about the buy and sell
orders. To say that the increased density of the network and the digitizing of
information have increased the information-processing capacities of capital
markets is almost an understatement. The strong increase in labour productivity in the finance sector, from an average of +3.18 per cent per year
between 1980 and 1995 to +6.76 per cent per year between 1995 and 1999,
bears witness to the very favourable nature of this development.

Lastly, the introduction of pro-shareholder governance within firms
has been facilitated by the development of ICT. Indeed, the doctrine of
shareholder value insists on the benefits of a network organization within
firms that breaks with the very hierarchized structure so typical of the
Fordist era (the 1950s and 1960s). Thus, for example, EVA should be applied
in a decentralized manner, in profit centres. The new technologies facilitate
the management of these more complex units in that, according to Petit

(1998), the new information and communication technologies are characterized precisely by their dual capacity to create networks and to facilitate the central control of lower economic units.

NOTES

1. We also refer to this ideology as shareholder sovereignty or shareholder primacy.
2. 'Fordism' corresponds to the growth regime centred on mass consumption specific to the 'Golden Age of Capitalism' after the Second World War. For a precise definition of the concept, see in particular Aglietta (1997), and Boyer and Saillard (1995).
3. The term 'institutional investors' groups together pension funds, mutual funds and insurance companies.
4. The bond market, unlike the stock market, has always been dominated by 'institutional' players because of the strong presence of insurance companies.
5. In the United States, corporate law is not legislated at a federal level. The States of the Union therefore compete with one another to attract companies. Delaware is by far the most attractive.
6. For a clear, precise presentation of this approach, see Baudchon and Brossard (2003).
7. See, for example, Greenan and Mairesse (1996) on French data, Hempell (2002) on German data and Bresnahan *et al.* (2002) on US data.

2. A critique of the foundations of shareholder value

> Despite the apparent divergence in institutions of governance, share ownership, capital markets, and business culture across developed economies, the basic law of the corporate form has already achieved a high degree of uniformity, and continued convergence is likely. A principal reason for convergence is a widespread normative consensus that corporate managers should act exclusively in the economic interests of shareholders. [. . .] Since the dominant corporate ideology of shareholder primacy is unlikely to be undone, its success represents the 'end of history' for corporate law. (Hansmann and Kraakman, 2001, p. 439)

In Chapter 1, we emphasized the role of institutional investors in the promotion of shareholder value: concerned with making their portfolio of securities as profitable as possible, these investors have taken advantage of their rising power in capital markets to increase demands on corporate executives. The quotation above, written by two of the foremost representatives[1] of US law and economics, shows the extent to which shareholder value has become a resonating theme in academic debates on corporate governance. Today, the large majority of theoretical publications uphold this form of governance, more or less explicitly. What, however, are the foundations of this position? One possible answer is that the theorists are simply repeating the legal order, the very function of which is to pronounce what the community recognizes as being legal or just. The question which immediately arises, then, is the following: is it true that the legal order, if assumed to express the norm, is favourable to shareholder value? The answer, just as immediate, is no, not in all countries. Chapter 3 demonstrates that neither Germany nor France grant much credit to this conception of power within quoted companies. For the United States, the answer is not so clear. After British law, US law is, out of all the developed countries, without a doubt the most favourable to shareholders. However, it does not follow automatically that this law upholds the idea that the sole responsibility of executives is to serve the interests of the shareholders.

In this respect, the thesis of Hansmann and Kraakman has the merit of defending a clear-cut point of view: both US law and practices tend to support shareholder value. Moreover, these two authors predict that the other models of governance (French, German, Japanese, etc.) will converge relatively quickly to US standards. This widely accepted prediction is based on the belief that the dynamic of institutions is driven by a logic of efficiency due to the growing intensity of competition on world markets. The confrontation between different models (German, Japanese, American, etc.) that was characteristic of the 1980s is now a thing of the past, heralding the 'end of history' as regards governance.

This thesis appears to us profoundly erroneous, in both its normative and positive (empirical) foundations: shareholder value is not a good principle of governance, nor is it establishing itself throughout the world.

At the normative level, we propose a critical examination of the theoretical arguments put forward in favour of shareholder value. That is the object of the present chapter. Our examination demonstrates the fragility of the normative and theoretical foundations of shareholder value. This conclusion enables us to put forward another conception of corporate governance, a conception that will run throughout the entire book.

At the positive level, we attempt to evaluate the extent to which Europe really is drawing closer to the US model. This question, known as the 'problem of convergence', is logically distinct from the preceding one. Thus, it is not because shareholder value is considered optimal that it will necessarily become dominant throughout Europe. Conversely, one can affirm that shareholder value is a bad principle while believing at the same time that Europe will gradually adopt it. This question is the subject of Chapter 3.

Our critical examination of the normative dimension of the 'end of history' thesis comprises two stages. In the first we retrace the intellectual genesis and construction of shareholder value in the United States. In the second we examine more analytically the arguments put forward in defence of this conception of the firm and of the role of its executives. Before concluding, we present the main lines of a coherent, alternative vision of the governance of listed companies.

THE INTELLECTUAL GENESIS OF SHAREHOLDER VALUE

In the United States, reflection on the position of shareholders and the responsibility of firms has been profoundly influenced by the seminal work of Berle and Means, first published in 1932. A presentation of their thesis, often misunderstood, is therefore an indispensable preliminary to grasping the genesis and construction of the agency model, which today constitutes the intellectual foundation of shareholder value.

A Reinterpretation of the 'Separation of Property and Control'

Few books have caused as much stir as *The Modern Corporation and Private Property*, by Berle and Means. The thesis put forward by these two authors, one (Means) an economist, the other (Berle) a legal specialist, in 1932 was immediately and very favourably received by the scientific community. This success can be explained by its date of publication, at the height of the US economic and stock market crisis, and by the quality of the demonstration, combining empirical studies with a meticulous analysis of jurisprudence.

The deterioration of private property

Berle and Means examined the way in which the rise to power of the stock company, the equity capital of which could be freely traded in financial markets, had affected private property, the main driving force of US economic dynamics in the nineteenth century. This issue led them to draw a distinction between two concepts – legal property and control. The latter is defined as the capacity to influence the board of directors, the executive body of the firm. From this definition, the two authors drew up a typology of existing forms of control. They distinguished the five following forms:

1. 'Control through almost complete ownership': these are entrepreneurial firms (in economic terms), for which the non-tradability of equity capital enables one individual or family to direct the company.
2. 'Majority control': one or more shareholders possess a sufficiently large proportion of the equity capital to control the board of directors by legal means.
3. 'Control through a legal device without majority control': a group of shareholders has real control of the company, without possessing a majority of the capital. This control can be achieved through different devices, such as pyramid or cross-shareholdings, or the possession of shares with multiple voting rights.
4. 'Minority control': small shareholders delegate their voting rights in general assemblies to professionals by means of proxies.
5. 'Management control': the equity capital is so dispersed that shareholders have little opportunity or incentive to get involved in the internal affairs of the company. For each shareholder possessing an insignificant fraction of the capital, the effort necessary to get management to adopt their views is much greater than the expected gain, thus giving rise to 'free-riding'. Consequently, the managerial team enjoys great freedom and *de facto* power over the board of directors.

The importance of each of these forms of control was deduced from a survey of the 200 largest, non-financial corporations in the United States, conducted by Means in Book I. The result was that 44 per cent of firms were under managerial control (compared with 21 per cent under control through a legal device and 23 per cent under minority control). Berle and Means drew the following conclusion: because of the tradability of equity and the development of the stock markets, the US economy had arrived at a new stage in its development, one characterized by a 'separation of ownership and control'. The traditional (liberal) concept of private property (Honoré, 1961) – where the owner was both the beneficiary of the wealth created by the object owned and the sole person capable of transforming (controlling) its substance – no longer applied to the *real* and *legal* situation of shareholders. According to Berle and Means, shareholders were owners of an equity stake in a company, much like they are today. This ownership gave them certain rights: in the United States, for example, the right to vote in general assemblies on the nomination of members of the board of directors. Nevertheless, these rights were no longer sufficient to provide shareholders with control of the company (the free-rider problem). In practical terms, therefore, the shareholders were no longer owners of firms.

Deficiencies in the law

Book II is devoted to an analysis of the jurisprudence of the time, conducted by Berle. This analysis demonstrates that US jurisprudence did not apprehend the full measure of the transformations presented in Book I. Thus the US judicial system continued to cling to the traditional (liberal) concept of ownership, continuing as if shareholders were still the owners of companies. The legal order therefore reaffirmed shareholder sovereignty, in other words the primacy of equity owners over the company. The discrepancy with reality was evident, as these same shareholders no longer possessed the prerogatives that constitute property in its classic conception. This discrepancy also underscored the failure of the legal system to discipline corporate managers. Indeed, detailed analysis of the jurisprudence demonstrated that the stacking of legal measures, with the aim of ensuring shareholder control despite the dispersion of ownership, was totally insufficient for restoring shareholder power:

> As the power of the corporate management has increased, and as the control of the individual has sunk into the background, the tendency of the law has been to stiffen its assertion of the rights of security holder. The thing that it has not been able to stiffen has been its regulation of the conduct of the business by the corporate management. And this omission has resulted, not from lack of logical justification, but from lack of ability to handle the problems involved.

> The management of an enterprise is, by nature, a task which courts can not assume; and the various devices by which management and control have absorbed a portion of the profit-stream have been so intimately related to the business conduct of an enterprise, that the courts seem to have felt not only reluctant to interfere, but positively afraid to do so. (Berle and Means, 1932, p. 296)

This quotation clarifies the reasons behind the legal system's incapacity to control effectively the misappropriation of corporate wealth by managers: these misappropriations proceed, for the most part, from the very process of management itself. It is, for example, by choosing to take over a given firm or to invest in a given market that the executives increase their wealth and power at the expense of the shareholders. Managers can always justify their choices by invoking industrial strategy, a justification that is practically impossible for the law to contest. Indeed, by definition, the law has neither the means to interfere with this management nor the capacity to substitute itself for the managers. Ultimately, cases of pure embezzlement, objectively perceptible by the law (insider trading, for example, or misuse of corporate property), are relatively rare.

Possible solutions
These two *positive* studies – one on the structure of ownership, and the other on the state of jurisprudence – are followed by a normative assessment, which concludes *The Modern Corporation*. Book IV opens with the following passage: 'The shifting relationships of property and enterprise in American industry [. . .] raise in sharp relief certain legal, economic, and social questions which must now be squarely faced. Of these the greatest is the question in whose interests should the great quasi-public corporations [. . .] be operated (Berle and Means, 1932, p. 294).

As we have seen, US jurisprudence at the beginning of the 1930s gave the following answer: in the interest of the shareholders. From this stance came the desire to strengthen equity holders' rights in order to maintain a certain continuity with the old order founded on the liberal concept of ownership.

Another possible reply to the question of whose interests should be served is to take cognizance of the concentration of power in the hands of the managers, observing that it is the result of a strictly contractual process: the shareholders have accepted their loss of control of the company in exchange for greater liquidity. In other words, they have traded control for liquidity. Therefore, they can no longer legitimately demand control of the company. The doctrine of shareholder sovereignty, by seeking to return control to equity holders, refuses to acknowledge this trade-off between control and liquidity. According to managerial sovereignty, managers should be free to exercise power as they see fit. The company is an object of property, as described in the doctrine of shareholder value. It is the subjects of the property (the owners) that have changed: these are now the managers (instead of the shareholders), and they are free to seek personal enrichment in the running of their object of property – the company.

Berle and Means consider the first of these replies (shareholder sovereignty) preferable to the second (managerial sovereignty). Nevertheless, we have already underlined the reservations expressed by these two authors as regards the doctrine of shareholder sovereignty. They argue that the concentration of power in the firm cannot be fought against in the name of shareholder primacy or the defence of property rights unless shareholders agree to renounce capital market liquidity. The courts' inability to discipline managers illustrates the limits of this doctrine: legal mechanisms alone cannot re-establish the link between the subject of property (the share-holder) and the object of property (the firm), when liquidity *specifically* presupposes complete separation between the person and the property. Nevertheless, Berle and Means reject the idea of leaving this power unbri-dled, to be exercised in a subjective or arbitrary way by managers.

Their position is finally presented in the last chapter, entitled: 'The New Concept of the Corporation'. It begins with a long quotation from Walther Rathenau, industrialist, statesman in the Weimar Republic and social theorist, describing the German conception of the public limited company in the following terms: 'The depersonalization of ownership, the objectifi-cation of enterprise, the detachment of property from possessor, leads to a point where the enterprise becomes transformed into an institution which resembles the state in character' (p. 309). The solution recommended by Berle and Means is to set limits on managerial power, in other words to ensure that it is exercised, not in the interests of those who wield it, but in the interests of those affected by it. The concept of ownership presupposes exactly the opposite: the owner of an object has 'subjective' power over that object and thus has the right to do whatever he or she wants with it (see Robé, 1999). The reference to the state in Rathenau's quotation is signifi-cant at this level: the distinctive feature of a (democratic) state resides in the fact that the concentration of power within the state apparatus, necessary for its efficiency, is counterbalanced by limits placed on that power. The exercise of power is subjected, by means of various procedures, to the will of the people. The idea thus upheld by Berle and Means is that the liquidity of capital markets calls for a rethinking of the nature of power within large companies: this power should be exercised on behalf of the company's constituents. Managers should no longer be accountable solely to the shareholders; they must be made accountable to all the stakeholders in the firm. The firm is no longer an object of property, but an *institution* that must be governed as such. In this regard, Berle and Means observed a certain lead in Germany's legal, political and economic orders, in recognizing the specifically institutional nature of the firm.

Few authors agreed with Berle and Means on this normative thesis. Their diagnosis of the separation of ownership and control, on the other hand, was widely adopted. For nearly 30 years, works devoted to the study of large companies subscribed to this representation by considering managers as the main players in the US economy. Williamson (1964) and Marris (1964) examined the consequences of this distribution of power, notably in terms of investment, while Galbraith (1967) raised concerns about the growing influence of a 'technostructure' at the head of firms.

The Agency Relationship and Shareholder Value

The first serious criticisms of this work only appeared much later, in the 1960s, with the development of Property Rights Theory (PRT), and then in the 1970s with Positive Agency Theory (PAT). These two theoretic *corpora* conflict with every point in the analysis of Berle and Means. At the empirical level, the separation between ownership and control was questioned. At the normative level, the primacy of shareholders was (re)affirmed, in complete contradiction to the conclusions of book IV of *The Modern Corporation*.

Pioneered by the work of Coase (1960), and later developed by Demsetz (1967), Alchian (1969), Furubotn and Pejovic (1972), PRT set out to modify the neoclassical framework by connecting all behaviour to the property rights system, while accounting for transaction costs. On the subject which interests us, the loss of control by shareholders was minimized by taking into account the disciplinary role of the market. Thus, for Alchian (1969), the leader of this movement, 'ignoring or denying the forces of open competitive market capitalization is [. . .] a fundamental error in the writing about ownership and control and about the modern corporate economy' (1974, p. 136). PRT theorists underline particularly the role of hostile takeovers (Manne, 1965). The idea is simple: the market will punish management that is overly unfavourable to shareholders by depreciating share prices, thus threatening managers with the risk of a takeover. Berle and Means are considered to have underestimated this mechanism, which limits managers' room for manoeuvre.

Positive Agency Theory (PAT) puts forward an even more radical criticism of Berle and Means's thesis. PAT, in which the most influential figures have been Jensen, Meckling, Fama and Klein, constituted the theoretical basis for the return to power of shareholders during the second half of the 1980s. The work of Jensen, at the time professor of management at

Harvard, contributed to legitimizing hostile takeovers in the United States (1986) as well as certain complicated financial structures, such as leverage buy-outs (1989), the proliferation of which between 1984 and 1989 marked the renewal of shareholder value.

Two major differences can be observed between PRT and PAT. The first difference is that whereas the concept of ownership is the central element in PRT, it is excluded from the very start by PAT in relation to the firm: 'We [...] set aside the typical presumption that a corporation has owners in any meaningful sense' (Fama, 1980, p. 289). Thus shareholders are no longer portrayed as hierarchically superior to the other stakeholders, but identified instead for the services they render: providing liquidity and assuming risk. This rejection of the concept of ownership is bound to a conception of the firm as a nexus of contracts between the factors of production. By definition, one cannot possess a contract (or contracts) as one can possess an asset. This position also has the advantage of concurring with microlegal studies, which have underlined the distance between the shareholders and the firm: shareholders own equity stakes, but not the material and immaterial assets which make up the firm's wealth. The company, as a legal entity, is the sole owner of these property rights.

The concept of 'agency relationship', on the contrary, is systematized to describe the nature of the relationship between shareholders and managers. This concept has been borrowed from legal analysis, where it designates 'a relationship in which the principal retains the power to control and direct the activities of the agent' (Clark, 1985, p. 56). Likewise, for Reuschlein and Gregory (1979), 'the agency relation differs from other fiduciary relations in that *it is the duty of the agent to respond to the desires of the principal*' (p. 11, our italics). The costs generated by the dispersion of shares are described as 'agency costs': these are all the costs connected to the fact that the principal (the group of shareholders) does not succeed in perfectly controlling the action of the agent (the managers of the firm).

Today, the number of authors who still explicitly espouse PAT is limited. The lack of formalization in this literature has undoubtedly contributed to its decline. Nevertheless, economists continue to privilege the agency relationship concept when addressing the question of corporate governance. These works most often lie within the scope of what can be called, following the terminology of Jensen (1983), Normative Agency Theory. This theory draws on rational choice theory, by examining the optimality of contracts in situations of informational asymmetry. Unlike Positive Agency Theory, Normative Agency Theory makes great use of microeconomic modelling. The review of the literature on corporate governance, now considered a classic, by Shleifer and Vishny (1997a) is a good example of this reliance on the concept of the agency relationship:

'Our perspective on corporate governance is a straightforward agency perspective' (p. 738). It must be noted that reliance on this concept leads to the adoption of shareholder value as the reference model. Qualifying the relationship between shareholders and managers as an agency relationship entails the belief that it is the duty of the latter to satisfy the desires of the former, in other words, that the managerial team has been hired by the shareholders to best serve their interests. As with any act of qualification, adopting an agency perspective is not neutral: it serves as a vehicle for a normative representation of the situation in which the two parties are involved.

The economic translation of this agency perspective is the following: the objective of the firm or its managers is reduced to maximizing the utility of the group of shareholders. Nevertheless, the hypothesis of opportunism, at the heart of contemporary microeconomics, requires analysts to acknowledge that managers will do everything in their power to divert (misappropriate) value. Shareholders must therefore ensure that incentive contracts are signed, in order to reduce conflicts of interest to the lowest possible level. If we denote V as the utility function of the group of shareholders, U the utility function of the manager, U the manager's reserve utility, w his or her salary, and $e(w) = \{e^+; e^-\}$ his or her effort ($e^+ > e^-$), then the firm's programme can be written as follows:

$$\begin{cases} \underset{w}{Max}\ V(w) \\ s.c.\ U(w; e^+) \geq \mathrm{U} \qquad\qquad \textit{participation constraint} \\ \quad\ U(w; e^+) \geq U(w; e^-) \quad \textit{incentive constraint} \end{cases}$$

To simplify, the stock market price is often used to represent V, as it incorporates, in theory, expected gains in capital and future distributions in dividends. From this model we can deduce that the firm behaves in an optimal (second best) way when it maximizes the well-being of the shareholders.

The analytic framework of Positive Agency Theory is losing ground, but its central message about the firm has become omnipresent: managers are shareholders' agents. All the mechanisms which favour aligning managers' interests with those of the shareholders will improve the efficiency of the firm (drawing closer to the first best solution).

The second difference between Property Rights Theory and Positive Agency Theory lies precisely in the identification of these mechanisms. The role of markets as disciplinary instruments is central to PRT and is re-affirmed by PAT.[2] The latter also focuses on the *internal* mechanisms of corporate governance, and in particular the board of directors. Fama and Jensen (1983) analyse the board as an institution whose function is to reduce agency costs by monitoring and ratifying the actions of the managerial team on behalf of the shareholders. Exclusive control of the board of directors by the stockholders constitutes an efficient arrangement. Following publication of this article, the question of the composition of this board became a central issue in debates on corporate governance: the defence of shareholder value, or of an agency representation of the shareholder/manager relationship, has subsequently often been associated with a vision of the board of directors as an instrument of the shareholders. Promotion of another doctrine of governance, on the other hand, goes hand-in-hand with a call to open up the board of directors to non-shareholders.

A Philosophy of Dispossession

Positive Agency Theory has had a profound influence on corporate governance debates. This theory has shaped the framework of interpretation that now predominates: corporate governance deals primarily, if not exclusively, with the relations between shareholders and managers, and these relations are conceived in a strictly hierarchical fashion. Managers are the obligees of the shareholders; the duty of the board of directors and hostile takeovers is to guarantee the quality of managers' services. This conception has structured most academic studies in the United States and has infiltrated the large majority of reform proposals with regard to governance. We therefore believe that it is essential to identify more clearly the moving forces behind this conception. Essentially, it is founded on two cornerstones:

- The first cornerstone is an orientation firmly in favour of shareholders. We shall not go into the sociological foundations of this orientation, which is rooted in the politico-economic history of the United States. We shall simply observe that it goes hand-in-glove with the belief that private property constituted a central vector of the national dynamic in the nineteenth century (the conquest of the West, industrialization).
- The second cornerstone stems directly from the work of Berle and Means. It is the diagnosis of the loss of control by shareholders, resulting, as we have seen, from the dispersion of stock ownership. Different authors ascribe different levels of intensity to this loss.

The juxtaposition of these two cornerstones immediately brings to light a tension, which constitutes the matrix of US corporate governance: shareholders are the legitimate possessors of power within the firm, but this power is being wrested from them by the top echelon of a hierarchy internal to the firm. From this situation comes the exclusive focus on the question of control: how can this lost control be recovered? The answer is by encouraging managers (with their potential for misbehaviour) to act in the interests of the shareholders and by establishing safety mechanisms capable of detecting and curbing managerial misconduct. In other words, 'the dominant corporate ideology of shareholder primacy' (Hansmann and Kraakman, 2001) is rooted in a philosophy of dispossession.

Analysing the board of directors as a strictly 'disciplinary' tool (Charreaux, 2000) in the hands of the shareholders, and not as a strategic body accompanying management in its choices, is characteristic of this conception. Directors' independence from the firm has become a cardinal value, the only one thought to guarantee the disciplinary role of the board. Almost all codes of good governance attempt to define the 'independence' of directors and the proportion of independent directors that a board should contain.[3] On the other hand, nothing is said about these directors' competence.

> If you own a business, and you want to improve its ROE, there are two ways of going about it, one of them good, the other not so good: the first is to improve your products, services, marketing, etc.; the second is to install a camera to make sure the manager is not putting his hand in the till. It appears that governance is more interested in the camera than in managing the shop. (our translation)

This metaphor, proposed by Batsch (2003a), illustrates clearly the philosophy of this approach.

Under these conditions, the strength of the agency model is easy to understand. This model deals precisely with a situation in which power is delegated and with the difficulties then encountered in securing that delegation. The penetration of agency theory, and, beyond that, of contract theory, into the domain of corporate governance, bears witness to the close correspondence between the US conception of governance and an analytical framework, first developed in the 1970s, which puts the emphasis on the incentive dimension of coordination.

THE THEORY OF THE FIRM
AND SHAREHOLDER VALUE

The key question remains to be answered: in the agency model, what are the theoretical foundations for the preference given to shareholders? In other words, why are corporate executives designated as the agents of the shareholders? Or, put in another way, why should the board of directors – the central organ of the firm – be reserved exclusively for shareholder representatives? What economic arguments are put forward? The simplest replies refer to profit maximization or risk-taking. The problematic nature of these arguments has led to the creation of a new path of research, focusing on the question of the incompleteness of contracts.

The Profit Argument

This argument is founded on the idea that in a market economy a firm's objective is to maximize its profits. If we add that these profits are the remuneration of capital providers, shareholder value would be justified. It would be, in some way, inscribed within capitalism itself. This analysis may be correct in the case of an entrepreneurial firm, but it is, on the contrary, much more problematic in the case of a managerial firm.[4] Let us explore this point in more detail.

Entrepreneurial firms are unique in that one and the same person (the central agent) fulfils the following four functions: entrepreneur (knowing the trade, the markets, managing uncertainty, etc.), manager (organizing the firm), capitalist (owning the means of production) and worker. The share of total revenues which comes back to him or her, once the (other) factors of production have been remunerated, can be considered as the profit. This profit is composed of various elements, deriving from the different functions: wages for managerial and non-managerial work, interest for capital contribution, and a 'pure' profit for the entrepreneurial activity – a mix of risk-taking and a capacity to lead the business in the midst of uncertainty. In the case of a managerial firm (or listed company), these functions are separated and performed by collective units rather than individuals. The functions of entrepreneur and manager are grouped together within the executive team, which is salaried. The company itself, as a legal entity, is the owner of the means of production. The shareholders receive residual earnings in the form of dividends by virtue of their contract; this function has no equivalent in the entrepreneurial firm. What then is profit? For the entrepreneurial firm, we have identified it in terms of its destination (the share that comes back to the central agent) and not by its origin (which is diverse, as we have seen). For the managerial firm, this attribution is no longer possible. The very concept of profit becomes muddled: it no longer designates the remuneration of a specific agent. Different stakeholders in the firm may be remunerated on the basis of the book profits. Thus shareholders receive part of it if dividends are paid; so may employees, if their remuneration includes an incentive scheme. Finally, it may be reinvested. In no case, either legally, contractually or statutorily, does profit belong exclusively to the shareholders. Bernstein

(1953) highlighted the distance between the concept of profit in the cases of managerial and entrepreneurial firms in the following passage:

> [in the case of a large corporation] the profit has an 'impersonality' about it, whereas in the case of small business, the relationship between the entrepreneur and his company's earning is very intimate indeed. [. . .] In brief, while conceptually small business profit seems to accrue to people, big business profit belongs to 'the corporation'. (1969, p. 243)

This makes it easier to understand the mistake made in basing shareholder value on the concept of profit maximization: the fact that the objective of the firm is to maximize its profit does not imply that the firm must be managed in the exclusive interest of its shareholders; profit is not reserved for their exclusive remuneration. In other words, in the case of a managerial firm, the principle of profit maximization does not, in itself, convey any criterion for the distribution of profit between the different constituents (shareholders, employees or the firm itself).

The Risk Argument

From an economic point of view, the second argument is the most widely used to justify shareholder value: it is because the shareholders are the risk-bearers in the firm that they should take precedence in the distribution of power and profit. The idea that the shareholders are the party which incurs the risk is very widespread: it derives from the fact that the remuneration of equity holders is not specified beforehand in the contract which binds them to the company, unlike the remunerations of wage earners and creditors. An allocation of power in favour of shareholders is the only one that respects the basic principle of externality management, according to which the capacity to impact the income from an asset should be conferred on the person receiving those revenues. All institutional mechanisms which contribute to returning control to the risk-bearers thus make it possible to draw closer to the optimum. They participate in the internalization of externalities. On this subject, Easterbrook and Fischel (1993), promoters of contract theory in the economic analysis of law, wrote:

> voting rights are universally held by shareholders, to the exclusion of creditors, managers and other employees. [. . .] The reason is that shareholders are the residual claimants to the firm's income. [. . .] As the residual claimants, shareholders have the appropriate incentives [. . .] to make discretionary decisions. (pp. 67–8)

Nevertheless, this link between risk-taking and the right to control is a fragile foundation on which to base shareholder value. In fact, the intensity of the risk taken by shareholders can be challenged as soon as we move away from the question of the residual nature of their remuneration as defined in their contract. First, their liability is limited: the losses they sustain in the event of bankruptcy of the firm are limited to the value of their capital contributions. Second, the tradable nature of their assets and the growing liquidity of stock markets provides them with a capacity for exit and diversification without equal, in any case much higher than that of the employees. Current developments tend further to reduce the risk incurred by shareholders, reinforcing our scepticism about the validity of risk as a justification. One example of this trend is the spread of the principle of the creation of value for the shareholder, the logical foundations of which were presented in Chapter 1. Thus Economic Value Added (EVA) affirms the idea that there exists a minimum remuneration for the shareholder, namely the cost of capital as evaluated by the market. Only financial profitability over and above this cost is considered to create value. The pursuit of a strategy oriented towards the creation of value for the shareholder thus necessitates the (internal) setting of a profitability threshold which must be exceeded. Obviously, the application of this principle remarkably modifies the status of the shareholder (Lordon, 2000): from a residual creditor, the shareholder is transformed (thanks to EVA) into a secured creditor, similar to lenders. Shareholders acquire guarantees of return on their investment, which may not be legally binding (contractual), but which are nevertheless very real. To observe this change, we need to go beyond the contractual clauses and examine the *actual* unfolding of the relationships. The reduction in the risk incurred by shareholders is necessarily accompanied by an increase in the risk incurred by the other stakeholders, and notably by the employees. The development of the individualization of remunerations, for managers, white-collar workers and blue-collar workers, forms part of this movement of the transfer of risk (Coutrot, 1998; H. Petit, 2003). Increased work flexibility throughout all Western countries has also been part of this movement: the growing use of specific forms of employment (short-term and temporary contracts), along with the generalization of subsidiary and outsourcing strategies, make it possible to adjust the wage bill to suit industrial requirements. In short, the rise to power of the doctrine of shareholder value is turning the traditional roles upside-down: employees are incurring an ever greater share of the risk as the shareholders succeed in taking advantage of a favourable balance of power to guarantee partially their income.

The statistics for the evolution of dividends as a proportion of profit in the United States give an idea of the scale of this movement (see Figure 2.1). During the 1980s, while profits remained globally stable, the

size of dividends rose as pressure from the capital markets increased:
dividends as a proportion of profit doubled, from 24.7 per cent in 1980 to
50.1 per cent in 1990. From 1992 to 1997, dividends continued to rise, but
with profits climbing as well: the share of dividends settled at around
50 per cent. In 1998, a new trend began to form, one that would appear fully
in 2001, 2002 and 2003: profits fell, yet dividends continued on their upward
movement started at the beginning of the 1980s. Consequently, dividends
as a proportion of profits exploded, reaching 87.3 per cent in the second
quarter of 2003. Thus, for more than 20 years, we have been observing a
regular rise in dividends, completely detached from movements in profits.
This ratcheting up, which appears to exclude any possibility of a reduction
in the cash flow paid to shareholders, clearly highlights the developments
described above: for the last two decades shareholders have succeeded in
partially guaranteeing their income against trading fluctuations, thus significantly reducing the risk they incur. Consequently, the argument that the
firm should be managed in the exclusive interest of its shareholders
because they are the ones incurring the risk loses a lot of its validity.

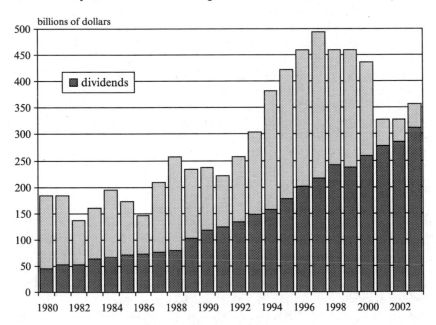

Source: Flow of funds (Federal Reserve), Tables F.102.

Figure 2.1   *Evolution of dividends as a proportion of total profits*
              (before tax) for non-financial companies (excluding farming)
              in the USA

The Incomplete Contract Approach

The above discussion underlines that the relative position of a given stake-holder should not be evaluated exclusively through the contract between that party and the company; the actual development of their relationship must also be taken into account. If shareholders are sometimes judged to be the only residual creditors of the firm, that is because analysis has focused exclusively on the equity contract. As we have seen, conclusions are substantially modified when we take into account the *ex post* dimension of contracts, in other words their actual unfolding. This observation has led to a renewal of the normative approach to corporate governance, focusing analysis on the question of contractual incompleteness. The hypothesis of incompleteness represents the translation of the above idea into the syntax of contract theory: affirming that we need to analyse the actual realization of the relationship means recognizing that contracts signed *ex ante* do not cover this relationship exhaustively. In other words, we consider that these contracts are incomplete; certain decisive elements of the relationship cannot be contracted at the start, giving it an indeterminate character from the outset. In terms of governance, the importance of the hypothesis of contractual incompleteness is particularly evident, as Hart (1995) points out: 'Governance structure matters when some actions have to be decided in the future that have not been specified in an initial contract' (p. 679).

The securing of investments in financial and human capital

The hypothesis of contractual incompleteness lies at the heart of the contemporary theory of the firm. It is one of the foundations of trans-action cost theory, pioneered by Williamson (1975, 1985), and of modern property rights theory, developed by Grossman and Hart (1986). These two approaches both explore the way in which parties to a transaction secure their reciprocal investments when contracts are incomplete. In this context, protection of specific, non-redeployable investments cannot be achieved beforehand by the establishment of a contract providing for every possible contingency. Consequently, the parties to the contract are led to establish institutional devices, enabling them to appropriate a share of the organizational quasi-rent as a return on their investment. When applied to corporate governance, this schema considers rights on the board of directors as a tool for securing investments. Thus Zingales (1998) writes of the 'incomplete contracts approach to corporate governance'.

This path was first explored by Williamson in Chapter 12, entitled 'Corporate Governance', of his seminal 1985 book *The Economic Institutions of Capitalism*. His argument is taken up and furthered in two articles, one by Williamson and Bercovitz (1996), the other by

Romano (1996). These works recognize that shareholders are not the only risk-takers within the firm. This assertion, however, is not based on the observation, made above, of a transfer of risk from shareholders to employees, but on the development of a risk that is *internal* to the workforce. This new risk derives from a trend, noted by many observers, of an increase in the specificity of human capital (see also Blair, 1995). This increase does indeed constitute a risk-taking factor: workers' payoff depends on the future distribution of the quasi-rent generated by the investment in human capital, which is fundamentally uncertain. This risk is all the stronger as the specificity of capital, in other words its non-redeployable nature, places employees in a disadvantageous position at the time of (re-)negotiation of the allocation of the quasi-rent. Reflection is thus focused on the measures capable of efficiently protecting those parties which incur the greatest risk (shareholders and employees), whereas contracts are incomplete. These authors reach the following conclusion: shareholders should be protected through rights of control over the board of directors. As for employees' investments, they should be secured by means of various devices: a pre-defined system of promotion, severance packages and procedures for settling internal disputes. Employee participation on the board of directors, however, is not envisaged. One may be surprised by this asymmetry between the treatment of shareholders and that of employees: in one case, the recognition of a weakness gives the right to control; in the other, it gives the right to protection against the arbitrary nature of decisions. The conclusion of Romano is clear: 'Transaction cost economics offers no analytical support for expanding board representation to non-shareholder groups, and indeed, cautions against such proposals' (1996, p. 293). The German model, in which employee representatives sit on the supervisory board,[5] is deemed to be inefficient.

Towards a questioning of shareholder value
The work of Zingales (1998, 2000) and of Blair and Stout (1999) has developed the incomplete contract approach to corporate governance pioneered by Williamson. This work offers, following Blair (1995), a new conception of the process of value creation within the firm. Thus it is observed that the quasi-rent created by the firm derives from the pooling of complementary factors of production, in the form of tangible, intangible, human and financial capital. Compared with the work of Williamson, more emphasis is placed on the incomplete nature of contracts and on the synergies that come into play between the investments of the different stakeholders. The firm is conceptualized as a 'nexus of specific investments'. The allocation of rights of control over the entity thus created plays a decisive role, in that this allocation will determine how the value created is divided up. Consequently,

each stakeholder will be more or less motivated to commit to the firm, and this will influence the very level of the organizational quasi-rent.

Taking into account the complexity of the relationships formed between the different stakeholders and the plurality of centres of value creation, Zingales (1998) and Blair and Stout (1999) propose a solution that moves away from the doctrine of shareholder value: the stakeholders should delegate their powers to an independent third party – the board of directors – whose objective is to best serve the interest of the constituted entity. In this context, the directors are no longer simply the agents of the shareholders; their fiduciary duties must be exercised towards the whole firm, in accordance with what is today the most widely accepted analysis of the contents of these duties in US corporate law. Thus the productive assets of the firm must be managed in the interest of the firm itself. This point is new compared with the work of Williamson, for whom the role of the board of directors was to serve the interests of the shareholders. In short, the primacy of shareholders is partially challenged.

For Zingales (1998) and for Blair and Stout (1999), however, ultimate control of the board of directors should remain in the hands of shareholders, because of their contractually weak position. Here, we find a mode of reasoning analogous to that of Williamson who, after recognizing the importance of employees in terms of the creation of value (through their specific investments), excludes them from board-level participation. This conclusion, it must be noted, upholds the optimality of the US model of governance, in which the managers, while having their fiduciary duties extended, are exclusively controlled by their shareholders through the board of directors.

Zingales (2000) goes one step further in an article of a very prospective nature entitled 'In Search of New Foundations'. This title reveals his ambition: in terms of corporate governance, he seeks to grasp the implications of transformations in forms of coordination, which have become more flexible, and in methods of value creation, which are more closely focused on workers' skills. His conclusion moves even further away from the doctrine of shareholder value: 'In the current environment, where human capital is crucial and *contracts are highly incomplete*, the primary goal of a corporate governance system should be to protect the integrity of the firm, and new precepts need to be worked out' (p. 1645, our italics). Despite this call for further reflection, Zingales offers no 'solutions'; his article is essentially devoted to describing the limits of existing theories.

The issue of contractual incompleteness
Examination of the contributions of Zingales (1998, 2000) and of Blair and Stout (1999) brings out a remarkable principle: the stronger the emphasis on

contractual incompleteness, the more managers' responsibility is extended. Zingales (2000) thus calls for reflection on new principles of governance in light of the current situation in which contracts are 'highly incomplete'. The corollary of this increased incompleteness is an affirmation of the collective nature of the firm: from a form strictly centred on shareholders (Williamson, 1985), principles of governance were first extended to collective management of productive assets (Zingales, 1998; Blair and Stout, 1999), before finally embracing protection of the integrity of the firm (Zingales, 2000).

It should be noted, however, that this principle, by which the widening of the field of incompleteness is accompanied by an extension of the responsibility of managerial power, raises its own problems. The widening of the field of incompleteness progressively reduces the validity of the contractual analysis on which the work of Zingales and of Blair and Stout is founded. To say that contracts are incomplete is to acknowledge that the 'off-contract' plays a role in coordination. As this incompleteness increases, the scope of contractual analysis therefore tends, by definition, to shrink (Favereau, 1997). The less we understand the nature of the interactions at work within the firm, the more *ad hoc* becomes the description of any particular model as efficient. Consequently, we may consider that Zingales (1998) and Blair and Stout (1999) give voting rights to shareholders less for analytical reasons specific to their model and more for shaping this model to fit the US reality. In doing so, they give 'scientific' credit to this model of governance.[6] Indeed, this difficulty is recognized implicitly by Zingales (1998), for whom 'at the current state of knowledge the [incomplete contracts approach to corporate governance] lacks theoretical foundations' (p. 502). The author adds by way of conclusion: 'Without a better understanding of why contracts are incomplete, all the result are merely provisional' (p. 502).

We can draw two conclusions from this presentation of the incomplete contract approach to corporate governance, one negative and the other positive:

1.   As it stands, this approach appears to display a certain conservatism. These works conclude that the model under consideration (the US model) is efficient, to the exclusion of every other model. This conclusion is all the more fragile because it relies on strictly microeconomic and contractual reasoning, placing the emphasis precisely on the massively incomplete nature of contracts. The risks of '*ad hoc*ness' are heightened as a result.

2.   On the other hand, this approach highlights the specifically collective dimension of the firm as a locus of coordination and actualization

of specific and complementary skills. This coordination cannot be reduced to a set of contracts, except in the case where these contracts are assumed to be largely incomplete. This ultimately amounts to concluding that intra-firm coordination is partially outside the realm of contractual order. In terms of governance the conclusions of this recognition of the collective nature of the firm are also interesting, in that they represent a move away from the doctrine of shareholder value.

For a Partnership Theory of the Firm

The 'discovery' of the collective nature of the company (beyond the sphere of contracts) by the contractual theory of the firm is all the more remarkable in that it rejoins a whole tradition of thought which has been largely ignored for nearly 40 years. This tradition, having more of a legal origin, fell into oblivion through a curious turn of history that saw its message attacked by both neoclassical and Marxist theorists.

In the United States, Berle and Means (1932) can be connected to this tradition, which proposes a holistic conception of the firm. By 'holistic', we mean a conception of the firm that focuses on its autonomous and collective nature. The firm exists in and of itself; it cannot be reduced to a set of inter-individual relationships. We have already described the way in which Berle and Means's analysis of the changes in private property, subsequent to the growth in capital market liquidity, led them to argue for an 'empowerment' of the firm in relation to its shareholders. We have also pointed out that this thesis, contrary to that of the 'separation of ownership and control', was carefully buried by firm theorists from the 1960s onwards.

The point of view upheld by Berle and Means has also been espoused by certain legal theorists in Europe. In France, the 'institutional theory of the firm' (*théorie institutionnelle de l'entreprise*), developed just after the Second World War, provides a particularly rich interpretation of the nature of the firm and the conclusions to be drawn in terms of corporate governance.

To understand the foundations of this 'institutional' theory, the first thing to bear in mind is that *the firm does not exist in law*. Only the corporation, grouping together the shareholders, has a legal existence. This is because the only methods of coordination recognized by the law are contracts and associations (Ripert, 1951): the firm remains hidden behind a network of contracts (corporate and labour).[7]

In response to what they saw as a lack, different legal specialists have sought to unveil the collective nature of the firm: first, by observing the existence of a sociological and economic reality of the firm; and second, by detecting, within current legislation, the premises of a recognition of the substance of the firm, and calling for further progress in that direction. This unveiling of the firm as an autonomous collective – which deserves to be treated as a person in the eyes of the law – has been based, in France, on German legal scholarship and on the 'theory of the institution' developed in public law:

- German legal culture established a 'labour relations doctrine', conceiving of employment relations as a relationship founded on the personal commitment of the employee, and not as a purely contractual relationship. This approach was extended into a community vision of the firm in the work of Gierke (1874).
- The 'legal theory of the institution', developed in France by Hauriou (1910), analysed an institution as an activity or idea which becomes autonomous in relation to its creator. Its management is thus driven by the search to satisfy the general interest of the institution, which reaches beyond the specific (and sometimes divergent) interests of the different parties involved. This analysis is very close to that of Berle and Means, for whom the concentration of power in the hands of managers was only acceptable when that power was 'contained', in other words given objectives distinct from the interests of those wielding the power.

The 'institutional theory of the firm' was born out of a synthesis of these two approaches through the work of Durand (1947) and Ripert (1951). Durand saw the firm as a 'grouping organized in relation to a common purpose' (vol. 1, Section 339, our translation), while Ripert proposed to 'bring to light the collective action, the solidarity between all the members of the same firm, the natural society created by the community of work' (p. 275, our translation). The key idea in this theory is that intra-firm activity is based on the cooperation between the different stakeholders (employees and capitalists), and that this cooperation aims at a common objective. Consequently, the firm displays the characteristics of an institution: it is autonomous in relation to its members, and the objective defined by its management must be to satisfy the general interest, which both synthesizes and transcends the motivations of its different constituents. The closeness of this thesis to the principles upheld by Berle and Means in Book IV of *The Modern Corporation* can be clearly observed on reading the following passage from *Aspects juridiques du capitalisme moderne* ('Juridical Aspects of Modern Capitalism') by Ripert (1951):

> In the grouping of forces constituted by the firm, the end pursued becomes of capital importance. This end is the common good of all the people who cooperate in the firm. It is no longer solely the limitless remuneration of capital through the profits made, it is also the guarantee of the livelihood of the people

who work in the firm and the families of these people. Capital and labour must each find satisfaction in the firm, but of a different nature, and if the firm cannot provide this, it does not deserve to survive. (p. 279, our translation)

Thus, for Ripert (1951), 'it is essential to render management independent of capital. We should not consider managers and directors to be the agents of the shareholders' (p. 285, our translation). Note that the foundations of the legal concept of the 'interest of the firm', which plays a key role in the French legal framework of collective layoffs, are found in institutional theory.

The progressive obliteration of this 'holistic' vision can be attributed to its awkward positioning, out of plumb with the two dominant post-Second World War conceptions of the firm – the neoclassical approach (in economics) on the one hand, and the Marxist approach (in labour law) on the other (see Box 2.1). The neoclassical approach has appeared in numerous variations (normative and positive agency theory, property rights theory, etc.), but these variants are unanimous in reducing the firm to a nexus of contracts agreed between autonomous agents. This vision is clearly antithetic to the holistic approach, which confers primacy to the entity over the stakeholders. Paradoxically, the Marxist approach also claims to adopt a 'contractual' approach (see Lyon-Caen, 1955). In this context, the term 'contractual' is used in opposition to the institutionalist (holistic) approach, of which the community connotations run counter to an analysis in terms of class struggle. If we add that the paternalistic character of institutional theory evoked, for certain authors, too much of the principles of Vichist ideology, it is easy to understand why holistic theory was struck by an 'anti-community taboo' after the Liberation (Segrestin, 1992). This taboo can also be observed in Germany and Italy.

BOX 2.1   THE MARXIST THEORY OF THE FIRM

The 'traditional' Marxist approach emphasizes a contradiction in labour relations. These are both a market relationship, which can be interpreted in contract terms, and a subordinative relationship of the employees to the managers in the performance of the contract, in other words in their work. The contract is therefore highly incomplete, and this fact is also recognized by neoclassical efficiency wage theories.

We need to go further by rethinking labour relations in a monetary economy. In this case, they are clearly not a market relationship. They are in fact a social division which deprives employees of the possibility of becoming autonomous producers. Not being owners, employees cannot be the subject of contracts. This means that labour relations are not only an incomplete contract, in the sense of an agreement between two subjects who are formally equal because they are both traders, but also a *sui generis* institution resulting from the private appropriation of the means of production. This institution is a mediation which establishes, enforces and legitimizes a system of rules concerning wages, working conditions, labour mobility, and so on. Thus conceived of, labour relations correlatively build the capitalist firm into an autonomous entity capable of subordinating employees through the power of labour coordination.

This structure is reflected in the access to money enjoyed by firms and employees. Firms have the monetary initiative to be able to produce. It is their access to monetary creation, either directly through the banks or indirectly through share issues, which enables them to draw resources from society, foremost among which are the human capacities of employees to produce in order to sell. It follows that the monetary initiative of firms is built on the anticipation of the accumulation of capital gathered in the collective entity and considered as a whole. This confers strategic power on the managers of the firm, because the definition of a global objective is indispensable for access to credit, as the model in Chapter 4 will demonstrate. Access of the employees to money, on the contrary, depends on the firm. This validates the mediation (role) of labour relations in the formation of the monetary wealth of the economy.

Economic analysis of the firm, in its most modern developments, is tending to return to the central message of these theories. We have already described the way in which emphasis on the incomplete nature of contracts has driven the contractual approach to consider the firm as an entity in itself, whose management must be oriented towards the satisfaction of a transcendent interest. This is all the more true for cognitive approaches to the firm. Unlike contractual theory, for which the firm is above all an incentive structure, cognitive approaches explore the way in which the firm constructs, maintains and develops tacit and collective productive knowledge. The competitiveness of the firm depends on the quality of the 'cognitive' process. The economics of conventions focuses particularly on the conditions for realizing these processes of collective learning (Favereau, 1994; Eymard-Duvernay, 2001): the concept of cooperation, around an objective shared by both the employees and the shareholders, is given a central role. This underscores the 'partnership' dimension of the firm. A partnership is defined generically as an association which has the aim of performing a common action. Today, this concept, rather than the term 'holistic', lies at the heart of different analyses seeking to define the essence of the firm. These analyses, be they British (Wheeler, 1997) or French (Charreaux and Desbrières, 1998), share the idea that the firm is collective in nature, in the style of Berle and Means or Ripert. As things stand, this term appears to us to be both the most illuminating and the most unifying, if an alternative has to be found for the contractual qualifier of the firm.

Clearly, the firm is not a pure partnership, and much work remains to be done in this direction. One cannot deny the existence of power struggles, asymmetries, and so on, just as one cannot deny all partnerial foundation to the firm. The firm has a partnerial dimension because it develops on the basis of cooperation oriented towards a common goal.

While the current movement towards employment insecurity has led certain authors to refuse to accept the partnerial dimension of the firm, it is also possible, conversely, to treat this movement as an opportunity to reaffirm the partnerial essence of the firm – from a reformist point of view (Kay and Silberston, 1995). We believe that the following remarks by Catala, in the introduction to the fourth volume of the general survey of labour law directed by Camerlynck in 1980, are more relevant than ever:

> The view we adopt concerning the nature of the firm is therefore lacking neither in practical implications nor in political repercussions. As things stand, it may be illusory or premature to detect an institution therein. However, to deny that the interests of those who contribute their energy, skills or capital converge, at least partially, within the firm, is not only to deny a reality, it is also to condemn *a priori* any institutional participation, any social organization of the firm, any effort to construct within the firm, by means of bodies and mechanisms that may be imperfect but are perfectible, a balance that respects the vested interests. (p. IX, our translation)

CONCLUSION

The conclusion of this chapter, which set out to assess the normative dimension of the 'end of history' thesis, is clear: shareholder value, or the agency perspective of corporate governance, is less a theoretically founded model than a position of principle. Contrary to the affirmations of its champions, it cannot lay claim to any scientific legitimacy: no economic reasoning can justify the assertion that the firm should be managed exclusively in the interest of its shareholders. Attempts at justification come up against the distributed nature of risk within the firm. Moreover, instead of the 'widespread normative consensus' (see above, Hansmann and Kraakman, 2001) on the intrinsic qualities of shareholder value, the most recent works (Zingales, 1998, 2000; Blair and Stout, 1999) propose a more contrasting, if not contradictory, conclusion – although one may observe the fragility of these results. Study of the creation of value within the firm thus brings out the collective nature of this process, which combines a group of specific productive resources under the authority of managers and directors. The implications in terms of the organization of power within the firm are noteworthy: management of the firm must be oriented to satisfying the interests of the entity itself, and not the interests of one of its constituents. In other words, the holistic, or partnerial, conception of the firm and its governance are reaffirmed by an economic analysis of the processes of value creation in the firm. The shift towards approaches which focus more on the cognitive dimension and less on the incentive dimension of the firm strengthens this conclusion.[8]

Economic analysis has yet to produce any argument capable of challenging the analysis of Berle and Means (1932), despite the efforts made in this direction ever since the success, during the 1970s, of agency theory. It could even be argued that current economic theory is moving towards the normative conclusions of *The Modern Corporation and Private Property*. In this work, Berle and Means provided a dual interpretation, both positive and normative. On the positive level, they diagnosed a fundamental transformation in the concept of property due to the growth in capital market liquidity. Although this diagnosis was very widely accepted, the remedy proposed was, on the contrary, firmly challenged and/or progressively forgotten by the dominant economic approach (contract theory). While the mainstream reaffirmed shareholder sovereignty, thus founding the set of themes of corporate governance on a logic of dispossession and control, Berle and Means called for a redefinition of the nature of power in the firm, this power to be exercised in the name of the firm as a collective. The intuition of these two authors, which has been taken up in France by Ripert, is therefore that shareholder value is not inscribed within capitalism. For them, the choice of liquidity made by the shareholders should logically be paid for by relinquishment of control over the wealth-creating entity, which becomes autonomous. This intuition has stronger foundations today than it had in 1930, due to the rise to power of institutional investors in the stock markets. By definition, these investors are only interested in the (relative or absolute) return on their portfolios. Investment in a firm is neither guided by a desire to get more involved with the entity, nor concerned with understanding its business or strategies. Financial profitability in relation to the risk taken is the unique criterion of choice. Consequently, the idea that the firm is an autonomous entity is today even more obvious than during Berle and Means's time.

Finally, the tradability of shares and the liquidity of stock markets call for a form of governance that emancipates the firm from the grip of its shareholders. The partnerial dimension of the firm must be reaffirmed: this dimension comes from bringing together the strategic, cognitive and financial skills necessary for the development and competitiveness of the entity thus constituted. Central power is conferred on the managers and directors, entrusted with the task of setting this productive force into motion in the temporal dimension. However, this power must be given objectives, in other words it must be exercised in the interest of the entity, which both synthesizes and transcends the interests of the main stakeholders (shareholders and employees). Making managerial power binding thus calls for a form of governance quite different from that championed by the doctrine of shareholder value, where managers must act in the strict interest of the shareholders, under the watchful eye of a board of directors composed exclusively of shareholder representatives.

In addition to a new normative vision of the governance of listed companies, the analysis conducted in this chapter argues in favour of a second shift: the reintegration of the wage–labour nexus into positive discussions on governance. There is nothing to justify the fact that debates on governance are focused exclusively on institutions relating to capital markets. This type of analysis, particularly used to examine the convergence of national models, confirms the partition between *corporate governance* on the one hand, lying within the scope of stock market law and corporate law, and *labour governance* on the other, lying within the scope of labour or industrial law. The next chapter, on the contrary, proposes an analytical framework which takes into account simultaneously the influence of the financial sphere and labour relations in the exercise of power in large companies.

NOTES

1. Hansmann is professor of law at the Yale School of Management and Kraakman at Harvard Law School.
2. Fama (1980), for instance, underlines the role of the managerial labour market and reputation effects, which contribute to reductions in agency costs.
3. In France, for example, the Viénot I report recommended the presence of two independent directors; this grew to one-third of the Board in the Viénot II report and to one-half in the Bouton report.
4. The term 'entrepreneurial firm' is commonly used to designate individual companies, or unlisted companies. The term 'managerial firm', on the other hand, designates all firms established on the basis of a public limited company.

5. Here, the difference between the board of directors and the supervisory board is of little importance. In both cases, we are dealing with the central strategic organ of the firm.
6. In the process, the French model, which is identical to the US model from this point of view, is seen as efficient. The German model, on the other hand, is once more perceived as being sub-optimal.
7. 'Association' is a legal technique which is, by nature, foreign to intra-firm coordination, as it designates a gathering or a group brought together with the view of satisfying non-financial interests.
8. For developments on this point, see O'Sullivan (2000) and Rebérioux (2003b).

3. The convergence of the European model in question

The previous chapter led us to reject the 'end of history' thesis from a normative point of view, in its designation of shareholder value as the optimal form of corporate governance. In the present chapter, we examine this thesis from an empirical perspective. At present, according to Hansmann and Kraakman (2001), it should be possible to observe an international convergence of governance towards the US model, favourable to minority shareholders. The continental European model in particular is claimed to be losing its specificities, drawing closer to the standards prevalent in the United States. It is this diagnosis, widely shared by theorists, that we subject to critical examination. We limit our analysis to the German and French cases, as they are characteristic of the continental European model. The period studied is the 1990s, during which the rise of financial markets, supposedly at the origin of transformations in forms of governance, was most prominent. In the first part of this chapter, we present the US, German and French models and underline their principal differences.[1] We aim to highlight the elements that make up these models, as brought out by the comparative literature on this subject. In the second part of the chapter, we appraise the way in which current transformations in the financial sphere are reshaping these elements. We also focus our attention on movements outside the financial sphere that may either reinforce or weaken the continental European model. It is on this basis that we are finally able to pass an overall judgement on the thesis of convergence.

THE EMPIRICAL DIVERSITY OF THE MODELS OF CORPORATE GOVERNANCE

The distribution of share ownership is the first factor of distinction between the US and continental European models of governance. The comparative literature most often puts forward the legal environment as the explanation for this difference. In the next section we use this principle, granting a determinant role to the legal order, to develop a method for the analysis of convergence. Taking this method as our basis, in the following sections we then present the US model of governance, followed by the German model and finally the French model.

The Distribution of Share Ownership

Before analysing the national models, it is important to note the differences in weight that capital markets have in different countries. A simple indicator of this weight was presented in Chapter 1: the ratio of national market capitalization to GDP. For the year 1995, for example, this was 0.95 in the United States, compared with 0.32 in France and 0.26 in Germany (see Table 1.1). The number of companies listed on the stock market constitutes a second, equally revealing index (see Table 3.1).

However, the essential factor of distinction between the US model and the continental European model lies in the distribution of share ownership, both from the quantitative (degree of concentration) and the qualitative (identity of shareholders) point of view.

The results of the comparative study carried out by La Porta *et al.* (1999) on the distribution of ownership in the three countries concerned are reproduced in Table 3.2. Thus, whether we look at the biggest companies or those of average size, we can see that widely held firms (in other words, without any single shareholder possessing more than 10 or 20 per cent of voting rights) predominate in the United States, contrary to France and Germany. The study conducted by Barca and Becht (2002) confirms this result through the calculation of the mean size of the largest blocks of shares in different countries. Whereas this mean size is lower than 5 per cent of

Table 3.1   Number of companies listed on the different stock markets

	United States		France	Germany
	NASDAQ	NYSE		
1995	5127	2242	904	–
1996	5556	2476	891	–
1997	5487	2626	924	–
1998	5068	2670	1097	662
1999	4829	3025	969	851
2000	4734	2488	966	983
2001	4063	2400	1195	983
			(Euronext)	
2002	3649	2366	1114	934
			(Euronext)	

Source: FIBV.

Table 3.2   Number (percentage) of widely held firms

	Biggest companies Ultimate owner at		Medium-sized companies Ultimate owner at	
	20%	10%	20%	10%
United States	80	80	90	50
France	60	30	0	0
Germany	50	35	10	10

Note: This table indicates the proportion (in %) of widely held firms for two different samples: the 20 biggest companies (in market capitalization, at the end of 1995), and ten medium-sized companies (the ten smallest companies with market capitalization of at least $500 million, at the end of 1995). A company is said to be widely held when it has no ultimate owner, that is, a shareholder possessing either directly or indirectly more than 20 per cent or more than 10 per cent of the voting rights in the companies, depending on the choice of threshold. Thus, 80 per cent of the biggest companies in the United States are widely held when the reference threshold is defined at 10 per cent.

Source: La Porta *et al.* (1999).

Table 3.3   Distribution of ownership (% of outstanding corporate equity held by sectors)

	United States	France	Germany
Banks	6	7	10
Insurance companies and pension funds	28	9	12
Mutual funds and other financial institutions	13	14	8
Non-financial companies	–	19	42
Households	49	23	15
Non-residents	5	25	9

Source: OECD (1998).

voting rights in the United States, the figure rises to 52 per cent in Germany and 20 per cent in France.[2]

The qualitative distribution of ownership also displays a very distinct configuration (Table 3.3): while institutional investors (mainly pension funds) are the principal holders of shares in the United States (alongside households), the German and French landscapes are dominated by non-financial companies.

We can see that the US model is characterized by wide dispersion of ownership and by liquid capital markets, dominated by investment funds. The essential properties of the continental European model, on the contrary, are relatively narrow capital markets, the presence of large blockholdings and cross-shareholdings between firms.

The Importance of the Legal Framework

The origins of this dispersion of ownership in the United States are currently the subject of a rich and lively controversy. Box 3.1 retraces the arguments of the main authors in this debate: Roe (1994) on one side, and La Porta *et al.* (1998) on the other. Over and above the differences which oppose the two sides, this debate is marked by a common approach, today unavoidable in comparative studies: to understand the most significant facts in terms of corporate governance requires detailed analysis of the legal environment.

BOX 3.1   DISTRIBUTION OF OWNERSHIP AND THE LEGAL FRAMEWORK: THE ROE VERSUS LA PORTA *ET AL.* DEBATE

In 1994, Mark Roe presented an innovative approach to the structure of US ownership in his book entitled, *Strong Managers, Weak Owners; The Political Roots of American Corporate Finance*. He developed the following thesis: far from being the result of a process of selection through efficiency, the 'Berle and Means' type firm, characterized by a wide dispersion of ownership, is the product of a legal framework which has fragmented financial institutions. This framework, largely introduced before the Second World War due to the pressure of public opinion and certain lobbies, discourages or prevents institutional investors from amassing large blocks of ownership (see, for example, the *Glass-Steagall Act* of 1933 for banks, or the *Investment Company Act* of 1940 for mutual funds). A presumption of inefficiency therefore weighs on the US model: in the absence of this over-regulation, large blockholdings could have developed, as they did in Europe, making it easier to monitor and control management.

In 1998, La Porta *et al.* (see also La Porta *et al.*, 1999) challenged this thesis, observing that the UK also has a widely dispersed ownership structure, but with no question of laying the responsibility for this at the door of a severe legal framework *vis-à-vis* financial institutions. They suggest another explanation for the existence of the two main governance models, an explanation which has been widely taken up today. According to these authors, the level of dispersion of ownership increases in direct proportion to the level of legal protection accorded to minority shareholders. Now, the quality of this protection is a direct function of the legal tradition of each country. Thus common law countries (the United States, the UK, etc.) provide much stronger guarantees to small owners than civil law countries, which make up for this shortcoming by a concentrated structure of ownership. This thesis, backed up by a very large body of data, takes a view diametrically opposed to that of Roe: it is not the US model that errs through an *excess* of regulation, but the continental European model that errs through a *lack* of regulation.

Following this comparative method, the legal environment and legal foundations of these models are given a position of foremost importance in our analysis. In other words, we connect the constituent elements and the most significant changes of each model as closely as possible with the legal order and its transformations. There is no question of affirming that legal rules are the sole determinants, at any given time, of the way in which the large listed companies are governed. Indeed, many practices without any legal foundation also play a part in shaping the exercise of power (the reproduction of an elite in France through the *grandes écoles* system, for example). In addition, a distinction must be made between the pronouncement of a legal rule and its practical application. We can, however, consider that the legal order sticks closely to the practices and conceptions of the players, whether preceding or following them. Thus, for instance, the existence of blockholdings is widely associated with legal measures that authorize their constitution. The dispersion of ownership, on the other hand, is often connected with the prohibition of certain mechanisms that would facilitate the formation of large blocks. However, as far as possible, we attempt to evaluate the influence of the legal order, by supplying indications of the degree of application of certain rules.

We therefore start our analysis by picking out a set of legal mediations which help to distinguish relatively clearly between the exercise and aims of managerial power in each of the two models, US on the one hand, and continental European on the other. At this stage, it is important to identify the legal fields which play a part in shaping the exercise of power. The analysis carried out in the previous chapter serves as a support in this. We demonstrated the way in which rejection of shareholder value as an efficient form of governance argued in favour of a reintegration of workers into governance debates. Labour relations should be on a par with the financial sphere as a prime subject of study in the matter of governance. There are therefore three legal fields which should be taken into account.[3]

1. Financial market regulation: this *corpus* comprises all regulations covering share issues (primary capital market), and subsequent transactions involving these shares (secondary capital market). The aim of these regulations is both to reduce informational asymmetries between investors and players inside the company, the 'insiders', and to prevent misappropriation of value by these insiders (Black, 2001). In the first case, the regulations aim to increase the financial transparency of companies, by obliging them to disclose standardized information. In the second case, the principal targets are insider trading and internal transactions.

2. Corporate law: these are the legal rules defining the relations between the different constituents of the company, that is the shareholders, directors, managers and employees. Typically, these rules deal with the nature of voting rights granted to shareholders, the power of the general meeting of shareholders, the composition and functioning of corporate boards, the accountability of managers and directors, and so on.

3. Labour law: this field can affect corporate governance directly when it favours the involvement of workers in decision-making processes. Following Turner (1993), we use the term 'negotiated participation' to describe this intervention by employees.[4] Negotiated involvement marks the recognition of workers as a constituent element of the firm, over and above their supply of service (working force). As a constituent element, they have the right to be informed and consulted about the main points involving the functioning of the firm (weak involvement). Possibly, they may be granted a power of co-determination on a more or less wide range of subjects, through elected representatives (strong involvement). This concept of negotiated involvement may create confusion: there is obviously no question of managers being absolutely controlled by the very people they are supposed to manage. Rather, the concept refers to a body of positive rights which induce (or force) managers to take the interests of employees into account when making their decisions (Streeck, 2001). Corporate governance is thus directly affected: these rights to information, consultation and co-determination contribute, when they exist, to the definition of a specific aim for the exercise of power within companies, in which the

maximization of the well-being of shareholders is not taken to be the required norm (Rebérioux, 2002).

The classification proposed here clearly tends to oversimplify. It is sometimes difficult to determine whether a particular rule lies within the domain of financial market law or corporate law (for example, shareholders' obligation to inform the market authorities when they possess a certain amount of voting rights). In France, financial market and corporate law are brought together within the *Code de commerce*. Likewise, the participation of employees in corporate boards may fall within the scope of either corporate law or labour law. Lastly, it should be noted that the regulation of public offers (takeover bids or exchange offers) touches simultaneously on all three legal fields. Nevertheless, it is useful to adopt this representation to appreciate the main differences between national models of corporate governance.

The US Model: Shareholder Value and Market Liquidity

The United States is characterized by highly developed financial market law. This law, of federal origin, imposes a set of procedures on managers to guarantee the disclosure of relatively standardized information to the capital markets. It also regulates share operations carried out by insiders, whose position within the firm provides them with private information. Lastly, financial market law also encroaches on internal relations within the company, as it regulates the use of proxies in general meetings. The Securities and Exchange Commission (SEC), the capital markets' regulating authority instituted by the Securities Exchange Act of 1934, plays a key role in this area: it supervises the whole informational chain, from the harmonization of accounting standards (the principal sources of financial information) to auditing and financial analysis.

Compared with financial market law, corporate law is relatively little developed; these laws are mainly produced by individual states, which compete with each other to attract companies.[5] The legislation of the United States therefore provides firms with a great amount of flexibility in the internal organization of their governance, in the name of contractual freedom. Only a few measures, such as the establishment of a board of directors, are of a constraining nature. Corporate law also introduces certain measures to guarantee the protection of minority shareholders, of an intensity which varies from state to state. The fiduciary duties of the managers and directors constitute the keystone of corporate law in the United States. The fulfilment of these duties is controlled *ex post*, with a high risk of litigation that is specific to the US system. Jurisprudence thus plays a decisive role, in that it specifies the responsibilities of managers.

The nature of the fiduciary duties of directors and managers is the subject of a great deal of controversy; but many commentators agree that these duties should be exercised in the name of the shareholders *and* of the company. Therefore, just as it lacks normative foundations (see Chapter 2), the agency model also lacks legal foundations. Thus Clark (1985) concludes: 'A review of elementary corporate law shows that this power of the principal to direct the activities of the agent does not apply to the stockholders as against the directors nor officers of their corporations' (p. 56).

Consequently, shareholders are protected more by financial market law than by corporate law.[6] Nevertheless, the legal framework still offers managers potential room for manoeuvre, all the more so since intense pressure from management circles led to the reinforcing of anti-takeover devices at the beginning of the 1990s. The freedom of managers is further strengthened by the absence of internal, non-shareholder counterbalancing powers: the employees in particular have no rights in terms of governance.

The US model of governance is therefore characterized by the importance it accords to the liquidity of financial markets. Neither corporate nor labour law really affects the discretionary power of managers; control of these managers therefore relies decisively on the regulatory force of the capital markets. From this point of view, two types of actors play a crucial role: first, the SEC, responsible for the good functioning of these markets; second, the institutional investors who, because of their weight in the capital of companies, today exert considerable influence on strategies. Therefore, if shareholder value is winning ground in the United States, it is thanks to the rise to power of these investors in a legal environment that is globally favourable to their wishes.

The German Model: A Compromise in Management

In first analysis, the German model of governance appears to be diametrically opposed to the US model, at least until the mid-1990s (Donald, 2003; Cioffi, 2005). The most recent changes will be examined at the end of this chapter.

Financial market law is traditionally little developed, and specific to each state. Capital markets are not very active and ownership is concentrated. The quality of financial transparency is distinctly lower than the standards prevalent in the United States. The logic of intermediation far outweighs market finance. Banks play a major role: at one and the same time, they are suppliers of liquidities, owners, proxies for the voting rights of their customers and active members of supervisory boards.

Corporate law, on the other hand, regulates strictly the internal organization of companies. This law is of federal origin. Contrary to the monistic structure that prevails in the United States (the board of directors), German companies have a dualistic structure with a board of directors (*Vorstand*) in charge of management, and a supervisory board (*Aufsichtsrat*), responsible for monitoring the managers. The functioning of shareholders' general meetings is also the subject of a large number of legal measures.

Without a doubt, the most characteristic trait of the German model is the position reserved for workers in the matter of corporate governance, through the co-determination system, the *Mitbestimmung*. This co-determination, guaranteed both by corporate and by labour law at a federal level, is based on two pillars. The first pillar is integrated into the dualistic structure of German companies. Worker representatives sit on the supervisory board, alongside shareholder representatives elected during the general meeting. This form of co-determination has three faces. In the iron and steel and mining industries, the co-determination law of 1951 provides for parity between the shareholder and employee representatives (i.e. an equal number of seats on the supervisory board). The board member in charge of labour-related questions is named by the employee representatives alone. The co-determination law of 1976 imposes 'sub-parity' for all firms employing more than 2000 workers. Although the number of seats reserved for the representatives of each party is equal, the president of the supervisory board, whose vote counts double in the event of a deadlock, is elected by the shareholders. Finally, the constitutional law of 1952 extends the principle of co-determination to all companies with a workforce of between 500 and 2000 employees. This structure does not have equal representation of both sides, as only one-third of seats are occupied by worker representatives. The law of 1976 is the most important of the three, as it affects 4.5 million workers, compared with 1.5 million for the law of 1951, and 1 million for the law of 1952 (Müller-Jentsch, 1995). The works council (*Betriebsrat*) constitutes the second pillar of German co-determination. This council possesses a right to co-determination concerning the consequences, both social (principles of payment and working hours) and personal (systems of promotion, recruitment and individual layoffs), of the economic and financial orientations of the company. For these orientations, the *Betriebsrat* only has the right to information and consultation.

Taken as a whole, the German system produces a compromise in management between shareholders, workers and creditors, through the medium of a considerable *corpus* of corporate and labour law. Transparency and capital market liquidity, on the other hand, are weak, and the regulatory bodies for these markets are very fragmented. Shareholder value enjoys neither practical nor legal legitimacy. German law tends to conceptualize the company as an autonomous entity, the running of which is subject to strong procedural constraints obliging the stakeholders to negotiate.

The French Model: An Intermediate System

The French model occupies the middle ground between the US and German systems. Corporate governance is regulated more by corporate law than by financial market law, but this latter is richer than in Germany. Capital markets are also more developed. Created on the model of the SEC in 1967, the *Commission des Opérations de Bourse* (COB – the stock market regulatory body) has played an important role in the development of these markets. The state's disengagement from productive capital (privatizations) carried out in the 1980s and 1990s, followed by the explosion, from 1996 on, of the 'hard cores' (Morin, 1998), have dramatically altered the landscape of French governance, which had been characterized by the importance of the public sector and cross-shareholdings.

The great majority of companies have a monistic structure (board of directors), but corporate law provides for the possibility of adopting a dualistic structure, which is being chosen by a growing number of big companies.

As in Germany, employees intervene in matters of governance, but to a lesser extent. They possess rights to information and consultation through the intermediary of the works council. However, this council does not enjoy any right to co-determination, and the directing board (board of directors or supervisory board) is reserved for shareholder representatives.[7] Nevertheless, the powers of the works council, inscribed in the Labour Code, are important. Article L.431 of the Labour Code, for example, requires the employer to provide the works council with the information it may wish to obtain on the general functioning of the company. This information also plays an important role in the *ex post* control, conducted by judges, of the legal validity of economic layoffs. Another important right is the possibility for the works council to call in an expert accountant, in order to obtain a counter-valuation of the information communicated by the employer. This right challenges the '*employer's monopoly on legitimate expertise*' (Grumbach, 1995). This is particular to France. Grumbach (1995) thus perceives in France the outlines of a veritable '*system of co-supervision*', rather than co-determination, conducted jointly by the judge and the works councils.

Lastly, French law reproduces a holistic vision of the company as an autonomous entity. In this, it is much closer to the German model than to the US one. Managers must act in the name of 'corporate interest', which, according to certain authors (see in particular Paillusseau, 1984, 1999), is synonymous with the interests of the firm.[8] This is also the position adopted in the Viénot I report on corporate governance. Commissioned by the MEDEF (French Business Confederation) and the AFEP (French Association of Private Businesses) and published in 1995, the section devoted to 'The objectives of the mission of the board of directors' notes:

> In Anglo-Saxon countries, the emphasis is primarily placed on the objective of fast maximization of share value, whereas, on the European continent in general and in France in particular, it is placed rather on the corporate interest of the company. [. . .] The corporate interest can be defined as the greater interest of the body itself, in other words the company considered as an autonomous economic agent pursuing its own ends, distinct notably from those of its share-holders, employees, creditors (including the tax authorities), suppliers and customers, but which correspond to their common general interest, which is to ensure the prosperity and continuity of the company. (p. 8)

The French system therefore presents the characteristics of an intermediate model, as regards both the financial transparency of companies and the degree of worker involvement in the decision-making processes. It is customary to present French managers as enjoying very wide discretionary powers, although this vision sometimes verges on caricature.[9]

This discussion has enabled us to bring out the diversity of corporate governance models, rooted in distinct conceptions of the firm and its inscription in the capitalist system. Heuristically, it is useful to distinguish between two main types of model.

1. The US model is characterized by an orientation resolutely favourable to shareholders through strong regulation of capital markets. Disclosure requirements are high and interventionism on the part of the authorities (principally the SEC) is considerable. The direct regulation of intra-firm relations through corporate law is, on the contrary, weak. The integration of employees into decision-making processes is non-existent. This particular configuration of power within the firm, where control is ultimately intended to be exerted from the outside by minority shareholders, is often described as the 'outsider' model;

2. The continental European model favours internal regulation of the firm: corporate and labour law thus organize the deliberative structures between the main players in the firm. Controlling interests protect management from capital market fluctuations. A holistic or partnerial vision (see Chapter 2, p. 45) of the firm prevails, finding expression in the concepts of corporate interest and/or worker involvement. Financial market law is less ambitious. This situation can be referred to as the 'insider' model.

CONVERGENCE OR DIVERGENCE? THE OUTLINES OF AN ANSWER

We therefore have two principal and opposing systems of corporate governance. The US system considers the firm to be the object of property rights; the submission of this object to the interests of the shareholders is achieved in the first place by the depth and liquidity of stock markets. The continental European model, on the contrary, is founded on a holistic or partnerial vision of the firm; company management is partially protected from the stock market by the stability of large blockholdings and by employee participation.

The thesis of convergence, with its underlying apologetic vision of shareholder value, sees in current developments a gradual abandonment of continental specificities in favour of an alignment with US standards. Besides the development within business circles of a rhetoric focused on the creation of value for shareholders, there are three empirical elements underpinning this thesis. Taken together, these factors are said to be contributing to a shift in the centre of gravity of the continental model of governance, away from 'inside' control towards 'outside' control.

- The first and most obvious factor is the significant increase in the weight of stock markets, in terms of both the traditional indicator of stock market capitalization as a proportion of GDP, and the daily volume of exchanges carried out in the different stock markets;
- Following this movement, banks are investing more in capital markets to the detriment of their traditional role as both lender and controlling shareholder;
- Lastly, US and British institutional investors (pension and mutual funds) have steadily asserted their presence in the capital markets, to the point where, today, these institutional investors are the second most important shareholders in France. The penetration of foreign investors in the capital of German companies also appears to have accelerated since the second half of the 1990s (Gehrke, 2002).

In the first analysis, these developments do indeed represent a weakening of the characteristic traits of the continental model, but they are insufficient to justify any affirmation of convergence towards the US model. It is difficult, for example, to grasp the impact of market liquidity on the exercise of power within companies without examining the performance of the takeover market. Likewise, the weight of institutional investors in equity capital is not enough to assert that these investors are running the companies. We now present an overall appraisal of the thesis of convergence, concentrating on the transformations that affect the structures of owner-ship and the legal environment. The current movement appears to us to be much more complex than that announced by the 'end of history' thesis.[10]

Financial Market Law as a Factor of Convergence

Parallel to the very favourable development of capital markets, financial market law is the domain which has undoubtedly drawn closest to US standards.

First, obligations in terms of the disclosure of information and financial transparency have greatly increased. The European Union has been a driving force behind this increase. The 1988 directive on financial trans-parency, aiming to develop information about the identity of shareholders, gave impetus to this movement, even though its transposition into national law took time: Germany only became compliant in 1994. The 2001/34/EC directive, which strengthens publicity norms and standardizes information connected with share issues with the creation of a unique prospectus, also constitutes an important step in the transformation of European capital markets. In this field, France has appeared as a model, with two major texts: the 1989 law relating to the security and transparency of the capital market, and the 1996 financial activity modernization law.

Second, there is a tendency towards the centralization of market author-ities, along the lines of the SEC. The German case is particularly striking: in 1994, the second law for the promotion of capital markets instituted a federal market authority, the *Bundesaufsichtsamt für den Wertpapierhandel* (BAWe), thus breaking with the fragmentation of German stock market authorities. Centralization was further strengthened in April 2002 with the FinDAG law, which replaced the BAWe by the BAFin (*Bundesanstalt für Finanzdienstleistungsaufsicht*), a body of which the prerogatives exceed even those of the SEC. In France, the law on 'new economic regulations' (NRE), passed in May 2001, gave more powers to the COB, while the Financial Security Act, passed in July 2003, took a further step forward with the creation of the Financial Markets Authority (AMF), a merger of the COB and the Financial Markets Council (CMF, created in 1996). In the field of financial market law, the signs of convergence are therefore evident: the transparency of information given to shareholders as a whole has progressed greatly, while the role of market authorities continues to grow.

Corporate Law and Controlling Interests: Overall Stability

In corporate law, on the contrary, it is impossible to draw such a clear con-clusion. Certain signs of convergence can be observed. Most notably, the

risk of litigation, characteristic of the US model, is tending to increase as
the accountability of managers and directors and the possibility of bringing legal actions against them grow: the NRE law in France (Frison-Roche,
2002) and, to a lesser extent, the KonTrag law in Germany, passed in 1998,
both move in this direction. As for the protection of minority shareholders
and the stability of blockholdings, it is difficult to make a final judgement.
Certain measures favouring these blocks are losing ground: in Germany,
the KonTrag law has forbidden multiple voting rights and voting caps and
has restricted the banks' use of their voting rights. However, the most recent
studies (Barca and Becht, 2002; Becht and Mayer, 2002; Faccio and Lang,
2000; Boutillier *et al.*, 2002) show that these devices, which are constituent
of the continental European model at the same time as they reveal national
specificities, remain widespread. For example, it appears that voting caps
are on the increase in France (Magnier, 2002). The existence of blockholdings remains the situation of reference in various continental European
countries, despite the increase in market liquidity. The massive presence of
US and UK institutional investors in the capital of European companies
does not call this observation into question: essentially, these investors have
taken their place in the 'float' of company equity, in other words outside the
structures and controlling interests (Boutillier *et al.*, 2002). Furthermore,
given the size of the blocks they possess individually (rarely exceeding 2 or
3 per cent), the ability and desire of these investors to impose their views in
a foreign context is doubtful.

Worker Involvement: Affirming the European Model

The existence of forms of 'negotiated involvement' in Germany and France
has already been mentioned in the sections on the German and French
models of governance. This participation, which can be found in various
forms throughout continental Europe, constitutes an original, specifically
European model of corporate governance. It is possible, at the present time,
to observe a movement of consolidation of the rights of employees to participate in the affairs of their company, not only on a national level[11] but
also, and above all, on the level of the European Union. This movement is
putting a brake on the process of convergence of the European model
towards the US model.

The adoption, in September 1994, of directive 94/45/EC on European
works councils can be interpreted as the first step in this process. Since it
came into force in 1996, companies of 1000 employees or more, with a
minimum of 150 workers in at least two member states, must have established a 'European' works council, representative of the international composition of the workforce of the firm and endowed with information and

consultation rights. While there were only about 30 such structures in the European Union in 1994, and about 400 in 1999, today there are nearly 800, out of a total of a little more than 1800 companies concerned. The directive appears to have succeeded in developing what used to be a minority practice, by imposing employee representatives as legitimate partners. Its success can also be appreciated in terms of the spreading effects it has provoked. Thus, even before the UK signed the Maastricht social protocol, within the framework of which the directive had been adopted, a large number of British multinational companies had established European works councils through voluntary agreements (more than 150 in 1999), exceeding even the most optimistic predictions (Jobert, 2000, p. 161). This phenomenon also seems to have influenced non-transnational companies, which have adopted information and consultation bodies after observing these practices within firms subject to directive 94/45 (Streeck, 2001).

This movement of consolidation of a European model of governance through legislative action, based on the 'negotiated involvement' of employees, accelerated significantly with two EU legislative advances following the Nice summit (December 2000).

The first step forward was the adoption, in October 2001, of regulation 2157/2001 relating to the status of European Company Statutes and of directive 2001/86/EC, which completed this statute in terms of worker involvement. A European company (EC) is a moral person possessing an original, specifically EU status. It must be registered in one of the member states of the European Union, with the obligation of establishing its central administration in that state. We shall see the importance of this point later. An EC cannot be created *ex nihilo*, but through one of three different paths: (a) the conversion of a national company possessing subsidiaries in another member state for at least two years; (b) the merger of companies from at least two different member states; and (c) the formation of a holding company by companies established in at least two member states.

The diversity of European practices with regard to employee participation (information, consultation and co-determination) has represented an obstacle to the adoption of a European partnerial structure for more than 30 years. In particular, the question of board-level participation (supervisory boards or boards of directors) has crystallized these conflicts, with certain countries fearing the import of this practice (Spain, the UK and Ireland), and others seeing in this statute the means to avoid strong national requirements in this domain (Germany). The *tour de force* of this directive was to overcome these disputes, thanks to an original legal technique, which, however, also added to the complexity of the text. Box 3.2 presents the main points of this directive.

BOX 3.2   WORKER INVOLVEMENT IN THE EUROPEAN COMPANY (DIRECTIVE 2001/86/EC)

The provisions for worker involvement in European companies (EC), drawn from the recommendations of the Davignon Report, are the object of a separate directive – as the regulation is a form relatively unsuited to questions of labour law. This directive does not directly define the conditions of employee involvement – given the differences between member states on this question, that would have been impossible – but establishes a protocol of negotiation between employers and worker representatives of the future entity on the forms of participation that will be implemented. Thus the directive requires the constitution of a Special Negotiating Body (SNB), representative of the international composition of the labour force, entrusted with leading these negotiations with the employers to a fruitful conclusion. In addition to the conditions of negotiation (parties involved and agenda), the directive sets fall-back statutory provisions on information/consultation and on board-level participation. These reference provisions can be applied if the parties so wish, and must be applied if agreement cannot be reached in the negotiations. The provisions of this model, relatively favourable to employees, have the aim of encouraging management to come to an agreement. The protection of acquisitions in the matter of board-level participation was one of the main stakes in this text. Thus the agreement reached must not, when an EC is created through conversion of a national company, result in a lower level of participation (number of representatives sitting on the board) than in the previous situation. In the case of creation of an EC by merger or holding (see above), a lower level is possible if and only if it is accepted by a two-thirds majority of the SNB, representing at least two-thirds of the total workforce. This point was introduced to avoid, for example, an EC resulting from the merger of a big company not practising participation with a small German firm, being required to introduce co-determination.

The directive distinguishes clearly between fall-back provisions (obligatory in the event of unsuccessful negotiations) relating to information/consultation and those relating to board-level participation (in an annex to the directive). The former provide for the establishment of a representative body, closely modelled on the

SNB, endowed with information and consultation rights slightly higher than those possessed by European works councils, in accordance with the directive 94/45. As for the measures concerning staff representation on governing bodies, these depend on the way in which the EC was formed:

(a) In the case of *conversion*, the measures previously in force continue to apply.

(b) In the case of *merger*, the EC will have the level of representation (in the proportion of seats) of the merging company the most advanced in the matter. However, this obligation only applies if at least 25 per cent of the workforce were previously covered by board-level participation. This fall-back provision relating to board-level participation in the case of merger presents one particularity: it is not obligatory, but *optional*, in the sense that a member state can choose, when the directive is being transposed into national law, not to accept it. In this case, no company created out of a merger and concerned by this measure (i.e. with more than 25 per cent of the workforce previously involved in this form of co-determination) can register in this country, nor can it establish its head office there. This option had to be introduced to obtain agreement from the Spanish, who were the last obstacle to adoption of the directive: Spanish employers feared spread effects resulting from the installation of companies with board-level participation on Spanish soil.

(c) Lastly, in the case of creation of an EC by *holding*, the EC will possess the highest level of representation from among the companies at the origin of the EC, if and only if 50 per cent of the workforce was previously concerned by the participation. Contrary to the previous case, this measure is not optional.

Sources: Moreau (2001); Goetschy (2002); *Journal officiel* (2001).

This text, while preserving national differences, clearly moves towards a strengthening of employees' rights in terms of governance (Bordogna and Guarriello, 2003): not only do the rights accorded in the field of information/consultation go further than those provided for by the directive 94/45 on European works councils, but the rights of employees previously covered by board-level participation have, essentially, been preserved. This latter requirement is to guard against the use of the directive to weaken labour rights. Moreover, spread or contamination effects, depending on how one judges them, are to be expected from the installation of companies with a strong participative structure in countries where this form of governance does not exist. We have already remarked on the occurrence of such effects concerning the directive on European works councils. These processes of diffusion are hard to contain in the present case, as an EC cannot be registered in one country and transfer its central administration to another. It is precisely to avoid this 'shock wave' that Spain obtained the right not to transpose the fall-back provision for board-level participation in the case of a merger (Moreau, 2001, p. 975); consequently, no company that falls under this measure can register in Spain (see Box 3.2). We can therefore expect this text to lead to a certain generalization of worker participation on boards throughout Europe.

The adoption of directive 2002/14/EC, establishing a general framework relating to information and consultation of employees throughout the Union, in March 2002, represented the second step forward in the consolidation of employees' rights in Europe. This directive is to be applied, depending on the choice of the member states, to all companies with more than 20 or more than 50 employees. Three types of subjects must be covered: economic and strategic questions (solely in the form of information), employment evolution within the company and the organization of work. The changes are particularly significant for Ireland and the UK which, apart from directives 98/59 and 77/187 (see above), had no regulations in this field. The directive does not specify particular conditions within this general framework, but defines a protocol for negotiation of these measures. Here again, fall-back provisions are set out in case negotiations fail. This text completes Union legislation on information/consultation, composed, at the national level, of directives 98/59 (collective layoffs) and 77/187 (establishment transfers), and, on a supranational level, of directive 94/45 on European works councils.

Labour law therefore represents an even greater thorn in the side of the convergence thesis than corporate law.

The Regulation of Takeovers: Chaotic Development

The question of exchange offers and takeover bids[12] – at the intersection of financial market law, corporate law and labour law – crystallizes the oppositions running not only through Europe, but also through each country, concerning the way in which companies should be considered. The questions of managerial accountability and the nature of the firm arise forcefully at the time of takeover offers (Deakin and Slinger, 1997). For agency theorists, these operations represent the ultimate weapon of small shareholders against management (see Chapter 2). Yet in the United States, most states adopted anti-takeover measures at the beginning of the 1990s. The repeal of these measures, alleged to reduce the stock market valuation of companies, is one of the traditional demands in the activism of institutional investors

In Europe, the history of the thirteenth directive, concerning takeovers, does not correspond to the predictions of the convergence thesis (see Box 3.3).[13] This history is a good illustration of the two opposing conceptions of the nature of the firm present within the Union. According to the liberal economic conception, the firm 'belongs' to the shareholders. This is the conception underlying the proposition of the directive in its initial version. The continental conception, on the contrary, seeks to implement the idea of the company as a community. There are two ways to do that. First, management could be authorized to act in the name of a greater interest (the corporate interest). Second, the employees could be integrated into decision-making processes. That would mean partially merging the corporation, as a moral person, and the firm, as a productive entity. In fact, the text voted on by the European Parliament on 16 December 2003, leaves considerable freedom to member states in their choice of the rules that are to apply to companies within their jurisdiction. In this respect, the text constitutes a certain setback for the advocates of the creation of an active and integrated takeover market into the European Union.

BOX 3.3   THE EVENTFUL HISTORY OF THE THIRTEENTH TAKEOVER BID DIRECTIVE

On 4 July 2001, the European Parliament rejected the proposition of a corporate law directive on takeover offers, with 273 votes for and 273 votes against. Formulated by the Commission as early as 1985, this directive has had an eventful history. The objective of this text was to facilitate the restructuring of companies in Europe, the idea being to harmonize the takeover market within the Union. After a series of closely argued negotiations between the Commission, the Parliament and the Council, the text was structured around three articles.

- Article 5 provided for the obligation to make a takeover bid once a certain level of voting rights had been acquired (with each member state free to choose this threshold). This measure aimed to prevent takeovers without the agreement of minority shareholders, in other words by the gradual and discreet purchase of shares in a company. The price of the bid (referred to as an 'equitable price') was not defined in the directive.

- Article 6 obliged the company targeted by the takeover bid to inform employee representatives of the conditions of the operation, once this had been made public by the bidder.
- Article 9 prevented, according to the principle of 'neutrality', the managers and the board of the targeted company from interfering with the free choice of the shareholders. For example, it should be impossible for the board of directors to take defensive measures once a takeover operation has been started, without submitting them to the general meeting for approval.

The last two articles were the subject of debates which led to rejection of the text. With regard to article 6, many members of Parliament considered that the measures proposed in favour of employees were highly insufficient and should go beyond a simple procedure of information. It was article 9 that proved to cause the biggest problems: the principle of neutrality – the heart of the directive – derives straight from the doctrine of shareholder sovereignty. According to this article, only the shareholders have the right to decide the fate of the company in the event of a takeover bid, despite the fact that such an operation has major consequences for the future of the firm: the restructuring that generally follows such operations bears witness to this. According to article 9, management cannot use corporate interests or the interests of the firm as grounds to oppose a takeover, a measure which goes against the holistic vision of the firm.

In response to this failure, the Commission nominated a group of experts in corporate law, chaired by law professor Jaap Winter. This group was entrusted with the task of producing a report on the drafting of a new directive to harmonize the law concerning takeovers. This report, delivered in January 2002, shaped the drafting of a second directive project; the most controversial elements of the first text were kept. Notably, article 9, setting forth the principle of neutrality, was not changed. It was in fact reinforced by article 11, forbidding the use, during general meetings convened to decide on the adoption of defensive measures, of devices to restrict voting rights, as well as the use of double and multiple voting rights: this article prevents management from taking advantage of mechanisms that could be used to adopt anti-takeover measures undemocratically, thus bypassing the principle of neutrality. Moreover, although one article (article 13) was added concerning the information of employees, it only refers back to labour law directives already in existence. This is a way of leaving workers out of the debate, all the more so since managers cannot intervene to take worker interests into account (in accordance with article 9). This raises the question of the usefulness of consultation of the employees by the managers, if these latter subsequently have no power to intervene.

After many negotiations, the second directive project was finally adopted on 16 December 2003, by the European Parliament (321 votes for, 219 against and 9 abstentions), accompanied by numerous amendments which considerably reduce the impact of the text. Among these amendments, three are particularly important:

- Article 9 is optional: each member of the Union can decide, when the directive is transposed into national law, to keep this article or to drop it. In addition, each state can authorize a company within its national jurisdiction not to respect article 9, if this company is targeted for a takeover by a company that is not subject to this article ('reciprocity' clause).
- Article 11 is also optional: nothing obliges a member state to restrict the use of double and multiple voting rights during hostile takeover operations.
- Lastly, obligations in the field of information/consultation have been strengthened. The worker representatives of the targeted company and of the assailing company must be consulted for the procedure to be considered legitimate.

These optional clauses are shifting the focus of debates to national borders. Although it is still too early to appreciate fully the impact of this text, the fact that articles 9 and 11 are not obligatory clearly deprives this directive of some of its substance. The perspective of a unified takeover market in Europe – a factor of competitiveness and modernity according to the champions of shareholder value – has been, if not definitively dismissed, then at least postponed. On the other hand, the fact that article 9 has been conserved (its abandon being optional) is a relative failure for the advocates of a holistic or partnerial vision of the firm.

Within national jurisdictions, the construction of legal frameworks to regulate takeover bids has revealed similar tensions – to such an extent that it is difficult to observe any alignment with the standards of the outsider model. Thus France, since the end of the 1980s, has adopted a series of measures that have considerably improved the functioning of the takeover market. The year 2001 was marked by particularly effervescent legal activity, with no less than four successive reforms, the most important of which was part of the law on the 'new economic regulations' (NRE). Current developments do not all go in the same direction. The NRE law established the obligation for the company making the takeover offer to inform and consult the works council of the targeted firm about its industrial projects; if it does not, the voting rights acquired during the operation will be cancelled. This text, which increases the number of measures, does not come out clearly in favour of either a pro-shareholder vision or a more institutional vision of the firm. It can also be observed that the recent generalization of voting caps and multiple voting rights is tending to seize up the takeover market. For Becht and Mayer (2002), the growth in anti-takeover devices is a specifically European phenomenon.

In Germany, we can observe a strengthening in anti-takeover devices. One week after the rejection of the thirteenth European directive in July 2001 – partly ascribable to German MEPs – the *Bundestag* adopted a law on takeover bids. The text, initially very close to the proposition of the directive, was heavily modified, to such an extent that its final contents appear to combine opposites. As in article 5 of the European directive, a takeover offer becomes obligatory when a shareholder exceeds a threshold of 30 per cent of voting rights. In addition, the principle of neutrality is validated, preventing the directors (*Vorstand*) from taking defensive measures once the takeover bid has been launched. At the same time, however, the law increases the possibility for managers to adopt anti-takeover measures *in advance*. This point is decisive, certainly more so than the acceptance of the principle of neutrality: hostile takeovers can thus be effectively slowed down. The position of employees has been improved considerably. First, the role of the supervisory board, on which worker representatives sit in accordance with co-determination laws, is increased during these operations. Second, both the assailing firm and the target firm are required to inform and consult the works council (*Betriebsrat*) of the latter.

Taken as a whole, recent developments in the legal framework covering hostile takeovers, and in particular the failure to introduce a specifically European takeover market, are incompatible with the thesis of convergence. The continental European treatment of this issue is certainly changing. However, rather than strictly imitating US standards, the changes taking place in Europe are the result of the confrontation between European specificities and capital market requirements.

CONCLUSION

We are now in a position to present an overall appraisal of the thesis of convergence. Table 3.4 summarizes the main points of convergence, resistance or divergence of the continental European model of corporate governance. The developments related in this table illustrate a movement of considerable complexity. The diagnosis of a one-dimensional movement, such as that put forward by the thesis of convergence, is proved to be erroneous. It is possible to break down recent developments in the following manner.

- Financial market law constitutes a strong factor of convergence, both in content and form. In terms of content, the strengthening of the transparency of European capital markets is a movement towards the affirmation of shareholder power. In terms of form, the centralization of capital market regulatory authorities, with the creation of the AMF in France and the BAFin in Germany, tends to reproduce the US model, embodied in the SEC. Equally, from an institutional point of view, even if we stray somewhat from financial market law towards corporate law, the growth in the risk of litigation in Germany and France brings them closer to the US system.
- Corporate law, at least the branch dealing with measures of control, displays a certain inertia. Germany, where the KonTrag law abolished double voting rights and voting caps, represents an exception in this respect.
- Lastly, labour law is a factor of resistance, even of divergence. Directives on European works councils, the information and consultation of workers on a national level, and worker involvement in the European Company all strengthen the European model of governance, founded on 'negotiated involvement'. The symbolic dimension of these directives, particularly the directive on employee involvement within European companies, should not be underestimated. By reminding European players, notably managers, of the foundations of the conception of the firm which prevails in Europe, this directive is capable of favouring European integration and social cohesion.

It therefore appears that convergence becomes ever stronger as we draw closer to the financial sphere, the spearhead of globalization. On the contrary, the institutions connected with labour relations, in other words the

Table 3.4　Principal transformations of the continental European model of governance

Domains	Main changes	Degree of convergence
Financial market law	Improvement of financial transparency: + + • EU: directives of 1988 and 2001 • France: 1996 law on the modernization of financial activities	+ +
	Centralization of market authorities: + + • Germany: BAWe (1998) followed by BAFin (FinDAG law, 2002) • France: AMF (financial security law, 2003)	
Corporate law	Rise in risk of litigation: + • France: NRE law (2001) • Germany: KonTrag law (1998)	+
	Blockholdings: 0 • France and Europe: stability and blockholdings • Germany: KonTrag law forbidding multiple voting rights and voting caps	0/+
Takeovers	XIIIth European directive: 0 France: NRE law: 0 Germany: law of 2001: −	0
Labour law	Directive on European works councils (1994) Directive on information / consultation of employees (2002) Directive on employee participation in European Companies (2002)	− −

Note: The '+' sign signifies that this field of governance contributes significantly to the convergence of the European model towards US standards. The '0' sign indicates stability. The '−' sign represents affirmation or divergence of the European model.

way in which internal company relations are conceived of and codified, act as a brake on convergence towards the US model or, alternatively, are no longer a factor of inertia, but a factor of divergence. Corporate law, which occupies a position in between these two spheres (financial and labour) is globally the most stable (Cioffi and Cohen, 2000). Lastly, the regulation of takeover bids, at the intersection of financial market law, corporate law and labour law, is marked by the contradictory evolutions specific to each of these corpora. It is therefore very difficult to pass a definitive judgement on the direction taken.

There is, however, one element which makes a significant contribution to the destabilization of the European model: the ideological domination of the Anglo-American world. The rise to power of US and British investment funds, the liberalization of European capital markets, and so on, are accompanied by the spread of a discourse or culture that is globally favourable to shareholder value. This redefinition of the conceptions underlying entrepreneurial activity, described by Boltanski and Chiapello (1999) as the 'advent of a new conception of the firm', constitutes one of the facets of shareholder power. There are several factors behind this domination, including the superiority of US expertise in accounting (see Chapter 5), the power of US audit firms (the Big Four), the attractiveness of the US university system and the country's macroeconomic performances of the last decade. The consequences are clear: national and international codes of good conduct are, to a large extent, champions of shareholder value and the agency model is omnipresent in scientific publications on corporate governance. On the scale of the European Union, the British influence reveals this disequilibrium: despite the fact that only two (the UK and Ireland) of the 15 EU countries (prior to 2004 enlargement to 25 countries) give no credence to the partnerial vision of the firm, this vision has failed to become established – as evinced by the Thirteenth Directive on takeovers, and the two Winter reports, the first on takeovers (see above), the second on corporate law (see Chapter 8).

The 'end of history' thesis of corporate governance, besides the fact that it adheres blindly to the doctrine of shareholder value, is the product of a faulty interpretation of globalization, according to which the model that appears to have dominated during a given period (the US model of the second half of the 1990s) is imposing itself on an international scale. On the contrary, we have demonstrated that globalization involves a process of confrontation of supra-national phenomena (in this case the integration of financial markets) with more local, continental, national or regional regulations. In this respect, the convergence of the European model of governance is far from established: although certain elements are indeed moving closer to the US model, factors of resistance, or even of divergence, are equally identifiable – particularly in the field of labour relations.

NOTES

1. The British model does display certain differences from the US model, but it also has some characteristics in common with the latter. As we are primarily interested in the

     evolution of France and Germany, we have chosen not to deal with the British model
in detail.

2.   For companies in the CAC40, which have more dispersed shareholdings than other
firms.

3.   For a similar approach, see Cioffi and Cohen (2000).

4.   This form of involvement contrasts with financial participation, which introduces a variable element in the payment of salaries, and 'managerial-type involvement', which covers
a group of organizational innovations aiming to increase the autonomy of employees
(see Rebérioux, 2003a).

5.   The state of Delaware is the runaway winner in this competition, as more than half of
the biggest US companies are registered there.

6.   This conclusion thus counters the thesis of La Porta *et al.* (see Box 3.1), who appraise
the protection of minority shareholders solely through corporate law (see Coffee, 2001,
note 7).

7.   Worker representatives may sit on these boards, but with no more than a consultative
role.

8.   The classic reference in this matter is the *Fruehauf-France* ruling of 22 May 1965.
However, Cozian *et al.* (1999) argue that the impact of this ruling should not be exaggerated, as it is relatively isolated and associated with very specific conditions.

9.   Fanto (1998) writes, in an article of reference in the Anglo-American world on the
French corporate governance system: 'chief executives in large French companies have
almost dictatorial power' (p. 53).

10.   For a similar conclusion in relation to the British case, see Armour *et al.* (2003).

11.   Germany, for example, strengthened the co-determination powers of the works council
(*Betriebsrat*) in a law passed in 2001.

12.   These operations can be carried out either using liquidities (takeover bids) or shares
(exchange offers).

13.   For a detailed analysis of the history and contents of this directive, see Beffa *et al.* (2003).

4. Corporate governance regimes

Chapter 2 presented a critique of the theoretical and normative foundations of shareholder value. We described the reasons for the difficulties generated by shareholder control over managers. This brought out the idea that the firm is a collective entity coordinating numerous different skills and functions that are very imperfectly contractualized. Because there are multiple interests vested in the firm, the search for a collective interest is essential for directing the coordination of its activities. The managerial firm necessarily possesses a centre of policy management. This is the seat of power, and it is subject to the influences of the interests connected with the firm through different types of incomplete contracts. A range of different governance regimes therefore exists, depending on the configuration of the interactions between the different interests vested in the firm.

In Chapter 3, we demonstrated that this diversity does indeed exist. The connection of interests in the firm is codified by three sources of law: financial market, corporate and labour. Their relative influence differs greatly between the United States and continental Europe. Any serious study must therefore distinguish between the rhetoric of shareholder value and the governance principles that are actually implemented by firms. It is the legal rules underlying these principles which give each country its dominant characteristics.

The extraordinary rise in stock market prices during the 1990s enriched shareholders enormously. However, finding a causal link between the concomitance of the stock market boom and the doctrine of shareholder value displays a surprising confusion. How can it be affirmed that the stock market rises because shareholders are imposing discipline on firms? We now know that the truth lies elsewhere. Company managers have exploited equity markets to obtain extravagant payments, completely disproportionate to the alignment of their interests with those of the shareholders. This has become strikingly apparent since the disorderly collapse of the markets. While the markets were rising, shareholders benefited, whether companies were well-managed or not. The inflow of capital was such that managers were able to indulge in an orgy of external growth operations, of doubtful economic rationality, with the blessing of shareholders.

The same question is raised by the other side of the coin. Is the enormous hole in private, defined contribution pension funds ($300 billion in the

United States, $100 billion in the UK) the result of corporate management in the interests of the shareholders? It may be in the interests of certain shareholders, in collusion with managers, and to the detriment of the majority of shareholders; it is certainly in the interest of the investment banks and financial consultants of all kinds. We must therefore put the ideology of shareholder value into proportion and take a serious look at the constellation of powers exerting their influence within and on firms.

To do so, we must consider corporate governance as a form of institutional mediation which participates in the orientation of managers' strategies. The present chapter therefore aims to create a bridge between the microeconomic foundations of corporate governance described in Chapter 2 and the financial reasoning presented in the following chapters, devoted to accounting, financial valuation and the dynamic interdependencies between finance and firms.

In the first section, we identify the different parties involved in the constellation of powers, which make the firm an organization endowed with a strategic aim. In the second section, we present a theoretical model to formalize this strategic aim within the field of constraints resulting from the constellation of powers. We then deduce a series of propositions concerning the influence of different financial logics on the accumulation of capital in firms. In the third section, we return to the pivotal role played by equity value in the development of innovation and in the allocation of income associated with the different poles of power.

FINANCIAL PLAYERS
AND TYPES OF GOVERNANCE

The rapid expansion of capital markets has strengthened the participation of players capable of exploiting the power of evaluation and the freedom of action resulting from greater market liquidity (Orléan, 1999). Asset management mobilizes a whole chain of intermediaries. Among these, investment banks play a predominant role. They intervene at critical points in the intermediation of the market. They bring together armies of financial analysts who are particularly active in the evaluation of merger/takeovers. They advise institutional investors and managers. They introduce firms onto the Stock Exchange and sell the issued shares through their investment networks. They are the main players in over-the-counter (OTC) derivatives markets.

These financial players did not enjoy so much influence in the financial systems of the 1960s and 1970s, in which there was a separation between credit and shares. The stock market had little importance in the valuation of firms. The control of free cash flow gave company managers considerable independence. Their external financial relations were protected by stable capital shareholdings. The strategies pursued by these controlling groups were only restrained by their indebtedness to the commercial banks.

This brings out the fact that there are several modes of control of firms (Albert, 1991). When the financial systems are hybrid, these modes can coexist, depending on the sectors in which the firms operate. It is therefore appropriate to identify the financial players involved in governance according to the modes of control they exert (Prowse, 1994).

Control by Debt

Control by debt is exerted when the solvency of firms is at stake. When the issue of equity capital in the form of shares is uncommon, commercial banks are pre-eminent. German capitalism and Japanese capitalism have nurtured governance regimes in which this form of control exerts great influence (Jackson, 2001).

However, control by debt is only one component of a system of governance. It only becomes predominant when the constraint of debt is active, thus giving banks the means and incentive to influence the decisions of company managers. When relations between the bank and the firm are passive, in the sense that they are long-term relationships guaranteeing regular financing, this maintains a system of governance in which the active pole lies elsewhere.

Thus the German post-war system displayed great stability and impressive longevity. The solidity of the ties between banks and industry was only one of the pillars. The other pillars were cross-shareholding and co-determination. Together, these measures protected firms from the pressures of capital markets. They rendered the existence of a takeover market impossible (Streeck, 2001).

Control of solvency is asymmetric, and this provides managers with a large degree of independence. They dispose of free cash flow once those entitled to a share of the value added have been paid. The allocation of free cash flow is the heart of strategic power.

Control of solvency depends on the evaluation of the credit risk, an area in which banks have made great strides. They analyse expected and unexpected risk separately. Expected risk is passed on to firms through the cost of credit. Unexpected risk forms the basis of the determination of the economic capital required of the banks by their supervisory bodies. The lower the quality of the credit, the higher the unexpected losses and the greater the required amount of economic capital. The increased level of expected losses is reflected in a higher risk premium.

Under these conditions, each bank determines a maximum credit supply linked to a marginal credit quality. It compares the rate of return on loans with the expected cost of deterioration in credit quality. These two variables are determined in the following way:

Rate of return on loans = rate of credit − cost of financing
− cost of constitution of economic capital

This rate of return forms a bell curve as a function of the deterioration in credit quality. It starts by increasing with the margin of interest and then decreases, because the rise in the cost of economic capital takes the lead with increased unexpected losses when the debtors are in high-risk credit categories.

Expected cost of deterioration in credit quality = risk-free rate of interest
+ risk premium

This cost grows continuously, following a convex curve as a function of the deterioration in credit quality. The marginal quality for the bank is such that:

Rate of return on loans = expected cost of deterioration in credit quality

For this marginal quality, there is a corresponding maximum rate of indebtedness imposed on debtor firms. The robustness of the control by debt, and therefore the ability of banks to prevent debtors from slipping into over-indebtedness, depends on the reliability of their evaluation of unexpected losses. Underestimation of these losses leads to excessive indebtedness, and consequently to the failure of control by debt.

Direct Control

Direct control can take one of three forms: internal control, state control and control by an arrangement of capitalistic alliances forming a majority shareholding group.

Internal control
Internal control corresponds most closely to the US model analysed in the famous work by Berle and Means published in 1932. The combination of dispersed stock ownership, a high rate of self-financing and a stock market oriented towards the liquidity of shares rather than the contribution of new financing has resulted in managerial self-governing. The interest of these

managerial groups lies in their entrenchment through the growth of the firm. This form of governance flourished in the United States after the Second World War. It was accompanied by a functional and operational form of managerial organization, which proved to be efficient in the delegation of responsibilities within highly complex, multi-divisional companies. The combination of a pyramidal hierarchy within each division, decentralized profit centres and centralized control over strategic decisions by higher management, proved to be effective in reinvesting profits. Nevertheless, it also provoked social segmentation between blue-collar workers, white-collar workers, technicians and executive officers, whose job security was guaranteed by regular growth.

One aspect of stable internal control, of management entrenchment, that appears paradoxical at first sight, is that managers had much less freedom to grant themselves extravagant payments and to generally misappropriate the cash flow of their companies than they enjoy under the control of shareholder value. In fact, the reason is simple. Managers were controlled by the technostructure of their companies. Managerial organization formed a pyramid of hierarchical grades with lines of communication running both top down and bottom up. This unwieldy structure allowed for no radical changes. Functions and responsibilities restricted each other. Salary structures were wedded to hierarchical position and only evolved slowly. Such structures resulted in high fixed costs. The common goal of the firm was the cohesion of the technostructure itself. It was tied to an operational objective of maximizing the growth of the firm, for this ensured the stability of relative incomes, the general growth in the incomes of all stakeholders and the absorption of the fixed costs of the technostructure (Chandler, 1962).

Majority control
State control was a characteristic of the French system of governance up until the end of the 1980s (Chabanas and Vergeau, 1996). Taken together, companies with autonomous management controlled 100 per cent by the state and companies in which the state possessed either majority control or a blocking minority formed a substantial proportion of the largest French industrial companies. The indirect influence of the state, through the mediation of the banking system, was even more important. At the height of its powers in 1982, the Treasury controlled virtually the whole flow of funds.

Control through an arrangement of capitalistic alliances is a standard model in Germany or Japan. The originality of post-war Germany was the association, within the governance system, of cross-shareholding, going back to the time of Bismarck, and co-determination, which endowed firms with a formal system of employee representation capable of influencing strategic decisions (Jürgens and Rupp, 2001).

Control by a majority shareholding may also originate in an old form of direct control (internal or state) to defend against the corrosive powers of minority shareholders. This was the case in France with the privatizations and the formation of 'hard cores' at the end of the 1980s (Morin, 2000). By privatizing state-owned companies, successive governments (of both the left and the right) adopted the following strategy: about 10 per cent of the shares were sold or given to employees, 15 per cent to foreign investors, 50 per cent in shares sold on the market and 25 per cent sold to major shareholders forming a hard core in the capital of the companies. These stable blocks were allocated through the medium of private investments (Goldstein, 1996).

According to Mayer (2001), the presence of majority shareholders capable of controlling the management by whatever process it comes about, is very widespread in modern capitalism. The concentration of ownership is a means of circumventing instability resulting from the free-rider problem, when there is both dispersed share ownership and an active stock market. The formation of majority shareholders has therefore been a conse-quence of the destabilization of the internal control of management under the impact of financial liberalization (Becht and Ailsa, 1999). Even if these shareholders have not been introduced through a political process with the deliberate aim of achieving stability, the share of capital they own restricts their ability to defect. A shareholder known to own a significant proportion of the capital of a company trying to sell a large number of shares in the company on the stock market would most likely trigger panic selling. The sale of shares by a shareholder reputed to be better informed than others may be interpreted as a sign of an unhealthy financial situation. The seller would cause the market to work against him or her. This type of shareholder is therefore necessarily more actively involved in governance than minority shareholders are.

Imposing the highest possible financial profitability on company man-agers in the form of a guaranteed return on capital is the mark of the power that these shareholders have acquired in governance (Morin, 2000). The connection of these financial returns with enticing payments for managers in the form of stock options creates a strategic alliance between the execu-tive officers and these favoured shareholders. Investment banks seal these alliances in their double role as shareholders themselves and as financial strategy consultants. We can therefore use the term 'controlling group' to characterize this type of governance.

Control by corporate governance charters
The commitments of institutional investors oriented towards long-term management take the form of contracts incorporating long-term guaran-tees for the beneficiaries. These are defined-benefit pension funds and life

insurance companies. Generally, they do not exert majority control over companies, and they do not participate in controlling groups. They prefer to keep their freedom of manoeuvre and to diversify their portfolios. However, their long-term aims lead them to try to enforce certain rules on firms (Coffee, 1991). These rules take the form of governance charters, which they draw up themselves or behind which they are the driving force. They may also intervene actively in general meetings to block initiatives by managers who do not respect the terms of the charter.

Governance charters are therefore consistent with a conception of control by voice without the shareholders involving themselves in the strategy of the firm. They are drafted to oblige managers to respect financial performance criteria, without taking part in the elaboration of the strategy intended to satisfy these criteria. They are constraints to be respected. They are expressed in terms of procedures to be followed rather than precise objectives to be attained: transparent communication, detailed explanation of prospective accounts, hypotheses of environment, organizational reforms, industrial choices, project horizons and transition costs. Based on such enriched informational content, institutional investors maintain their investments or reorganize their equity portfolios without any scruples about the firms in which they are shareholders (Baudru *et al.*, 2001).

Control by the Stock Market

Control by the stock market is a Janus. One face can be beneficial, when the market raises venture capital to finance innovation. The other is a particularly perverse form of the exercising of property rights, when hostile takeovers dismantle firms to realize capital gains.

In this type of control, the stock market plays a dual role. First, it supplies a permanent public valuation of firms. This valuation is the support for another category of transactions: the market for corporate control. Firms or sections of firms are treated as commodities (Bhide, 1993). They are bought and sold at prices different from the public stock market valuation through the exchange of blocks of shares for other shares or for liquidities obtained on credit. These operations are triggered on the initiative of potential controlling shareholders, rivals of the actual majority group in the firm.

The motives for takeovers are varied. It may be the desire to lay hands on the cash flows of companies that are well-managed, but located in sectors of relatively slow growth. It may be a pure effect of financial synergy on the initiative of investment banks to push up the value of the shares of companies acquired. By manipulating the sale of shares and by organizing the publicity of these operations, it is possible to exploit the credulity of stock market investors, even more so since asset managers are attracted by short-term returns. In this way, banks can combine lucrative commissions with capital gains on the shares they have kept on their own account, and which they will sell once the price has risen. In the best of cases, these mergers and takeovers represent investments in external growth. Takeovers are thus carried out at prices which reveal a private valuation of the future productive power of the firm acquired. In these cases, the initiative comes from the managers of the acquiring company, with the support, or at least the tacit approval, of its controlling group. Thus managers work on the hypothesis that once they have restructured the acquired company, its return will increase above the level currently predicted by the stock market (Gaughan, 1996).

This restructuring includes the carving up and sale of sections of the companies acquired. The consequences for employees often prove to be disastrous: layoffs, demotions, mismatches between the management structures of the two companies. Studies carried out by auditing firms show that more than half of mergers turn out to be industrial failures after a few years. This does not, however, prevent these auditing firms from being fervent champions of takeovers. They are among the beneficiaries of the financial godsend that these operations provide, to the detriment of shareholders when the stock market price subsequently falls.

This type of control produces very different governance from that of internal control or control by a stable group of majority shareholders (Blair, 1993). Its driving force is the instability, or threat of instability, created by the possibility of hostile takeovers. In this way, minority shareholders can indirectly bring pressure to bear on corporate executives in favour of the maximization of the stock market price. If companies judged by the investment banks to be undervalued are vulnerable to takeovers by corporate raiders or by other companies, the realization of this threat depends on the absence of shareholder loyalty. This is indeed the case for institutional proxy management shareholders, who have no attachment to the companies in which they invest. They exert a latent threat of exit in the event of a fall in the stock market price. Consequently, managers are led to re-orient the guiding lines of the company's development towards the objective of increasing the market value. One means of defence includes the use of cash flow to buy back shares from minority shareholders in order to reduce the dilution which makes them vulnerable. A second means of defence is the mobilization of company savings plans to encourage employee loyalty towards the incumbent managers. A third is the approval by the shareholders' meeting of rules of defence which reduce the chances of success of a hostile takeover bid by creating equity interests without voting rights (Beffa *et al.*, 2003).

Control by the stock market can only be observed in markets with high liquidity. Stock ownership must therefore be very wide and dispersed, and interested solely in the maximization of portfolios. The United States, where the ownership and control of companies are separated from the ownership and management of the financial wealth of households, presents an ideal environment. Waves of mergers have indeed been a characteristic trait of US capitalism since the 1870s. They accompany the large cycles of the stock market. Merger and takeover activity is particularly intense during the euphoria of peaks in the stock market cycle accompanying periods of intense innovation. The methods used are essentially share exchanges backed up by bonded debt issues. This activity also increases at the end of phases of depression in the stock market, but in a very different form. In this case, the motives are financial consolidation and the elimination of excess production capacity. As share prices are low, cash payments are used to finance these acquisitions. Companies with a liquid financial situation can absorb struggling victims (Bruck, 1988).

During the 1980s and 1990s, control by the stock market had a major impact on the structure of companies. Just as the technostructure of companies with internal control of management was cumbersome and impossible to split up, so that of companies frequently restructured by mergers and acquisitions was flexible. This is a horizontal structure in a modular network. It is composed of independent profit centres, consolidated by financial objectives and control of cash flow by a central office. Instead of managers entrenched in technostructures, this regime of governance creates and reinforces the power of a managerial elite. This elite moves within the circles of the biggest listed companies, investment banks, consulting firms and law firms. The source of their power is financial. It is the seizure of cash flow and its extraction from the company by means of different expedients: stock options, golden parachutes, preferential allocations of shares during mergers/takeovers.

These practices can easily slide into misappropriation during the realization of capital gains attached to external growth, and in collusion between senior managers and the princes of finance. This is an elite which has hijacked the doctrine of shareholder value and which manipulates dysfunctions in the capital markets to satisfy its desire for personal profit and its lust for the power of money. Such phenomena, analysed in detail in Chapter 8, are only possible when capital markets are highly imperfect.

FORMS OF CONTROL, CORPORATE STRATEGIES AND THE ACCUMULATION OF CAPITAL

Using the analysis of the main players' behaviour and modes of action in governance presented in the previous section, we can now define the regimes of corporate governance. These regimes combine different forms of control under one dominant characteristic. We have seen that control by debt as such cannot constitute a regime of governance on its own. Banks participate in all the regimes, but the role they play differs from one to another.

Three regimes can be distinguished. They coexist in one same country. However, in Chapter 2 we outlined a theory of governance in which the objectives of the firm depend on the influence of the groups of interest associated with it. In the present chapter, we propose to develop this theory further. Now, the influence of employees differs greatly depending on whether or not labour law codifies obligations for the firms, giving employees the right to information or responsibilities in the running of companies. Because these obligations derive from national law and favour one type of governance rather than another, we can observe dominant national characteristics. Furthermore, these characteristics may be strengthened by the heterogeneity of corporate law in different countries.

Given this, we can distinguish three types of governance regime. The first is internal control supported by the banks and constrained by debt. The entrenchment of managers through the internal growth of companies is the dominant strategy. The second is control by the formation of a majority shareholding group allied with the managers of the company and/or the presence of patient institutional investors. These institutional investors rely on governance charters. Majority shareholders exert their influence through the board of directors. The dominant strategy for these two categories of shareholder is the maximization of return on equity capital. The third type of regime is control by the stock market. The dominant strategy is maximization of market value, either to profit from external growth or to protect the company from the threat of hostile takeover bids. Table 4.1 summarizes these results.

The predominance of one of these regimes over the others depends essentially on the dominant financial logic. We must therefore study the influence of a change in the financial environment in a model which covers all three forms of control identified in Table 4.1 and described above.[1] Each player has his or her own objective and means of control over the firm. The performance of the firm is determined by the interdependencies between the strategy of the managerial team and the financial partners. Below, we discuss the economic significance of the structural equations of the model in relation to the preceding analyses, and we then draw conclusions from its solution. The whole model and its detailed solution are presented in a technical annex.

The firm has relations with the three types of financial agents indicated in Table 4.1: the banks, which are assumed to represent all credit markets; the controlling group of shareholders; and the shareholders and potential

Table 4.1   Corporate governance regimes

Forms of control	Internal and debt	Shareholding group	Stock market
Nature of control and basis of valuation	Solvent internal growth	Return on equity	Market value
Style of governance and constraints on the firm	Technostructure Long-term bank– company relations	Board of directors and/or charter Minimal constraint of financial profitability	Control market Threat of hostile takeover bids
Form of capitalism	Corporative	Patrimonial	Carnivorous

investors who are preoccupied by the dividend yield and the liquidity of their shares. The firm pursues its own objectives, which are those of its managers. The firm is not the agent of any principal. However, it takes into account the constraints imposed by the financial players. Its objectives are those which enable the managers to perpetuate their position and strengthen their power. The growth of the firm through the investment of its profit is the primary source of this power. Nonetheless, the threat of the market for corporate control obliges managers to concern themselves with their survival. This structure must now be formalized.

The Accumulation of Capital and the Use of Profit

Empirical observations confirm the analysis made above. The stock market is dedicated to the valuation of companies, the payment of shareholders and, possibly, the control of performances through mergers and takeovers. It makes no significant contribution to the financing of productive investment through the issuance of new shares (see Chapter 1, Table 1.2). Indeed, over the period 1982–2000, net share issues by private companies in the United States were negative. This was the period of the biggest ever stock market expansion. We therefore follow Mayer (2001) and Lazonick and O'Sullivan (1997) in affirming that, even in market-dominated financial systems, bank credit and self-financing are the almost exclusive sources of financing. In the model, which concerns all non-financial companies, we assume that there are no share issuances. Accumulation is financed by retained profits and by indebtedness to banks.

The strategic tool of managers is gross savings, which is the difference between gross profit on the one hand, and financial costs plus the dividends paid to shareholders on the other (tax is excluded from the model). The performance of the company from the point of view of the products and factors markets is the economic rate of return (ρ). This rate is the ratio of net profit to the stock of productive capital. It is exogenous in this model, which concentrates on financial decisions. As we shall demonstrate, these decisions influence growth through indebtedness, the distribution of dividends and, indirectly, the market value.

In the Annex, we demonstrate that on a path of stationary accumulation, the rate of accumulation (g) is a function of a leverage effect:

$$g = (\rho - Div - rd)\frac{1}{1-d} \tag{4.1}$$

The bracketed term on the right-hand side of the equation is the leverage factor. It is the difference between the economic rate of return and the weighted cost of capital. The latter is the sum of the rate of dividend distribution (Div) and the cost of indebtedness (r) weighted by the rate of indebtedness (d). The second term is the leverage ratio, an increasing function of the rate of indebtedness, which is the ratio of debt to productive assets.

This equation can be written:

$$g = r + (\rho - r - Div)\frac{1}{1-d} \tag{4.1'}$$

It can be noted that the distribution of dividends is a cost which weighs on the internal growth of the company. The relation between accumulation and the rate of indebtedness is more ambiguous. On the one hand, a rise in the leverage of indebtedness makes it possible to grow more through the contribution of additional financing. On the other hand, it increases the financial cost of capital. The positive effect is only greater when $Div < \rho - r$.

Therefore, it is in the interest of the company to indebt itself to the maximum level permitted by the lenders' risk management only if shareholder pressure is not too strong. The interdependency of financial constraints is clearly apparent.

The Dilemma of Indebtedness

There are circumstances in which indebtedness is the stake in a conflict of interests between banks and the controlling group of shareholders. Steady growth can only exist in the absence of this conflict.

Banks exert influence on the financial management of firms because they monitor their solvency. In this case, banks seek to evaluate and control the credit risk. Banks, subject to the general uncertainty of the economic cycle and the specific uncertainty of the companies to which they lend, only have imperfect information about the risk factors. Possessing a portfolio of loans to a number of companies, they adopt a strategy which consists in tolerating a level of loan losses which must not exceed a maximum probability of insolvency of borrowers (Π). Furthermore, they try to estimate, on the basis of past data and the information supplied by credit rating agencies, the parameters of the stochastic processes which drive credit events. This explains why we can acknowledge that the economic return on capital is a random variable of which the probability density f and the cumulative function F are estimated by the banks using their historic data bases or migration matrices supplied by credit rating agencies. Let $E(\rho)$ be the expected average return, then we obtain: $\rho = \varepsilon E(\rho)$ where ε is a random variable of unitary average.

By taking into account the maximum probable loss which banks do not want to see exceeding a residual probability, we demonstrate in the Annex that there exists a maximum rate of indebtedness acceptable to the banks:

$$d_{max} = \frac{1 + E(\rho)F^{-1}(\Pi)}{2 + r} \tag{4.2}$$

Let us now consider the point of view of the controlling group of shareholders, which is interested in the financial return on equity. Financial profitability (R or the return on equity) is connected with the economic return and the cost of indebtedness in the following way:

$$R = \rho + (\rho - r)\frac{d}{1 - d}.$$

The financial return is an increasing function of leverage. Therefore, if the shareholding group is capable of imposing a minimum financial return on equity that exceeds the rate of economic return, it *ipso facto* imposes a minimum rate of indebtedness.

$$d_{min} = \frac{R_{min} - E(\rho)}{R_{min} - r} \tag{4.3}$$

This rate of indebtedness is an increasing function of the financial return required and of the rate of interest on loans.

By juxtaposing (4.3) and (4.2), we can see that a growth regime can only exist if:

$$d_{min} \leq d \leq d_{max} \tag{4.4}$$

Now, the maximum rate of indebtedness imposed by the banks is a decreasing function of the rate of interest. The minimum rate of indebtedness required by the controlling shareholders, on the contrary, is an increasing function of the rate of interest. As d_{min} tends towards infinity when r tends towards R_{min} from rising levels, there necessarily exists a critical value r^* for which $d_{min} = d_{max}$.

This already gives us some idea of the tensions between the 'new economy', shareholder value and leverage. The destabilizing financial dynamic generated by these tensions is studied in Chapter 7, which deals with financial crises. The 'new economy' provoked optimistic expectations of the economic return on capital. A rise in $E(\rho)$ widens the range of viability of indebtedness by pushing down the threshold of insolvency. However, the interpretation of the 'new economy' made by the ideology of shareholder value has incited shareholders to impose an increased minimum return on equity (the famous 15 per cent). This financial requirement drives firms to increase their leverage, something which the banks are prepared to accept as long as the estimation of expected losses results in a rate of interest compatible with condition (4.4). The growth of indebtedness is consequently drifting higher and higher.

From the above, we can conclude that the determination of the interest rate plays a crucial role in resolving these tensions. We already know that the fall in interest rates in the second half of the 1990s was largely responsible for the speculative craze which boosted growth in corporate investment. Now, the rate of interest on loans has two components: the central bank, which determines the risk-free rate, and the banks, which determine the risk premium. Low interest rates may therefore result from monetary policy and/or the under-assessment of risk.

The calculation of the risk premium is presented in the Annex, where we demonstrate that two credit regimes are possible:

- A regime in which the constraints imposed by the banks are inactive: the rate of indebtedness sought by companies is lower than the rate determined by the banks. In this case, the risk premium is zero.
- A regime in which indebtedness is restricted by the banks. In this case, the risk premium is positive. It is an increasing function of the probability of company insolvency, as evaluated by the banks.

Consequently, if the probability evaluated by the banks is low, the leverage ratio can be very high. Now, the stock market provides an estimation of the value of companies. This is why the evaluation made by the banks is highly influenced by the stock market.

Market Value and the Takeover Market

Minority shareholders do not participate in the governing bodies of companies; they simply seek the best return on their investments. This return comprises dividend yields and capital gains or losses due to variations in the price of shares. These shareholders are therefore concerned with the judgement of the market, which influences share prices. They participate in this judgement by selling their shares when they are not satisfied. This judgement is encapsulated in Tobin's *q*, in other words the market value of companies as a ratio of the economic value of their productive assets.

In our model, all forms of profit distribution which contribute to the exit of cash flow from the company, and which influence share prices, are grouped together under the name of distributed dividends. This therefore includes stock options, which increase the dilution of capital when they are taken up, and the buying back of shares, which aims to compensate for this dilution. The distribution of dividends and their analogues has a negative effect on the growth of companies, and therefore on future profits. It follows that the personal interest of managers in extravagant payments weakens their control over the company as a group, in that the immoderate lure of personal gain represents pillage of net self-financing. However, the managers may argue that the threat of hostile takeover bids and opportunities for external growth oblige them to maximize the market value of their company.

The equilibrium price of the stock market in terms of Tobin's *q* is determined by a trade-off between the dividend yield and the return on debts in the same class of risk, as presented in equation (4.5):

$$q = \frac{Div}{r + p - g^a} \qquad (4.5)$$

where g^a is the expected rate of growth of future profits and p the risk premium on shares, which depends on the volatility of the stock market and the probability of company insolvency. Tobin's *q* also appears to be an increasing function of dividend distribution. This is in fact less obvious than it seems, as the dividend distribution has a negative effect on growth. We demonstrate in the Annex, however, that, under an independent condition of *Div* which guarantees that *q* remains finite and positive, share prices are indeed an increasing function of dividends.

The sensitivity of share prices to variations in dividend distribution depends on the market's evaluation of the expected growth of firms. We know that we need to take the interdependency of the participants into account, as this provokes a distortion in expectations compared with what would result from an unbiased rational expectation of the fundamental value. We can do so by writing the equation (4.6):

$$g^a = \beta g_{-1} + (1 - \beta)g \qquad (4.6)$$

where β lies between 0 and 1 and measures the degree of imperfection of the stock market. Uncertainty about the future growth of profits results in the interdependency of the expectations of the participants. This is coordinated around a focal point which represents a shared reference. We assume in (4.6) that this reference is the past growth in profits. Its incidence rises in direct proportion to β. Note (see Annex) that the sensitivity of share prices to variations in the rate of dividend distribution is lower when the expectation of future growth is higher.

We have demonstrated that market value exerts its influence on the strategies of managers through the medium of the takeover market. The threat of acquisition by a predator or the opportunity of being a predator oneself depends on the valuation of shares. In the model, we use a simple specification for the probability of being attacked by a hostile takeover bid. This is equation (4.7):

$$prob(TO) = e^{-aq} \qquad (4.7)$$

The probability of a takeover bid to the detriment of a company is a decreasing function of the share price of that company. The parameter a measures the virulence of the takeover market. When a tends towards infinity, the market does not exist – there are no hostile takeover bids. We have chosen a convex function to express the sensitivity of the probability of takeover bids to a fall in q for a given a.

Corporate Strategy and Lessons Drawn from the Model

The financial strategy of firms, defined by equations (4.1) through (4.7), is much more complex than a principal/agent relationship between managers and shareholders. In the absence of a control market, or even when this market is relatively inactive, managers are attached to the companies from which they draw their power. Maximizing the firm's growth is their natural objective. Managers seek to achieve this maximization under the constraints of indebtedness that are imposed by a controlling group of shareholders and, possibly, by banks.

When the takeover market is active, managers must ward off the danger of takeovers if they wish to survive. This objective, which consists in controlling market value, affects the quest for growth. To achieve this compound objective under the constraints described above, the managers have two means at their disposal: the rate of dividend distribution and the rate of indebtedness.

Ultimately, the financial strategy is expressed formally as follows:

$$\underset{Div,\, d}{Max}(ge^{-aq}) \tag{4.8}$$

under the constraints: $Div \geq 0$ and $d_{min} \leq d \leq d_{max}$.

In the Annex, we demonstrate that the constraint on dividends is never tight. Writing the first order conditions enables us to define two regimes of indebtedness: one is maximal and therefore restricted by the banks; the other is minimal and therefore imposed by the controlling group of shareholders. In each regime of indebtedness, dividend policy is determined by the maximization of the company's objective. The rate of the indebtedness/dividend pair enables us to calculate the equilibrium share price and the growth of companies.

Once the existence of the two possible optimal regimes has been demonstrated, obtaining a solution to the model consists in determining which regime the system is actually in, according to the exogenous parameters which designate the participation of the different players in the governance of the companies. These parameters are the average real return on productive capital and the probability distribution of this return, the minimum return on equity required by the majority shareholders, the rate of risk-free interest set by the central bank, the risk premium on shares and the degree of activity of the market for corporate control.

First, let us remember that balanced company growth is only possible within a range of viability of indebtedness which depends on the level of the interest rate on loans in relation to a critical threshold. A sudden change in monetary policy, such as the doubling of the interest rate in the United States between 1980 and 1982, creates a 'credit crunch' where companies unwind debt.

When a regime of balanced indebtedness can be sustained, the first order condition of the maximization of the objective (4.8) determines the optimal level of the dividend. Remember that an increase in the dividend reduces growth, but pushes up the market value and therefore reduces the probability of being subjected to a takeover. The optimal level of the rate of dividend distribution is such that the following equation is satisfied:

Marginal loss of utility for managers due to the reduction in growth
= Marginal gain of utility for managers due to their increased
chances of survival

This being the case, the regime of maximum indebtedness imposed by the banks is all the more likely when the takeover market is relatively inactive and stock market liquidity is high. Note that there is every chance of these two characteristics being contradictory. A liquid stock market favours the proxy management of share portfolios in terms of reallocations triggered by trade-offs on expected returns. The shareholders therefore become less attached to companies as the stock market becomes more liquid. They can be more easily attracted by takeover bids or exchange offers. On the other hand, the regime of maximum indebtedness is favoured by the drift of indebtedness caused by a concomitance between the yield requirements of the controlling group of shareholders and tolerance on the part of the banks through the underestimation of risk when they use market value as the basis for their estimation of the probability of insolvency.

The opposite results are valid for the regime of minimum indebtedness. As the presence of an active takeover market makes it more likely for this regime to appear, such a market strengthens the influence of majority shareholders. A corollary result is that the requirement of very high financial returns may cause companies to shift into the regime of maximum indebtedness, therefore constrained by the banks. It follows that banks preserve a very high degree of influence, even in a financial system driven by the logic of the market.

Finally, we can present the results of a local exploration of the model, when we marginally modify the exogenous parameters in each regime of indebtedness. In the two regimes, the rate of growth is all the higher when the takeover market is inactive and when stock market expectations are guided by the fundamental value, in other words when the obsession with liquidity does not predominate.

In the regime constrained by the majority shareholders, the impact on economic performance of an increase in the required financial return is ambiguous. In the regime constrained by the banks, the rate of growth is all the lower when the banks are more sensitive to the insolvency risk, when monetary policy is more restrictive and when the risk premium on shares is higher.

THE STOCK MARKET AS THE MAINSPRING OF GOVERNANCE

In the two preceding sections, we studied the effects of the development of stock markets on corporate governance. Nevertheless, the modelling of financial strategies cannot embrace the full diversity of situations in which the different sectors find themselves. The model, although highly complex, treats economic return on capital as an exogenous parameter. Yet the 'new economy' is essentially a phenomenon of innovation. It has given rise to an original form of financing through venture capitalism and the hi-tech shares market in the United States (the NASDAQ). This chapter therefore needs to be completed by a more detailed study of the multiple impacts of the stock market. This will enable us to demonstrate, in the following chapters, why the variety of capitalism in which growth is driven by the stock market is vulnerable to financial instability. The global financial cycle and control of companies by the stock market go together in this carnivorous capitalism.

We start by examining the US experience before presenting more general conclusions about the impact of the stock market.[2]

The 'New Economy' and Shareholder Value in the Euphoria of the 1990s in the United States

The innovations resulting from the marriage of information technologies and communication technologies have drastically changed systems of financing and the appropriation of rent from innovation. During the period after the Second World War, innovation was organized within the biggest companies, which controlled the whole chain: R&D laboratories, market prospection, development costs. The internalization of the externalities of innovation could be shared between two or more companies within joint subsidiaries, mixed public/private companies or more flexible agreements. In addition, military objectives involved the state in technological investment in aeronautics, space, electronics and chemistry.

The computer revolution in the service industries, followed by the opportunities of the Internet and the stock market bubble created a strange mixture for a completely different vision of innovation. In a new version of the American dream, two people with an idea and a garage can create a new worldwide company within the space of a few years under the magic wand of venture capitalism (Van Osnabrugge and Robinson, 2000). Microsoft, Cisco or Amazon, for example, have all fed this saga (Hirschey, 2001). The explosion of venture capitalism exceeded even the most optimistic predictions. Venture capital funds drained $56 billion in 1999, compared with $3 billion in 1990. How could such excesses come about?

It is true that the ideology of shareholder value spread throughout the United States without meeting any opposition. This ideology fits with the most deep-rooted beliefs of US society. The rapid rise to wealth of an individual without inheritance or past is held to be the highest form of success. Correlatively, bankruptcy is considered a normal event in the life of entrepreneurs. It represents a learning experience from which to bounce back. There is neither public disapproval nor financial discrimination against a bankrupt individual who wants to start up a new venture. The legal formalities required to create or liquidate companies are very simple. This social climate creates an abundant pool of entrepreneurs in which the desire to get rich quick meets the only means by which this can be achieved by those who do not wield power by inheritance or status: the stock market.

The high prices of shares, fed by the craze of investors, have upset the balance of power which used to exist in the governance regimes of established companies. The two processes responsible for this upheaval are payment in stock options and external growth.

In the 'old economy', stock options have resulted in the extremely fast growth of executive remunerations compared with the salaries of company employees. In the 'new economy', this form of remuneration has been used to recruit and keep top-level professionals. The distribution of stock options occurred on a wider scale, because the microcomputer revolution of the 1980s provoked the emergence of innovative start-ups and accelerated the mobility of scientists and engineers between different firms. The consequence was a dilution of shareholding. This had to be compensated for by share buy-back plans to encourage the continual rise in the market price of shares. Thus during the years 1997–2000 Microsoft only distributed $800 million in dividends, but bought back $12.4 billion in shares. During this time, R&D expenditure ran to $11.2 billion. These buy-backs were financed by incredible tax advantages ($11 billion in tax credits).

During the whole stock market boom, companies in the 'new economy' used the high values of their shares to acquire innovative capacities. These were located within specialized innovative companies which sold themselves to the highest bidder. Cisco Systems was the champion in external growth, becoming the leading world producer of network infrastructures. The four companies in competition in the optic network industry (CISCO, Nortel, Lucent and Alcatel) ran up a total of $109 billion in acquisitions between 1998 and 2000. Ninety-seven per cent of the value of these acquisitions was paid in the form of shares in the acquiring company. Under these conditions, it is easy to understand why increasing one's share price was the crucial means of establishing a company in a sector where the accumulation of skills is the decisive competitive weapon. It follows that stock market valuation became an integral part of technological competition. The issuance of new shares to obtain means of financing, on the contrary, played no role in these acquisitions. It was by pushing up the value of their existing shares that companies acquired the means to take over others, and thus to obtain crucial professional skills.

It is true, however, that the NASDAQ enabled capital increases and new stock exchange listings worth a total of $206 billion in 1999 and $233 billion in 2000, compared with $77 billion in 1995 and only $46 billion in 1991. The role of stock market speculation in these new share issues is undeniable. Between 1995 and 2000, a study conducted by Loughran and Ritter (2002) found 223 stock exchange listings of which the share price doubled on the day of entry, compared with 20 listings of this type for the whole period from 1975 to 1994. Stock market bubbles and share issues go together. This highlights the inefficiency of the stock market, which can be exploited by unscrupulous managers. The latter made instant wealth, while the companies themselves did not survive the turnaround of the market (Conyon and Murphy, 2000).

Nevertheless, these share issues were more than counterbalanced by share buy-backs. For private companies as a whole, net share issues were negative for every single year from 1994 to 2000. Debt represented the exclusive external means of financing, and for extravagant amounts. From 1995 to 1999, $5792 billion of bonded debts were issued by US companies to buy back shares and finance technological investment. To this figure must be added syndicated bank loans to finance mergers/takeovers: $530 billion were raised for this purpose in 1999, in other words 30 per cent of the total value of syndicated loans for that year. Three US banks (J.P. Morgan-Chase, Citibank and Bank of America) played the leading role.

Apart from these merger/takeover operations, syndicated loans were also actively used to finance the huge expenditure of telecommunications companies. Motivated by the absurd valuation of third generation patents, these loans are high-risk, as the companies are burdened by huge overcapacities. The crisis in this sector is worldwide, and the main lenders are European banks.

A First Appraisal of Corporate Control by the Stock Market

A virtuous circle can exist in an economy driven by the stock market on the condition that innovation is the major preoccupation. It must concern not only senior executives, but all managers and employees, universities and all the economic institutions of the state.

The United States presents an original model, which is far from being the only one. Thus Boyer (2004) shows that the Scandinavian countries have advanced to the forefront of innovation in information technologies, while preserving social welfare and a relatively fair income distribution. Nevertheless, the United States inspires fantasies throughout the world through its crushing hegemony over the media, which broadcast the culture of individualism.

The US model derives its dynamism from a source upstream from the companies themselves, by awakening the entrepreneurial vocations grafted onto different paths of life. There are university researchers who cross over into enterprise creation thanks to the bridges laid down by university offices of development. There are entrepreneurs who have already succeeded. Instead of retiring, they sell their companies and reinvest in new enterprises. Lastly, there are the executives of big companies fired in the financial game of mergers and takeovers.

On this fertile ground, the creation of innovative firms is perceived along the lines of a gardener's plan. Starting a new venture follows a process of sowing and germination of seeds in which the capital markets play no part. The characters that are essential at the beginning of the transformation of ideas into companies are the business angels. These are small groups of wealthy capitalists, often former entrepreneurs, who are organized into partnerships. They contribute the seed capital and above all the strategic skills lacking to the would-be entrepreneurs. The originality lies in their personal involvement in the affairs they deal with.

The next stage, when larger capital contributions are required to move into development and the start of marketing, brings venture capital funds into play. Created by hedge funds and mutual funds, they make private investments in companies that have not yet been listed on the stock exchange. It is only at a later stage that the few successful companies, among all those which have been created and which have quickly disappeared, enter onto the venture capital market (NASDAQ). The role of the NASDAQ is therefore essentially to enable venture capital funds to exit while making very high capital gains to compensate for their losses in failed ventures. Obviously, this presupposes that the market is globally buoyant. The origin of the virtuous circle resides in the fact that high yield shares are widely distributed in innovative firms, while at the same time they enhance the value of the savings of venture capital subscribers (Lazonick and O'Sullivan, 2000b).

The development of the virtuous circle, when it occurs, appears in the spread of innovation. By bringing new products onto the market and rapidly reducing their unit production costs, innovative companies are the source of an increase in income distributed to numerous economic agents. The governance regime in companies benefiting from the diffusion of innovation determines the distribution of the fall-out from innovation. It may be that the dramatic changes in the organization of companies that take on innovation will transfer the employees' gains to the shareholders, if the companies concerned move from internal control to control by the stock market. The employees will then suffer wage cuts or job losses, while the shareholders enjoy higher yields on their financial portfolios. These higher yields are partly the result of share buy-backs by company managers seeking to control the price of their shares. As we demonstrated theoretically in the second section, the objective of this strategy is to ward off the threat of a hostile takeover and acquire a sort of high-value currency of exchange for the purposes of external growth.

The whole process, supposed to be a virtuous circle as described above, depends entirely on the stock market valuation of companies. However, this valuation is speculative, as we demonstrate in Chapter 6. It is the result of a collective opinion formed by the interdependency of the judgements of those who participate in the market. What is essential here is to understand how the interaction of expectations can take into account a phenomenon as uncertain as innovation. If this interaction is expressed by a generalized craze manifesting unsustainable promises of future income, the regime of corporate control by the stock market is perverted by the speculative distortion of share prices. The exuberance of the market has real and disastrous consequences, which are brought on by the strategic decisions of companies tied to market value. The virtuous circle of innovation is transformed into a vicious circle of overinvestment and the undervaluation of risk.

It is in this way, according to Shiller (2000), that the use of stock options to remunerate managers incites them to push their share prices up by deliberately making risky investments in the activities most susceptible to stock market crazes. By buying back shares, they reinforce the excessive increases in equity prices in a way which disgorges the cash flow of their companies. They thus carry out real profit capture to their own benefit. Far from aligning their interests with those of the shareholders, managers in regimes of governance controlled by the stock market become the most voracious predators of their own companies. There is no need to go as far as the United States to find proof of this. The behaviour of the former management of Vivendi is a reminder that the lust for power, insatiable greed and economic adventurism transform capitalism into a nightmare for shareholders.

External growth is equally ambivalent. According to the credo of the champions of shareholder value, the use of shares as a currency of acquisition enables companies to accelerate the introduction of new technologies without being subject to liquidity constraints. It is therefore a vector of growth through innovation. However, if the prices paid for acquisitions through the exchange of shares are absurdly high in a context of unbridled stock market speculation, they destroy value for the shareholders. Prices that are out of all proportion to any reasonable valuation of fundamental value attract corporate raiders seeking immediate capital gains, rather than managers capable of integrating the productive capacities acquired within a stronger company. This is why the majority of mergers/takeovers carried out within a speculative climate result in economic disillusionment.

Finally, the turnaround of the stock market provokes a depreciation of the assets acquired at such excessive prices. The considerable capital losses which result from the deflation of asset prices burden the balance sheets of acquiring companies for many years. This financial deflation is an essential process in the fluctuations of capitalism driven by the financial markets. It provoked an economic depression that lasted several years after the market turnaround. Therefore, the analyses and judgements made on shareholder value are biased and very incomplete if they postulate perfect capital markets. Because modern capitalism gives a central role to stock markets, the study of their functioning and of their impact on financial systems is of primordial importance. Their influence weighs on the valuation of companies and even more heavily on the transformation of the very foundation of financial valuation: the principles of accounting.

ANNEX

The Accumulation of Capital

In this section the rate of growth is obtained as a function of financial decisions (indebtedness and dividend distribution), by using accounting equations. The gross savings of the company are defined by: $S_t = P_t - rD_t - DIV_t$, with P_t being gross profits, rD_t the debt service, and DIV_t the dividends paid. As investment is financed by bank debt or internal resources, net investment is: $K_{t+1} - K_t = I_t - \delta K_t = S_t + D_{t+1} - D_t - \delta K_t$, with δ the rate of capital stock depreciation.

By relating net profit to the capital stock, we can define $(P/K) - \delta = \rho = \alpha(Y/K) - \delta$ the rate of economic return, which depends on a parameter α of distribution, this distribution including the cost margin, the wage-profit share-out and indirect taxes. It also depends on the average productivity of capital and the rate of depreciation. ρ is assumed to be exogenous. Furthermore, we assume that the rate of economic return is higher than the interest rate, $\rho > r$.

We denote $Div = DIV/K$ the dividends paid per unit of capital, and $d = D/K$ the rate of indebtedness.

By relating net investment to the capital stock, we obtain a relation between the rate of accumulation of capital $g = (K_{t+1} - K_t)/K_t$ and the rate of indebtedness (equation 4A.1):

$$\frac{K_{t+1} - K_t}{K_t} = \rho_t + \frac{D_{t+1} - D_t(1+r)}{K_t} - Div_t$$

$$= \rho_t + (1+g)d_{t+1} - d_t(1+r) - Div_t. \qquad (4A.1)$$

The analysis will be restricted to regimes of stationary growth, for which the ratios are constant, $d_t = d_{t+1} = d$ and $(K_{t+1} - K_t)/K_t = (D_{t+1} - D_t)/D_t = g$.

By using (4A.1), the rate of growth, g is expressed by:

$$g = \frac{\rho - Div - r \cdot d}{1 - d}. \qquad (4A.2)$$

Therefore, the rate of growth is the product of the rate of profit (difference between economic return ρ and the weighted cost of capital $Div + rd$) and the leverage ratio $1/(1 - d)$. Equation (4A.2) shows that the distribution of dividends limits the rate of accumulation. A simple manipulation demonstrates that the effect of indebtedness depends on the level of dividends *Div*:

$$g = r + (\rho - r - Div)\frac{1}{1-d}$$

For *Div*<$\rho - r$, the leverage effect increases growth. For *Div*>$\rho - r$, the rate of accumulation is affected negatively by an increase in indebtedness. What is important is the total financial cost of capital, $r + Div$. The rate of indebtedness will therefore depend crucially on the behaviour of the financial players.

The Dilemmas of Indebtedness

The behaviour of banks

We assume that banks tolerate a maximum probability of insolvency on their portfolio of loans Π. This refers back to a threshold in the perception of risk. Consequently, the banks will be led to impose an upper limit on the indebtedness of their customers.

The rate of future economic return on productive capital is a random variable of average expected value $E(\rho)$. We write $\rho = \varepsilon E(\rho)$, where ε is a random variable of unit average, of which the probability density is f and the cumulative risk allocation function F. These functions are perceived by banks. We therefore posit that banks have uniform capacities of investigation to induce a common probability law on future returns from their monitoring of companies.

Under the hypothesis that equity capital can be used as collateral and liquidated for its balance sheet value, a debtor is declared insolvent when $(1+r)D>\rho K+(K-D)$. Dividing by K and rewriting the equation, we obtain $\rho \leq (2+r)d-1$, where $\varepsilon \leq \varepsilon_0$ with $\varepsilon_0 = ((2+r)d-1)/E(\rho)$.

Banks determine maximum tolerated indebtedness by accepting the maximum probability of insolvency Π on their portfolio of loans, $Pr\{\varepsilon \leq \varepsilon_0\} \leq \Pi$. By taking the reciprocal function of F, we obtain the upper limit d_{max}:

$$\varepsilon_0 = F^{-1}(\Pi) = \frac{(2+r)d_{max}-1}{E(\rho)}$$

hence

$$d_{max} = \frac{1 + E(\rho)F^{-1}(\Pi)}{2+r} \tag{4A.3}$$

Majority shareholders

The majority shareholders impose a minimum financial profitability in the form of a minimum return on equity (ROE):

$$R = \frac{P - \delta K - rD}{K - D} = \frac{\rho - rd}{1 - d} = \rho + (\rho - r)\frac{d}{1 - d}$$

By taking $\rho > r$, the financial return is an increasing function of the leverage of indebtedness. When shareholders are in a position to impose a minimum financial return greater than the rate of economic return, they impose a minimum leverage at the same time:

$$E(R) > R_{min} \text{ implies } \frac{d}{1 - d} \geq \frac{R_{min} - E(\rho)}{E(\rho) - r}$$

and therefore a minimum rate of indebtedness:

$$d_{min} = \frac{R_{min} - E(\rho)}{R_{min} - r}. \tag{4A.4}$$

A regime of steady growth can only exist when the equilibrium rate of indebtedness lies between two limits resulting from the two constraints which express the institutional layout of the powers of corporate control:

$$d_{min} \leq d \leq d_{max}.$$

We can observe that d_{max} is a decreasing function of r and that d_{min} is an increasing function of r. As d_{min} tends towards infinity for low values when r tends towards R_{min}, there exists a critical value r^* for which $d_{min} = d_{max}$. When $r > r^*$, there is no regime of growth which satisfies (4A.3) and (4A.4).

The risk premium and the monetary rates of interest

The interest rate r which comes into play in equations (4A.2) and (4A.3) is the credit interest rate. It is different from the monetary rate of interest i, controlled by the central bank, which is the marginal cost of bank liquidities. The risk premium $r - i$ is the result of bank behaviour and depends on the insolvency risk. We have seen above that for $\varepsilon > \varepsilon_0$, bank debtors are solvent and can service their debt at rate r. For $\varepsilon \leq \varepsilon_0$, they are insolvent and banks seize their disposable income and the sale of collateral for a total of $\rho + (1 - d)$ per unit of capital. Therefore, the interest rate on loans is such that:

$$1 + i = (1 + r)\int_{\varepsilon_0}^{\infty} f(\varepsilon)d\varepsilon + \int_{-\infty}^{\varepsilon_0}\left(\frac{\varepsilon E(\rho)}{d} + \frac{1 - d}{d}\right)f(\varepsilon)d\varepsilon.$$

If we take into account the value of ε_0 drawn from the constraint of solvency and if we write:

$$z = \int_{-\infty}^{\varepsilon_0} F(\varepsilon)d\varepsilon$$

then we can integrate by parts and obtain the relation:

$$r = i + \frac{zE(\rho)}{d}. \qquad (4A.5)$$

The risk premium is a decreasing function of the rate of indebtedness. It is an increasing function of the probable loss z on unserviced debt.

There are two possible situations, depending on whether or not the threshold is reached.

When the constraint of indebtedness is not reached, the rate of indebtedness only depends on the demand for credit expressed by companies. The interest rate on bank loans does not include any risk premium. In this case,

$$\begin{cases} r = i \\ d < d_{max} \end{cases}$$

When the constraint is active, banks ration credit, and the price includes a premium. In this case,

$$\begin{cases} r = i + z\dfrac{E(\rho)}{d} \\ d = d_{max} = \dfrac{1 + E(\rho)F^{-1}(\Pi)}{2 + r} \end{cases}$$

We can solve this system to determine the ratio of indebtedness and the bank interest rate on the basis of bank behaviour:

$$\begin{cases} r = i + zE(\rho)\dfrac{2 + i}{1 + E(\rho) \cdot (z - F^{-1}(\Pi))} \\ d = \dfrac{1 + E(\rho) \cdot [z - F^{-1}(\Pi)]}{2 + i} \end{cases}$$

Minority Shareholders and Stock Market Prices

The takeover market is the institutional mechanism through which minority shareholders collectively influence the behaviour of the company. This mechanism uses the threat of hostile takeovers and the resulting incentive for managers to push up the price of equities. We measure stock market valuation by Tobin's q, defined as the ratio of market value to the accounting value of capital. This valuation depends on the policy of dividend distribution and on market expectations about the growth of the company.

Expectations about the rate of growth have an adaptative component and a perfect component:

$$g^a = \beta g_{-1} + (1 - \beta)g \text{ with } \beta \in [0,1]. \tag{4A.6}$$

By denoting A_t the share price, and $N_t = N = 1$ the number of shares, $q_t = A_t N_t / K_t$. The equation of arbitrage on the stock market (with p the risk premium on equity) gives:

$$\frac{A_{t+1} - A_t}{A_t} + \frac{DIV_t}{A_t} = r + p.$$

On a path of stationary growth, dividends follow the rate of accumulation of the firm, because there are no new share issues: $DIV_t = DIV_0(1 + g)^t$. At each moment, the share price is in accordance with its fundamental value:

$$A_t = \frac{DIV_t}{r + p - g^a}$$

Similar equations determine Tobin's q:

$$\frac{\Delta q_{t+1}}{q_t} + g + \frac{1}{q_t} \frac{DIV_t}{K_t} = r + p$$

because:

$$\frac{\Delta q_{t+1}}{q_t} = \frac{\Delta A_{t+1}}{A_t} - \frac{\Delta K_{t+1}}{K_t} \text{ (in the first order)}.$$

The equilibrium value of q is therefore:

$$q = \frac{Div}{r + p - g^a} \tag{4A.7}$$

This equation (Gordon-Shapiro) only has economic significance when the rate of growth is lower than the discount rate of future dividends: $g < r + p$ (otherwise, Tobin's q takes an infinite value). By using equation (4A.2), we can demonstrate that this condition is satisfied for all values of dividends if and only if: $r + p(1 - d) > p$. To exclude an infinite value of q, we make the following assumption:

$$r - p + p(1 - d_{min}) > 0 \tag{4A.A1}$$

Equation (4A.7) demonstrates that q is an increasing function of the rate of accumulation and, at first sight, the dividend policy. However, a more active policy of dividend distribution slows down the accumulation of capital (equation (4A.2)). The overall effect of dividends on the valuation of assets must therefore be looked into in more detail. Let us measure the effect on q of a permanent modification of the dividend policy:

$$\frac{dq}{dDiv} = \frac{\partial q}{\partial Div} + \frac{\partial g^a}{\partial Div}\frac{\partial q}{\partial g} = \frac{1}{r+p-g} + (1-\beta)\left(-\frac{1}{1-d}\right)\frac{Div}{(r+p-g)^2}$$

$$\frac{dq}{dDiv} = \frac{1}{r+p-g}\left(1 - \frac{(1-\beta)Div}{(1-d)(r+p-g)}\right)$$

$$= \frac{1-d}{r-\rho+p(1-d)+Div}\left(1 - \frac{(1-\beta)Div}{r-\rho+p(1-d)+Div}\right)$$

$$\frac{dq}{dDiv} = \frac{(1-d)(r-\rho+p(1-d)+\beta Div)}{(r-\rho+p(1-d)+Div)^2} . \tag{4A.8}$$

By using (4A.A1), we can see that $dq/dDiv > 0$. A reduction in dividends reduces the market valuation, for the direct effect of dividend distribution dominates the indirect effect on expected growth. Note that the more perfect expectations are ($\beta \to 0$), the more the negative effect of dividends on growth is predicted correctly, which is expressed by a greater fall in market value ($dq/dDiv$ decreases with β).

The threat of takeovers can be formalized as a probability that decreases as q increases: $1 - \phi(q) = prob(TO)$ with $\phi' > 0$. The convexity (form) of $\phi(.)$ determines the force with which the takeover market constrains corporate decisions through the threat of hostile takeover. We take the following specification:

$$\phi(q) = 1 - e^{-aq}. \tag{4A.9}$$

The coefficient a measures the strength of the takeover market. When $a \to \infty$, there is no takeover market ($prob(TO) \to 0$ for all positive values of q); conversely, $a \to 0$ corresponds to a very active takeover market.

The Programme of the Company

In this complex environment, the firm interacts with several groups (majority shareholders, minority shareholders and banks) with claims on its strategic resources through the mediation of the credit market and the stock market, which supports the takeover market. The interests of these stakeholders determine a set of constraints that must be taken into account in the strategies of the managers.

In the absence of a takeover market, managers are more attached to their companies. It is reasonable to believe that their objective will be a natural long-term one of maximizing the rate of growth. When a control market does exist, however, the managers will remain in the company as long as no successful takeover bid occurs. Their objective is therefore to maximize long-term growth adjusted by the probability of remaining in the managerial team. We formalize this by $max_{Div,d}\ g\phi(q)$, with $\phi(q)$ the probability of survival (from the managers' point of view). Their financial decision (dividend ratio Div and debt ratio d) is constrained by the behaviour of banks and majority shareholders through the constraint on feasible indebtedness, $d_{min} \le d \le d_{max}$. Naturally, $Div \ge 0$ is also a constraint.

The firm seeks to solve the programme of optimization under constraints:

$$\max_{Div,\,d} g\phi(q) \text{ under the constraints}$$

$$d_{min} \le d \le d_{max}$$

$$Div \ge 0$$

$$\text{with } g = \frac{\rho - Div - rd}{1 - d} \text{ and } q = \frac{Div}{r + \rho - g}.$$

Accumulation is only possible when $\rho - Div - rd > 0$. Under this condition, the constraint on dividends is not tight (otherwise, q would be zero, and the probability of a takeover equal to 1). The Lagrangian can therefore be written keeping only the constraints on indebtedness:

$$L = g\phi(q) - \mu_1(d_{min} - d) - \mu_2(d - d_{max}).$$

The first order conditions are written:

$$\begin{cases} \dfrac{\partial L}{\partial d} = \dfrac{\partial g}{\partial d}\phi(q) + g\phi'(q)\dfrac{\partial q}{\partial g}\dfrac{\partial g^a}{\partial d} + \mu_1 - \mu_2 = 0 \\[2mm] \dfrac{\partial L}{\partial Div} = \dfrac{\partial g}{\partial Div}\phi(q) + g\phi'(q)\left[\dfrac{\partial q}{\partial Div} + \dfrac{\partial q}{\partial g}\dfrac{\partial g^a}{\partial Div}\right] = 0 \end{cases}$$

which gives

$$\text{(FOC 1)} \qquad \frac{\partial g}{\partial d}\phi'(q)\left[\frac{\phi(q)}{\phi'(q)} + (1 - \beta)g\frac{\partial q}{\partial g}\right] + \mu_1 - \mu_2 = 0$$

(FOC 2) $\quad \dfrac{\partial g}{\partial Div}\phi'(q)\left[\dfrac{\partial g}{\partial Div}\dfrac{\phi(q)}{\phi'(q)}+g\left(\dfrac{\partial q}{\partial Div}+(1-\beta)\dfrac{\partial g}{\partial Div}\dfrac{\partial q}{\partial g}\right)\right]=0$

with the signs: $\dfrac{\phi(q)}{\phi'(q)}>0, \dfrac{\partial q}{\partial g}>0, \dfrac{\partial g}{\partial Div}<0, \dfrac{\partial q}{\partial Div}>0.$

By examining the first order conditions on d (FOC 1), we can see that $d=d_{max}$ if $Div<\rho-r$, $d=d_{min}$ if $Div>\rho-r$ and can take any value in the interval for $Div=\rho-r$. The choice of indebtedness d affects the market valuation q through the expected rate of growth. Therefore, the decision concerning indebtedness does not lead to any trade-offs between growth and market valuation. The optimum debt ratio depends on the equilibrium level of dividends.

The first order condition on dividends (FOC 2) can be rewritten:

(FOC 2′) $\quad \dfrac{\partial g}{\partial Div}\phi(q)+g\dfrac{dq}{dDiv}\phi'(q)=0.$

This equates the marginal loss due to the fall in the rate of growth $(-(\partial g/\partial Div)\phi(q))$ with the marginal gain of a greater probability of survival $(g\phi'(q)(dq/dDiv))$. By using (4A.8) and (4A.9), this equation can be transformed to give (equation (4A.10)):

$$\frac{e^{aq}-1}{a}=(\rho-Div-rd)(1-d)\frac{r-\rho+p(1-d)+\beta Div}{[r-\rho+p(1-d)+Div]^2} \quad (4A.10)$$

with q being a function of dividends given by (equation (4A.11)):

$$q=\frac{Div}{r+p-g}=\frac{Div}{r+p-\dfrac{\rho-Div-rd}{1-d}}=(1-d)\frac{Div}{r-\rho+p(1-d)+Div}$$

$$(4A.11)$$

We denote LHS(Div) the left-hand side of (4A.10), and RHS(Div) the right-hand side of the equation, as a function of Div. LHS(.), being an increasing function of q, increases with Div. In addition, for the threshold value $Div=\rho-r$, we can calculate $g=r$ and $q=(\rho-r)/p$, and therefore LHS($\rho-r$) is independent of d. RHS(.) is a decreasing function of Div. However, the value at the threshold point depends on d:

$$RHS(\rho-r)=\frac{r}{p^2}[(\beta-1)(\rho-r)+p(1-d)].$$

By using (4A.11), RHS(.) can be rewritten in the form:

RHS(Div)

$$= \frac{\rho - Div - rd}{r - \rho + p(1 - d) + Div} (1 - d) \frac{r - \rho + p(1 - d) + \beta Div}{r - \rho + p(1 - d) + Div}$$

$$= \left[\frac{(1 - d)(r + p)}{r - \rho + p(1 - d) + Div} - 1 \right] \frac{q}{Div} (r - \rho + p(1 - d) + \beta Div)$$

$$= \left[(r + p) \frac{q}{Div} - 1 \right] \frac{q}{Div} (r - \rho + p(1 - d) + \beta Div)$$

Figure 4.1 represents the objective of the firm (above) and the two sides of the first order condition (4A.10) (below) as a function of Div. We can verify that the objective of the managerial team is continuous, and that the programme is piecewise convex.

There are at the most three local extrema. When it exists, the interior solution $d_{min} < d < d_{max}$ at (4A.10) is a local minimum. For this value, $\partial g / \partial d = 0$ or $Div = \rho - r$. We then have $q = (\rho - r)/p$ with $r = i$. The debt ratio determined by condition (4A.10) is d^{int}:

$$d^{int} = 1 - \left(\frac{p}{i} \frac{e^{\frac{a(\rho - i)}{p}} - 1}{a} + (1 - \beta) \frac{\rho - i}{p} \right).$$

For $d_{min} < d^{int} < d_{max}$, there are two local maxima, one for $d = d_{min}$ and one for $d = d_{max}$. The global maximum depends on the parameters. For each local maximum, the dividend policy is a solution of (4A.10), with $d = d_{min}$ or $d = d_{max}$ respectively. Therefore, it is not possible to determine the optimal situation analytically. Nevertheless, it does give us an overall view of the type of regime we are dealing with.

A Global Study

In this section, we seek to determine the type of regime, maximum or minimum indebtedness, according to the behaviour of the different agents. We shall use a global study to do this, following the existence of the local maxima described above. If the evolution of one parameter causes one of the equilibria to disappear, we can deduce that a threshold exists for this parameter (depending on the other parameters, of course), which causes the regime to change.

$$d_{min} < d^{int} < d_{max} \text{ is equivalent to}$$

$$1 - \frac{\rho - i}{R_{min} - i} < d^{int} < 1 - \frac{1 + i - E(\rho)F^{-1}(\Pi)}{2 + i},$$

in other words, by using expressions (4A.3) and (4A.4) and by rearranging:

$$\frac{1 + i - E(\rho)F^{-1}(\Pi)}{2 + i} < \frac{p}{i} \frac{e^{\frac{a(\rho - i)}{p}} - 1}{a} + (1 - \beta)\frac{\rho - i}{p} < \frac{\rho - i}{R_{min} - i}.$$

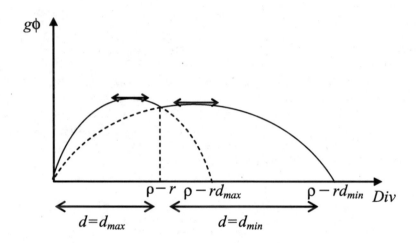

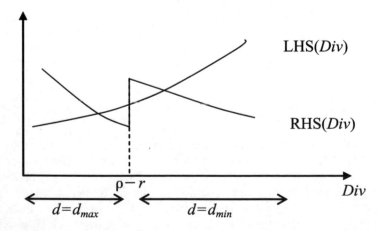

Figure 4.1   Equilibrium of the firm

For $d^{int} < d_{min}$, the only local maximum is the regime of maximum indebtedness. The choice of indebtedness is constrained by bank behaviour, $d = d_{max}$. A sufficient condition is:

$$\frac{p}{i} \frac{e^{\frac{a(\rho-i)}{p}} - 1}{a} + (1-\beta)\frac{\rho-i}{p} > \frac{\rho-i}{R_{min}-i}.$$

This regime constrained by the banks is all the more probable when

- a is high;
- β is low;
- R_{min} is high. An increase in d_{min} following a rise in the ROE requirements can cause a shift into a regime of maximum indebtedness constrained by the banks;
- Π is high (the banks accept higher risks);
- r is low;
- p is high (result of simulations).

For $d^{int} > d_{max}$, only the regime of minimum indebtedness is possible, $d = d_{min}$. Indebtedness is constrained by the behaviour of the majority shareholders. A sufficient condition is:

$$\frac{1 + i - E(\rho)F^{-1}(\Pi)}{2+i} > \frac{p}{i}\frac{e^{\frac{a(\rho-i)}{p}} - 1}{a} + (1-\beta)\frac{\rho-i}{p}.$$

This regime, constrained by the majority shareholders, is all the more probable when:

- a is low. An active takeover market reinforces the influence of the majority shareholders;
- β is high;
- R_{min} is low. ROE requirements which increase can cause a shift into a regime constrained by the banks;
- Π is low. A fall in d_{max}, through a rise in the threshold Π, can cause a shift into the regime of minimum indebtedness;
- r is high;
- p is low (simulation).

A Local Study

How can we characterize the effect of a variation in parameters inside each regime? For each regime, we analyse how the performance of the corporate sector, that is to say the rate of growth g and market valuation q, changes with the exogenous parameters (a, β, i, Π, R_{min}). The results are obtained by differential analysis or quantitative simulation.[3] Figure 4.2 illustrates the effect on equilibrium of some parameters. A rise

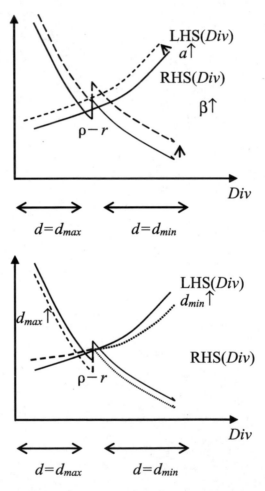

Figure 4.2   The effect of some parameters on the rate of accumulation and on the stock valuation of the firm

in *a* moves LHS upwards: as the control market is less active, a marginal increase in the probability of survival can be obtained with a lower market valuation. This therefore reduces *Div*, whatever the regime. *Ceteris paribus*, this can cause a shift to the regime constrained by banks. An increase in β moves RHS upwards. The less the negative effect on growth of the dividend policy is expected, the more the firm must distribute in dividends. More adaptative expectations favour the regime of minimum indebtedness.

Maximum Indebtedness: $d = d_{min}$

Div^* is a solution to equation (4A.10) with maximum indebtedness, *r* and d_{max} by the constraint of solvency by which the banks determine the credit supply and the risk premium:

$$\begin{cases} r = i + zE(\rho)\,\dfrac{2 + i}{1 + E(\rho) \cdot (z - F^{-1}(\Pi))} \\ d = \dfrac{1 + E(\rho) \cdot [z - F^{-1}(\Pi)]}{2 + i} \end{cases}$$

After the above analysis, $\partial Div^*/\partial a < 0$ and $\partial Div^*/\partial \beta > 0$. By using (4A.2) and (4A.11), we obtain the corresponding effects on the rate of accumulation and the market valuation:

$$\frac{\partial g^*}{\partial a} > 0 \qquad \frac{\partial q^*}{\partial a} > 0 \qquad \frac{\partial g^*}{\partial \beta} < 0 \qquad \frac{\partial q^*}{\partial \beta} > 0.$$

The simulations carried out suggest that $\partial Div^*/\partial p > 0$, and therefore $\partial g^*/\partial p < 0$.

An independent increase in d_{max}, through a greater degree of risk-taking by the banks Π, reduces dividends. The leverage effect and the reduction in dividends combine to increase the rate of growth. The effect on *q* is ambiguous.

Monetary policy has an ambiguous impact on dividend distribution (positive for low *i*, negative for high *i*), but in the simulations carried out, a rise in *i* had a negative effect on real and stock market performances ($\partial g^*/\partial i < 0$; $\partial q^*/\partial i < 0$).

Minimum Indebtedness: $d = d_{min}$

Div^* is determined by (4A.10) with $d = d_{min}$. The banks do not ration credit, and the debt ratio is determined by the ROE requirements of the majority shareholders:

$$\begin{cases} r = i \\ \\ d_{min} = \dfrac{R_{min} - E(\rho)}{R_{min} - i} \end{cases}$$

The impact of a, p and β is identical to the previous case $d = d_{max}$. Π has no influence (as long as we do not shift into the other regime). The influence of ROE requirements on dividends is ambiguous. Remember that a rise in R_{min} can cause a shift to the regime of maximum indebtedness. ($sgn(\partial Div / \partial R_{min}) = sgn(\partial Div / \partial d_{min})$) can be positive or negative. In this regime, the rate of growth decreases with indebtedness d and with dividend distribution Div. The effect on g should therefore be negative, but it can be positive following an increase in ROE requirements. The effect on q is ambiguous. The effect of monetary policy is also ambiguous.

NOTES

1. The model developed here was created by Michel Aglietta and Régis Breton in the research report for the *Commissariat Général du Plan*, directed by Michel Aglietta and entitled, *Régimes de Gouvernement d'entreprise: différences nationales et stratégies d'entreprise* (Corporate Governance Regimes: National Differences and Corporate Strategies), September 2001.
2. This section is largely drawn from the contribution of William Lazonick and Mary O'Sullivan to the research report for the *Commissariat Général du Plan: Régimes de Gouvernement d'entreprise: différences nationales et stratégies d'entreprise* cited in Note 1.
3. The details concerning the values of the parameters and the results of simulations can be obtained from the authors.

5. Accounting, finance and the firm

The preceding chapters focused on the question of corporate governance, that is to say, the power structures of listed companies. The rise to power of financial markets expresses itself in the opening up of these structures to a shareholder logic: the development of stock options and instruments for the measurement of shareholder value, the liberalization of the takeover market, institutional activism, emphasis on the independence of administrators, and so on. From a theoretical viewpoint, governance appears as the central mediation channel between firms and financial markets. We turn our attention next to a second mediation: corporate accounting. As a first-order cognitive resource on the activities of firms, accounting is essential to financial market information, which is interested in forecasting future corporate performance. Interactions play equally in the other direction: what happens in capital markets can influence the accounting representation of the company.

If the technicality of debates on governance often causes the importance of the underlying issues (definition of the company, capital–work relationship, etc.) to be lost from view, this is even truer of accounting. The adoption of one particular accounting language over another is the adoption of a corporate representation: the nature of the information that is produced about an activity depends very largely on the idea one has or wishes to convey of this activity. Thus in a complex syntax, which too often makes the theme accessible only to experts, there are hidden essential questions standing at the core of our work: What interests should a company serve? What is the place of the different stakeholders? What constitutes a performing company?

This chapter offers an analysis of the role played by accounting in the regulation of financial capitalism. We adopt first a theoretical point of view, seeking to highlight the importance of the accounting question. The following two sections are specifically devoted to the question of fair value. The success of this accounting valuation method is a marker of the process of financialization; its selection by the European Union is from this viewpoint open to criticism. The next section presents the broad features of the principle of fair value, and the one after provides a critical analysis of this principle. In the conclusion of the chapter, it will become apparent that the process of accounting standardization favours at the global level the penetration of enterprises by the logic of finance.

COMPANIES AND ACCOUNTING: THEORETICAL ELEMENTS

What is accounting? In its simplest terms, accounting can be defined as an instrument for recording and monitoring the activity of a particular entity – the company. This instrument has a performative character (Cartelier, 2004). A company's performance does not exist preview in any intelligible form until its accounts are made public.

In light of this definition of accounting, the following question arises immediately: what is a company? We have already answered this question (see Chapter 2). It involves an autonomous entity in which the activity of a number of stakeholders is coordinated. Beyond accounting, the quality of this coordination is sanctioned or validated by the market and consumer demand for the product or service provided. This productive logic is irreducible to a market exchange: intra-corporate coordination has a particular temporal dimension, unlike market allocation. The latter is by definition discrete. The notion of a 'going concern' is often used to reflect the temporalization of the activity specific to a company (see for example Commons, 1934). According to this view, the rationale of accounting is to take stock of the 'revenue' ('earnings' in accounting terminology, 'profits' in economic terminology) generated by an activity over a particular period, defined by convention. Accounting should establish the wealth and financial state of the going concern. To this end, two reporting documents are drawn up. The earnings statement records the products and the costs for the period, that is, any commitments which one considers to be linked to this period alone. For its part, the balance sheet rests on the matching of assets and liabilities. Assets are defined as the total of tangible, intangible and financial capital that has served as the substrate of the productive activity. Liabilities are made up of the total resources necessary to finance this capital. These resources are classified according to whether they come from equity capital or debt capital. Undistributed earnings from the period are added.

Two Approaches: Dynamic versus Static

Questions about asset and liability valuation and the way in which this valuation weighs on corporate performance (earnings) are evidently central for accounting. Referring to the work of Richard (Richard, 1996, 2002; Colette and Richard, 2000) and Biondi (2003), and following terminology introduced by the German theoretician Schmalenbach (1926), one can distinguish two broad types of response to valuation questions, instituting two polar accounting approaches. Since the construction of the first accounting systems regulated by law, in France in 1673 and in Germany (Prussia) in 1794, Western countries have oscillated, depending on the period, between these two approaches in their process of accounting standardization. This binary typology will be very useful for understanding current developments.

The first approach might be termed 'dynamic'. This conception of valuation endorses the specificity of intra-corporate coordination relative to market coordination.[1] The coordination specific to an enterprise mobilizes capital internally, that is, its assets, in order to create value via the launch of a product or service into the market. These assets result from past investments; they are the counterparty of expenditures linked to the acquisition of specific elements to ensure the temporal running of the company's commercial productive activity. *A contrario*, the costs are non-invested (or non-capitalized) expenditures, that is, they lack a dynamic dimension. The fundamental intuition of the dynamic approach is the idea that the capitalized elements (assets) have value not in themselves, but only insofar as they contribute to the company's activity. Their value cannot depend on elements external to the company, for example, their exchange value (market price). Hence it is logical to recognize these assets at their cost of entry[2] and to keep this valuation in the course of subsequent inventories, taking account nevertheless of their progressive wear and tear entailed by their use in production and commercialization. Asset valuation is at entry (so-called historical) cost with depreciation. In other words, once integrated in an entity, physical, intangible and financial capital will not vary except for reasons linked strictly to the activity to which they contribute (and these are mainly depreciations), but never for reasons external to this activity.

Here can be seen the logical foundations of the 'method of historical cost', as it is called by US and UK accountants. This method is not a technical choice: it is rooted in a particular vision of the company, which corresponds, in its broad lines, to the conception that we developed in Chapter 2.

The 'static' approach to accounting stands in opposition to the dynamic approach, which conforms to the method of historical cost. In the terminology of Colette and Richard (2000), the aim of static accounting is 'to measure the liquid value of a company's assets in order to verify the capacity of that company to repay its liabilities immediately' (p. 168, our translation). Thus accounting is put at the service of the company's creditors. As a theory of the firm, the static approach holds that companies are instruments for the valorization of creditor wealth rather than partially autonomous collective entities.

The consequences of this vision of the firm and of its accounting on asset valuation are immediate: assets are valued not so much for their contribution to intra-corporate coordination, as for their disposable value with its ability to guarantee the repayment of all debts at any precise moment. The value of a good envisaged in this way is nothing more than its market price, that is to say, the amount in accounting units resulting from its potential exchange. At each inventory, the balance sheet assets must be valued at their market value and not at their entry cost. Depreciations are recognized as costs and hence lower the earnings statement. *A contrario*, appreciations are recognized as profit and increase earnings. The term 'static' refers to this importance of market value in asset valuation, flowing from the desire for maximal creditor protection.

The choice of a static approach can equally also be felt in the definition (and not just the valuation) of assets. In fact, any elements which have only slight market value by reason of their specificity to the company cannot be considered assets at all: their disposal will not help to cover debts, which constitutes the criterion of ultimate judgement in the static approach. As a consequence, the application of this approach induces a certain reservation regarding the capitalization of expenses. The costs incurred in creating a brand or developing research in a field of activity are not capitalized and pass directly through as expenses in the accounting period, contrary to their definition in dynamic accounting.

The Empirical Diversity of Accounting Models

At the empirical level, observation of accounting systems as they emerge at the end of the accounting standardization processes undertaken in national territories reveals their diversity. This diversity results from the relative influence of dynamic and static approaches in each system. More recent trends will be studied in the next section.

The second half of the twentieth century saw the domination of the dynamic vision in France, the United States and the UK. The method of historical cost was very widely adopted as the principle of asset valuation. At the same time, expense activation remained fairly generous.

It would be an error, however, to analyse these systems as pure applications of the dynamic conception, since deviations from the principle of historical cost were systematic. Thus, whenever it became clear that some assets had become devalued on the market, companies could be invited to make provisions for depreciation, which would lower earnings by the same token. In this way, capital losses were recognized, contradicting a purely dynamic vision. On the other hand, potential capital gains were ignored, in accordance with what one might call the 'prudential principle'. If we take the case of France, this prudential twist to the dynamic dogma concerned essentially the value of financial assets kept for obvious disposal purposes, in the hope of realizing a capital gain. The fixed assets involved, both tangible and intangible, were by contrast not numerous and mainly concerned lands and goodwill.

In Germany, it is currently admitted that accounting is anchored in a valuation concept that is more static than dynamic (see for example Richard, 2002). The German accounting system is concerned with the best possible protection for creditors. Hence the penetration of market value is greater, and the policy regarding the capitalization of expenses is more conservative. Here again, one can observe a sizable twist to the dominant (static) dogma: potential capital gains are not recognized. In other words, when the market value is greater than the entry cost, no correction is made. If some commentators have seen in this deviation a manifestation of the dynamic conception, Richard (2002) suggests a different explanation: the non-recognition of potential capital gains avoids the distribution of unrealized profits to shareholders. In a limited company, the limited liability clause isolates the wealth of the shareholders from the wealth of the company. Consequently, in the case of liquidation, creditors are unable to recover any distributed but unrealized profits from the wealth of the shareholders. Thus an asymmetry is apparent between potential gains and losses. In the end, the standard valuation method in Germany retains the formula of taking the lesser of the depreciated cost and the market value. In the German case, one other point deserves to be mentioned: if the domination of a static vision tends to impose an external viewpoint on a company (namely, the creditor viewpoint), other enactments favour the power of managers and/or (stable) majority shareholders to a significant degree. The great freedom in managing earnings, often smoothed and/or massively reinvested, goes in this direction by privileging the continuity of the operating cycle over any redistribution of profit to investors.

From this contrast, we shall retain the idea that the prudential principle brings about the convergence of systems which are rooted in the beginning in polar accounting doctrines. Valuation adjustments are simply far more frequent in Germany than in France. In the United States or the UK, the traditional attachment to the method of historical cost has lessened over the last two decades. Thus a shift is operating towards a static conception of accounting. This conception, however, is very different from the static Germanic approach.

Accounting and the Representation of the Economic System

Private accounting defines the economic identity of subjects in a monetary economy. Thus one can view the economy as a system of accounts linked by flows of payments which are the counterparts of exchanges of economic objects valued in cash terms (goods and services, rights to unilateral transfers, items of wealth, credits). The effective exchanges of economic objects for cash determine their social value. The latter does not pre-exist exchange: payment is the operator of validation or social sanction of private activities. To sell a good or a service for a determinate cash amount is to accept the judgement of society which expresses its estimation of the contribution of the private agent to this cash-implemented abstraction called value.

It follows that accounting contains an irreducible tension between two aspects of reality: the values manifest through objective monetary exchanges on the one hand, and calculated promissory values on the other hand. To make this essential distinction in the continuous entanglement of monetary flows, accounting fixes a convention of temporal partition into accounting periods. There are working accounts and cash accounts which record objective flows over a period. There are accounts which give expression to promissory value to sales exchanges of the financial accounting period. These balance sheet accounts link financial reports together and allow one to give a quantified representation of the wealth of private agents or of the capital in the case of companies. Whereas the first type of accounts rests on payments that are beyond dispute if they are witnessed, the second type rests on conjectures, none of which is binding. These conjectures depend on the viewpoints of those using the balance sheet accounts. Thus dynamic accounting is in opposition to static accounting, without any possibility of a higher mediating viewpoint to disengage them. Rather than a unilateral alignment on a single viewpoint, it is better to acknowledge their irreducibility and organize their coexistence. In brief, accounting rules vary in time and space as a function of dominant interests. In that regard, accounting is an institutionalized valuation convention within a given space.

The only case where accounting standards are neutral is in the imaginary universe of general equilibrium. In this universe, the opposition between reporting periods and the inter-linkage of periods is abolished. When equilibrium occurs everywhere and always, no sale ever has a problematic valuation. There is no longer any distinction between objective value and promissory value. The value of private wealth is stripped of ambiguity. Correlatively, cash no longer has an essential role: it is neutral. The next parts of this chapter present the manner in which the shareholder viewpoint in its current embodiment disguises its interests: it puts accounting at the service of the financial management of private wealth, behind an ideological discourse borrowing from this image of equilibrium. The postulate is that it is possible to converge to this ideal universe of equilibrium by relying systematically on financial market indications in order to value balance sheet items and by simulating absent markets by models. This is precisely the meaning of the doctrine of fair value. We shall show that this pretension to get beyond ambiguity has no foundation. It expresses nothing other than an increased corporate awareness of the interests of market finance and of its principal actors.

What should one do if one accepts the ambiguity of accounting? One must admit that the value of a company depends on a host of easily manipulated attributions, as we shall show in Chapter 8 in studying the Enron-era scandals. These scandals reveal that the formal nature of the rules is no gauge of efficiency. Several undetectable embezzlements took place which complied fully with the accounting standards. This should be no surprise since the 'values' recorded on the balance sheet, and even more on the off balance sheet, are not values certified by the test of payment. Only a pragmatic viewpoint which achieves compromises between the interests of corporate partners could by trial and error result in a median conciliation. The right accounting standardization is that which enables corporate partners, in situations of disequilibrium, to make decisions which will be taken as satisfactory *ex post*.

As we shall see in the next section, international standardization is committed to a diametrically opposed path in attempting to make the balance sheet coincide with financial market valuations. That alternative imports market volatility into corporate earnings statements. If the payment principle is violated in order to determine reported earnings, because company directors have licence to recognize as current income the promises of future income incorporated in the fantastical asset valuations by presenting *pro forma* accounts, then financial reporting is seriously compromised. It is hardly astonishing that suspicion should spread to the reliability of the images that senior executives wish to give of their companies.

THE RENAISSANCE OF THE STATIC APPROACH: FAIR VALUE

With the static approach, the accounting function is not so much the representation of a particular activity (intra-corporate coordination) as the protection of a stakeholder group (the creditors). To these two functions at work in accounting, it is possible to add a third: the instruments of management. The use of accounting for management purposes has a long history, with the development of cost accounting aiming at internal knowledge of production costs. More broadly, general accounting constitutes the control panel of management: it provides a set of indicators allowing simultaneous corporate monitoring and orientation. As the economy becomes financialized, a different management need is felt with increasing urgency: portfolio management. Distrust of corporate accounting data is very widespread, or very solidly anchored, in the financial community (Cohen, 2000). These data are presented as relatively disconnected from stock market prices, and hence of little use in financial investments. It is on the basis of this distrust that the concept of EVA/MVA, which its advocates present as 'the' method enabling one to bring together accounting data and stock market valuations in the best way (see Chapter 1), has been developed.

Accounting and Stock Markets

The idea that corporate accounting is above all an instrument in the service of market efficiency owes its dynamism to the affirmation of market finance. A first explicit 'trace' of the assignment of this mission to accounting can be found in the US 'conceptual accounting framework' of 1973. This is not by chance, in that this date corresponds very exactly with the re-appropriation of accounting by the SEC, the guarantor of stock market transparency in the United States since 1934.

Up until the start of the 1970s in the United States, accounting standardization was the domain of the American Institute of Certified Public Accountants (AICPA), which represents the profession of accounting experts or auditors at the federal level. The collusion between accounting standardization and auditing, frequently denounced, led to the reorganization of the process of production of accounting rules. In 1973, the SEC took command: a new standardization body was created, the Financial Accounting Standards Board (FASB), placed under the tutelage of the SEC.[3] The latter was equipped with the legal power to establish accounting principles for the codification of current practice,[4] but it delegated this power very largely to the FASB (Walton, 2001). Since its creation, the FASB has sought to define a conceptual accounting framework. This framework can be defined as a set of coherent assumptions about the function and substance of accounting, serving to orient and legitimate the production of accounting principles (Anthony, 1987). According to Colasse (2000), it is 'an intellectual tool which serves as a deductive guide for the production of standards' (p. 94; our translation). The framework is fleshed out in a series of conceptual standards, the Statement of Financial Accounting Concepts (SFAC) – the seventh and last (SFAC 7) dating from February 2000. The first conceptual norm (SFAC 1), published in 1978 and devoted to the objectives of accounting information diffused by quoted companies, recognizes explicitly that the privileged users are the shareholders (current or potential) and creditors. Accounting must help them to evaluate the cash flow perspectives. The vision of accounting as working within a larger project of capital market transparency is very palpable in this first standard.

In continental Europe, until very recently, accounting standardization has remained sheltered from this re-appropriation by private institutions linked to financial markets. While there is no conceptual framework defining explicitly the parties concerned by accounting, it is clear that accounting information is destined *a priori* for a broader public than simply investors. In the French case, the process of accounting standardization is a process of partnership – preventing any deflection into the service of a single stakeholder (Colasse, 2000). The elaboration of accounting rules, which are designed for all companies (whether quoted or not), is the business of the National Accounting Council (*Conseil National de la Comptabilité*, CNC). The council has about 50 members, representing the accounting profession and public administration, but equally the various unions (workers and employers). In the absence of a conceptual framework, standards are produced in an inductive manner, according to the problems encountered. Thereafter, the elaboration of standards follows a process of negotiation between the different members of the CNC until consensus is reached. In Germany, accounting standardization is done at the federal level: German federal law has never been favourable to shareholders, as we saw in Chapter 3.

Thus, in opposition to the 'pro-shareholder' vision of Anglo-American accounting (as an aid to financial decision-making) stands a more partnership-oriented vision in continental Europe. The holistic corporate representation which prevails globally in continental Europe is mirrored in the way in which accounting is understood.

The Principle of Fair Value

How does the financial orientation of accounting translate into concrete terms? To regard accounting as a tool of financial management boils down to thinking that the rationale for accounting is to protect and inform shareholders. Thus the static conception is reactivated in an amended version: it is no longer so much the protection of creditors that is sought as the protection of holders of stock. Fair value accounting is the new buzzword. According to Biondi (2003), 'fair value can be considered as a synthesis of the possible alternatives to the principle of [historical] cost' (p. 446; our translation). Fair value presents itself as the antithesis of the method of historical cost, which dominated US and UK accounting for a long time.

Fair value is in some sense the older brother of EVA, born of the same father (the shareholder renaissance) and the same mother (an 'anti-accounting' rhetoric, hence anti-historical cost). The key idea of the fair value project can thus be defined in the following way: portfolio choices will be that much more judicious (or shareholder protection will be that much better), if assets and liabilities, that is to say, the set of items constituting the balance sheet, are valued without reference to the method of historical cost. Breaking with the method of historical cost takes the form of an alternative mobilization of two concepts of value, which only coincide, for a given asset, in the presence of liquid efficient markets.

The first of these two concepts is the *market value*, that is to say, the price that one would obtain for the asset in a 'normal' transaction with a correctly informed and autonomous party. This is just valuation by the market, characteristic of the static approach defending creditors, except that the prudential principle, customary in Germany, has been sidelined. From the viewpoint of investor rationality, it is necessary to be aware of potential gains as well as potential losses.

The second concept is the idea of *actuarial value* (or *value in use*), that is to say, the actual sum of revenue flows expected from the use or possession of the asset. This value appeals to two distinct assumptions, one about future profits and the other about discount rates. The recourse to discounting, and hence to expectation, in order to value balance sheet items, introduces a radical rupture from the idea of accounting as an instrument for drawing up accounts: forecasts are introduced massively into what is, let us recall, a performative language. Therefore the judgement pronounced by the accounting method on the company bears not so much on what the company has done, but on what the market thinks it will do. To calculate this actuarial value, partisans of fair value authorize recourse to theoretical models. These models are necessary when sufficiently liquid markets do not exist capable of providing an evaluation of the actuarial value. The models used may be private (personal), but their relevance must be made public. In this way, a shift takes place from marked-to-market to marked-to-model. The idea that the fair value of an asset refers to a value determined on a highly liquid market is not new: it is rooted in an apologetic representation of the market, as guarantor of justice and the common good. On the other hand, the idea that simulation of the market by theoretical models enables one to reach the market ideal is surprising.

In summary, the doctrine of fair value differs from the traditional static conception of accounting on two points. In the first place, fair value implies a symmetric treatment of potential gains and losses, a break from the prudential principle which has guided accounting practices until now.

In the second place, this doctrine appeals to a notion of actuarial value, constitutive of stock markets. As a consequence, the introduction of private theoretical models into accounting language is legitimized.

International Standardization and Fair Value

Various accounting standards of the United States are currently directly inspired by the doctrine of fair value, which pushes the traditional method of cost aside: this is the case, for example, of the standard SFAS 133, which recommends the use of marked-to-market and/or marked-to-model for the valuation of certain financial instruments. Even more than the US regulator, it is the international regulator, the International Accounting Standard Board (IASB, formerly the IASC; see Box 5.1), which has made fair value its warhorse.

According to Mistral (2003), 'from a conceptual point of view, fair value is without any doubt the cornerstone of the project led by the IASB' (p. 30; our translation). The conceptual framework of the IASB thereby favours shareholders since they have 'a reasonable knowledge of economic affairs and accounting and the desire to study the information in a reasonably diligent way' (IASC, 1998).

BOX 5.1   FROM THE IASC TO THE IASB: A BRIEF HISTORY OF INTERNATIONAL ACCOUNTING STANDARDIZATION

The International Accounting Standard Committee (IASC), a private company regrouping the professional accounting associations of the principal developed countries, was born in 1973. Its objective was to promote international accounting harmonization by offering accounting standards suitable for application on a grand scale. It is an agency without tutelage and lacking any coercive power. From its creation until the end of the 1980s, the IASC published some 30 standards, the International Accounting Standards (IAS), containing numerous options to facilitate their acceptance by different states. The slowness of this process can be explained by the necessity for the IASC to establish its legitimacy. Two new features mark a change of strategy (Klee, 2000). In 1989, the IASC equipped itself with a conceptual framework, in the style of the FASB. Then, in 1990, a declaration of intent reduced the number of possible treatments of the same problem to just two: a benchmark treatment, and an optional treatment. The rise to power of the IASC was sealed in a significant institutional reorganization, in April 2001, aiming at increasing its independence relative to the accounting profession. The regulator took the form of a council, renamed the International Accounting Standards Board (IASB). Composed of 14 members, including 12 full-time members, this council has its headquarters in London, and the standards that it produces are now called the International Financial Reporting Standards (IFRS). Council members are nominated on the basis of their competence and without nationality restriction by the IASC. The IASC Foundation, which also guarantees the financing of the IASB, is a private foundation, registered in Delaware in the United States. It is controlled by a committee of 19 administrators, whose president is a former governor of the Federal Reserve Board.

The *corpus* of 41 accounting standards (the IFRS) of the accounting system proposed by the IASB cannot be reduced to a simple schema. Thus this system combines a broad vision of expenses to capitalize, in the spirit of dynamic accounting, while at the same time promoting to the maximum the principle of fair value, characteristic of so-called static accounting. More precisely, as regards asset and liability valuation, the position of the IASB can be summarized in the following way.

- *Financial instruments* should be valued at fair value (marked-to-market or marked-to-model) when they are not clearly fixed assets held for strategic reasons (IAS 39[5]). The undisguised ambition of the IASB is to embed, with the shortest possible delay, 'full fair value', understood as valuation at market or actuarial values of the whole set of financial instruments, whether they be assets or liabilities, both for financial and non-financial companies. This project, as we shall see later, is currently at the core of a polemic.
- *Tangible and intangible fixed assets* can be valued either at depreciated historical cost, which is the benchmark treatment (see Box 5.1), or at fair value (IAS 16 and IAS 36). When the method of historical cost is retained, fixed assets must nevertheless be subjected to an impairment test at each inventory (IAS 36). This test appeals to the notion of recoverable value, which is the *higher* value of the market value and the actuarial value (possibly calculated with a model). The value test consists simply in comparing the accounting (book) value of an asset with its recoverable value. If the former is higher, if therefore there is depreciation, the fixed asset is recognized at its recoverable value and the earnings statement is negatively affected. On the other

hand, if the recoverable value is higher than the accounting value, no correction is made. This principle is close to the traditional method of the minimum of cost and market value characteristic of German accounting. It should be noted here, however, that the recoverable value may be increased by the bias of a model, which loosens the market constraint: if the market value of an asset is judged too weak at the time of the value test, it is sufficient to estimate a higher actuarial value. The recovery value will then be equal, by definition, to this latter; the corrections made at the end of the value test will be less.

Analysis of the different treatments proposed by the IASB, according to the balance sheet items, underlines the will of the international regulator to stick as closely as possible to the pro-shareholder static vision of accounting. As much as possible, reference is made to a market value or an actuarial value: if the benchmark treatment for fixed assets remains historical cost, its scope is lessened by the systematization of the impairment tests, in virtue of IAS 36. This analysis shows equally that we are still far from a generalized valuation at fair value. This valuation, carried by proponents of an accounting system entirely subject to capital markets, remains for the moment a very hypothetical project. Nevertheless, with the IASB, the tension which animates accounting between a partnership-based viewpoint on financial reporting and the private viewpoint of financial management weighs in favour of the latter. It is at this sale that the decision of the European Union to adopt the IASB as sole regulator for consolidated accounts should be judged. Having regard for the consequences of this decision, which cannot be minimized, a brief historical sketch is necessary.

In the framework of the Rome Treaty, anticipating the economic integration of member states, the Union committed itself in the 1970s to a process of accounting harmonization. This process, whose aim was to bring together rather than align the accounting methods of the different states,[6] permitted the adoption of two directives specifically devoted to the question of accounting. The Fourth Directive, ratified in August 1978, deals with the objectives, the presentation and the content of the annual accounts of capitalized companies. The Seventh Directive, dating from July 1983, is for its part devoted to consolidated accounts. At the end of the 1990s, nearly 20 years after the initiation of the process, the report was meagre. In parallel, the standards of US GAAP strengthened their acceptance as an increasing number of European companies chose to list on the US markets. The situation was becoming worrying, because the European Council of Lisbon fixed a deadline of 2005 for the implementation of the

Action Plan for financial services. The Plan, established in 1999, whose aim was the integration of capital markets, identified accounting standardization as one of the pillars of integration.

This collection of factors led the Commission to opt for a radically new approach to the accounting question: on 12 March 2002, a regulation was submitted to the European Parliament, anticipating the adoption of the IFRS accounting standards produced by the IASB, by the entire universe of European quoted companies (including banks and insurance companies), for their consolidated accounts by 2005. A member state may choose to extend this obligation to the annual accounts and even to unquoted companies. Contrary to the vote of the Thirteenth Directive on takeovers (see Chapter 3, Box 3.3), the 1606/2002/EC regulation was very widely adopted (by 492 votes out of a total 526).

A CRITICAL ANALYSIS OF FAIR VALUE

The European Union's abandonment of its accounting preferences has happened in a climate of relative indifference. The constitutive principle of the accounting framework produced by the IASB, namely the principle of fair value, has never been the object of a real critical examination.[7] To us it appears essential to underline the intrinsic defects of fair value, while also contesting the arguments most frequently advanced in defence of this principle. The ambivalence of accounting, examined in the first section, is irreducible. Accounts mingle numbers representing real transactions and future suppositions. The more that accounting contaminates objective numbers by fluctuating judgements about the future, the less reliable the interpretation of performance, and the greater the suspicion with which external observers regard the accounts. Furthermore, the putative advantages of fair value are perverted by a doctrinaire approach which attempts to deny the ambivalence. It is better to accept ambivalence and to organize the accounting system in a way that gives financial market valuations their legitimate place, while at the same time putting the users of the accounts in a situation where they do not confuse objective facts and estimates.

Criticisms of the Principle of Fair Value

There are three classic arguments in favour of fair value.

1. Fair value takes account of advances in accounting research. The following extract from an interview given by the vice-president of the IASB to the newspaper *Le Monde*, dated 31 October 2003, illustrates

this point of view. In response to a journalist's question whether the IAS did not amount simply to an imposition of the US model on Europe, the interviewee replied: 'It is not a matter of models! Since accounting research has advanced further in the United States, it seemed to us judicious to let Europe enjoy the benefits' (our translation).[8]

2.   Fair value facilitates investment decisions in financial markets.
3.   Fair value has the merit of simplicity and avoids managerial manipulations: the invisible hand of the market replaces the too visible hand of the company managers in the matter of valuation. Intentional distortions – such as the profit smoothing characteristic of the German model – are thus prevented.

None of these three arguments stands up to attentive examination.

Fair value as an advance in research?
The idea that fair value is the result of advances in research reduces accounting to an activity of purely technical problem solving. It is a simplistic vision, which is completely impervious to the fact that there is no neutral way to qualify and quantify an activity. The accounting language adopted drives necessarily a corporate vision, that is to say, a vision of the nature of a company's activity and of the place of its different stakeholders. Fair value, beyond the fact that it reactivates an old conception, matches perfectly the doctrine of shareholder value. However, one of the central messages of this book is that there is nothing natural about shareholder value: it is a political vision of the company which enshrines the domination of shareholders over other stakeholders. For Europe, the imposition of fair value is in total contradiction to the partnership approach to companies characteristic of continental European countries.

Shareholder value enshrines also the domination of financial markets over the company as a productive entity. Thereby it denies production and its associated temporality. As regards fair value, the stigmata of this negation are obvious: the volatility injected into balance sheets through the regular revaluation of assets and liabilities as a function of market value or as a function of a theoretical valuation of this market value contradicts the lengthy operating period characteristic of entrepreneurial activity. This contradiction is all the more violent because financial markets are, in the absence of profound reforms, inherently unstable, as we show in the next two chapters.

Fair value as a portfolio selection aid?
If one accepts that accounting stands at the service of shareholders (something that we refute), one must nevertheless contest the idea that fair

value represents progress along this path. Fair value does not constitute an improvement from the portfolio management perspective. Fair value valorizes balance sheet items one by one, according to their market value or stock market valuation. However, stock market players actually need to forecast the ability of a company, taken as a whole, to generate profit flows in the future (Colette and Richard, 2000). To say that fair value is necessary for investment choices or perfect markets is to think that the separate valuation of the set of elements constituting the company can help to forecast the latter's potential to create value. It is the negation of any holistic or collective idea of the company. The identity of a company, that which enables it precisely to create value, is to be found in the particular combination of material, immaterial and human capital, and not in a juxtaposition of capital.[9]

In summary, the application of fair value provides information not so much about the ability of a company to make profit in the future, as about what its immediate liquidation, that is, its dismemberment into units, would bring. Contrary to the assertions of its advocates, fair value is therefore less in harmony with a shareholder vision than with a liquidator vision. The IASB appears conscious of this problem. In fact, IAS 36 recommends, when calculating the recoverable value (see earlier), not to proceed only to asset-by-asset valuations, but to effect regroupings into coherent units, into 'cash-generating units'. The complexity of this operation is so evident that one may doubt its feasibility.

This discussion leads one to question the negative critique made by promoters of fair value: the idea that the method of historical cost is fundamentally inappropriate for stock market investments. Here one encounters a classical rhetoric, insisting on the structural inability of accounting to provide valuations correlated with those of the stock exchange. From a theoretical point of view, the foundations of this posture are nevertheless questionable. The ability of a company to generate revenue flows is perhaps better valued by a method giving information on the performance achieved by the entity than by a principle consisting of the introduction of forecasts produced by those very agents who are trying to do the valuation. The application of fair value can only strengthen the self-referential character of capital markets by refusing in principle the idea that portfolio selections do not rest on values defined outside the financial sphere.

Fair value as guarantor of the honesty of accounts?
The idea that fair value is simpler and hence less subject to manipulation than the model of historical cost is equally very debatable. The question of 'wealth generating units' of IAS 36 illustrates very well the difficulties that the application of this doctrine can entail. The use of models to value the

price of certain assets is an additional complicating factor, rather than a simplification: complexity in the choice of model, its implementation, parameterization, and so on. For Bois (2001) this would suffice to justify the constitution of 'provisions for model risk' to absorb the shocks linked to the errors of 'marking to model'. Beyond this complexity, marking to model encourages the creativity of managers, in the bad sense of the term: the selection of models and the forecasting of future revenue flows and discount rates open up opportunities for earnings manipulation that are far greater than the ultimately fairly rigid application of the method of historical cost. Chapter 8, devoted to the series of financial scandals that kicked off in 2001, develops this point in detail. Moreover, there is a concrete illustration in the next section, in which the treatment of goodwill is analysed.

Towards a dualist organization of accounting

The exigencies of corporate accounting, which are the true measurement of the performance achieved and the representation of future opportunities, are irreconcilable within a unified system of accounts. Accounting reform must take on board the fundamental duality between attested values, which are objective facts, and the estimates, forecasts and suppositions of every colour, which are conjectures. Instead of dissimulating this duality behind the standard of fair value, one solution would be to structure the accounts so as to highlight this distinction as clearly as possible. This means distinguishing central accounts and satellite accounts, alerting users that these categories of accounts are not to be put on the same level in order to infer a judgement about the performances of companies and their development potential. The central accounts would contain as few suppositions as possible in presenting the operation during the financial reporting period. The dimension of payments represented by cash flow would be clearly highlighted. Those tangible assets that can be handled within dynamic accounting without any extra hypothesis other than depreciation, the rules of which are explicit, could equally be part of the central accounts. Satellite accounts would then contain all the attributions of fair value in the balance sheet, intangible assets and off-balance-sheet elements.

Furthermore, it might be proposed that all accounting elements that are suppositions should be presented in the statistical form of confidence intervals. Their essential distinction from accounting numbers, which are the results of attested transactions, would thereby be visible to all users. There are therefore plenty of pragmatic dispositions in order to improve noticeably the recognition of accounting ambivalence. Unfortunately, the standardization currently underway has committed itself to a unilateral path which would prove very damaging if doctrinal blindness were taken to extremes. In this debate, the valuation of financial instruments assumes crucial importance.

Valuation of Financial Instruments

This question poses specific problems. If the relevance of fair value in the valuation of tangible and intangible fixed assets can be contested, this is certainly not true of certain financial instruments. It is clear that recourse to a market value makes sense for balance sheet items linked to market operations.[10] Financial assets, whether classical or derivative instruments (options, swaps and other term instruments), held in the sole hope of realizing capital gains on liquid markets, do not contribute anything to the creation of value through their association with other assets. For this reason, the dynamic conception of valuation at historical cost is problematic. The contribution of these elements to corporate activity is better recognized by revaluations in light of market price. This does not mean that the entire set of financial instruments is adapted to fair value.

IAS 32 and IAS 39: The Terms of the Controversy

Currently, the position of the IASB on the recording and valuation of financial instruments, contained in the standards 32 and 39, is that the following elements fall within the scope of fair value: elements linked to market activities (elements held in the very short term), derivative products, whether held for speculative reasons or hedging, and stable holdings. The treatment of goodwill is equally governed by a principle that breaks with the method of historical cost. Instruments linked to banking intermediation (credits and deposits) are excluded, however.

Profiting from the natural fit of fair value with certain financial instruments, the IASB makes no secret of its desire to extend this valuation method to the entirety of these instruments (assets and liabilities). This project, termed 'full fair value' is presented without equivocation in the report published in December 2000 by a group of experts set up by the IASB.[11] The project attracted some criticism in Europe, particularly within banking and insurance. The sensitivity of these two sectors to the generalized application of fair value is not surprising. By definition, the balance sheets of banks and insurance companies are essentially composed of financial instruments. The changes represented by the full fair value project would be considerable in the end.

For banks, intermediation activities would be hit directly, since the value of deposits (on the liability side) would change according to market conditions. On the asset side, the value of fixed rate loans would evolve with the interest rate curve, which determines the discount rate applied to expected repayment flows. Furthermore, and this is the object of the following section, the fact of applying fair value to derivatives used for hedging (which is effectively anticipated in IAS 39) is equally a significant factor of instability. Definitively, an indiscriminate application of fair value would promote a substantial increase in the earnings variability and thus in the volatility of equity capital. Hence, one may raise the question as to how banks will manage these new risks; a transfer of risks to households should perhaps be expected. Moreover, it should be noted that even the prudential principle of bank activity monitoring is called into question without any alternative solutions being proposed.

The full fair value project is equally troubling for insurance professionals. Insurance necessitates stable resources, which one can scarcely imagine varying with market fluctuations. Furthermore, the valuation of insurance contracts at their fair value poses a problem, to the extent that generally no liquid market exists for this type of product. The choice of discount rate retained in the models used (marked-to-model) can have dramatic consequences (Mistral, 2003).

Just as the Commission was anticipating a mass adoption of the 41 existing IASs, thereby marking its full and entire adherence to the philosophy of the international regulator, the first splits appeared on the subject of IAS 32 and IAS 39. A letter of 8 November 2002, signed by 20 presidents of the largest European banks, expressed openly concerns about the application of fair value to banking activities. Taking advantage of their lobbying power, as well as great expertise in these questions, the banking and insurance sectors opposed head-on IASs 32 and 39. Their opposition paid off. On 16 July 2003, the Accounting Regulatory Committee (ARC, responsible for ratifying the international standards on behalf of the Union) voted unanimously in favour of the adoption by the European Community of all the IFRS, with the exception of standards 32 and 39.

Credit risk accounting
A crucial question for banks is the calculation of credit risk provisions. When loans are recorded at their face value on the balance sheet, as long as a debtor does not default on his or her payment, their value does not change. Nonetheless, the credit risk profile can evolve over the term of the loan depending on the financial situation of the debtor. This is what ratings agencies attempt to capture, at least for rated debtors, by changing the grades expressing the credit quality of the debtor. These migrations from one credit class to another are not reflected, however, in the book value of the loan (the historical value). That means the accounting value of credits does not coincide with their economic value. Correlatively, credit risk,

which is a combination of the probability of default and expected losses if a default occurs, is not hedged continuously.

To improve provision for unexpected credit risks, banks distance themselves from the principle of historical cost in determining the economic value of loans.[12] Credit risk provision thus depends on the difference between the original accounting value (the depreciated historical cost of the credits on the balance sheet) and the economic value (present value of future cash flows from the credits). This economic value is contingent on variations in the financial situation of the debtors which change the credit quality. Accurate estimation of the risks must therefore enable expected losses to be hedged by risk premia. Unexpected losses resulting from extreme credit events must be hedged by the constitution of economic capital in the spirit of the regulatory capital requirements mandated by the supervisors (the Basel II ratio). In this way, a dynamic hedging of credit risk is achieved. Credit risk is recorded on the balance sheet (through the valuation of the economic value of the loan) and in the earnings statement (through the influence of the credit risk on the difference between the expected revenue flows and the contractual revenue flows) of banks before a credit event can materialize (Mathérat, 2003).

Still, the accounting in terms of economic value, which underpins these dynamic provisions, is different from fair value. The former is constructed in order to isolate pure credit risk, contrary to the latter. The dynamic provision can be written as follows:

$$\text{provision} = \max\{0, \text{depreciated historical cost} - \text{economic value}\}.$$

In its strict hedging of the credit risk stemming from the deterioration of counterparty (creditor) quality, provision is only positive if the economic value becomes less than the depreciated historical value. On the contrary, a valuation at fair value would lead to erratic fluctuations in loan values that would have nothing to do with changes in credit quality: for example, variations in market interest rates resulting from changes in monetary policy or fortuitous perturbations in market liquidity would affect loan values through the discounting of expected flows. In this way, an artificial volatility is introduced into the earnings and equity capital of banks. Far from improving the hedging of credit risk, this valuation, subject to the vagaries of capital markets, would perturb it.

Derivatives and hedging risks

The standard IAS 39 is categorical about hedging: hedging instruments must be derivatives (mainly options and swaps) exclusively, and all must be valued at market value. In other words, derivatives are, without any exception, subject to the regime of fair value, whether they are part of a market operation or of a hedging operation. This application of fair value to hedging instruments is very problematic, as we shall see.

There exist two kinds of hedge. The 'fair value hedge' (type I) protects against variation in the values of balance sheet items. These variations in value, necessitating a hedge, are due to departures from the method of historical cost,[13] whence the term 'fair value hedge'. For its part, 'cash flow hedge' (type II) protects against fluctuations in future earnings. Variations in the value of type I hedges must be recorded in the earnings statement. Variations in the value of type II hedges are handled in the equity capital.

To understand the problem posed by standard IAS 39, it is useful to note that the neutralization of risk, the objective of hedging, is only possible if the hedging instrument and the hedged instrument are valued in the same way (Mistral, 2003). In making the application of fair value obligatory for a derivative designed to hedge an element valued at historical cost, the IASB breaks with this principle. The common sense rule currently in effect will be turned on its head. As regards type II hedges, the problem is still more acute, to the extent that no underlying hedged elements exist. The very fact of having recourse to derivatives to hedge variations in expected earnings thereby injects parasitic fluctuations into the value of equity capital. In other words, the act of hedging itself becomes a bearer of increased volatility. Since the Basel regulatory ratio relates equity capital to risk-weighted assets, banks are caught in a cleft between the exigencies of two regulators each persevering with its own logic: the banking regulator and the international accounting regulator (Khallouf, 2003).

In brief, the extensive use of fair value is incompatible with prudence, which beggars belief since hedging risk is the issue. Further, generalized hedging using derivative products implies necessarily the use of complex products incorporating options. These instruments have no liquid markets. Marking to model is therefore necessary. The difficulty is that there is no benchmark model when hedging instrument markets are not perfectly liquid. As will be shown in the following chapter, the development of derivative markets for the transfer of interest rate risk and credit risk calls for techniques which exacerbate liquidity risk. However, this type of risk is essentially endogenous, interdependent, and hence impossible to hedge individually.

We arrive thus at a complete reversal of bank behaviour in risk management. Risk management consists in defining types of asset–liability portfolios containing financial instruments possessing relatively homogeneous risk characteristics, in calculating net positions, and in deploying macro-hedges for these positions. While this method is not always very precise, it is nonetheless compatible with the state of knowledge about risk valuation and the limits of information. This compatibility is possible when one is no longer dealing with high frequency data gathered on secondary markets in daily publicly traded securities. On the contrary, the IASB aims to impose the micro-hedging of financial instruments one by one. The uncertainty of hedging instrument prices causes liquidity risks against which individual financial agents are powerless.

Deconsolidation and the treatment of goodwill

The study of the financial scandals precipitated by the bankruptcy of Enron (see Chapter 8) reveals a systematic use of off-balance-sheet operations. The parking of assets and liabilities off balance sheet, linked to guarantees to the acquirers involving risk reversion to the disposer in the case of certain events, makes assessment of the financial situation difficult, even impossible. Therefore, the principle governing the authorization of disposals has crucial importance.

Currently, a formal legal approach is the norm. In France, for example, consolidation of an entity is subordinated to the existence of capital links. As soon as the disposal is made to an entity apparently independent of the disposer, the transfer is held to have taken place. In the United States, deconsolidation takes place if the assets disposed of are out of reach of the creditors of the disposer or if their management is not done in the exclusive interest of the disposer. This particularly permissive rule allowed frauds of massive magnitude to happen.

Two other approaches are possible. The first takes the viewpoint of risks and advantages. An asset can be taken off the balance sheet if and only if the disposer transfers the majority of risks and benefits attached to that asset effectively. Thus the notion of control, in substance if not in form, is dominant. The IASB proposes a median way resting on the notion of continued involvement. An asset is taken off balance sheet in proportion to the risks and rights to profits that are transferred. Therefore, if an asset is disposed of, but linked to a guarantee, a provision must be maintained in the balance sheet for the maximum amount guaranteed.

These two approaches are incontestable improvements on the current rules on both sides of the Atlantic, in order to prevent abusive asset moving through the use of Special Purpose Entities (SPE, see Chapter 8). They both try to reflect on the balance sheet the operations in which a company is involved in terms of risks and profits. They are more economic than legal. Nevertheless, they lead to quite different presentations of the balance sheet. The approach based on substantial control is the more restrictive and hence the more prudent. The approach enjoying the favours of the IASB is complex. It leads to quantification of the risks dependent on guarantees that are difficult to value, since they are linked to credit events whose definition is far more ambiguous than default.

The inverse phenomena of consolidation by merger and acquisition also pose arduous problems. Goodwill can provide the occasion for all kinds of manipulations, both in the determination of the takeover price and in the assignment of the gains to the balance sheet. In this field, there exists a certain convergence between the US accounting framework and the international regulator. When the economic life of intangible assets is undefined, as is often the case, depreciation of the goodwill is forbidden. Moreover, the goodwill must be the object of regular revaluation. The international regulator recommends the use of an impairment test, in light of IAS 36. These dispositions diverge from the French rules, which allow depreciation of goodwill over a relatively long period.

The ban on depreciation of goodwill and the obligation to revalue it on the basis of a market valuation, applying the IFRS, is ambivalent. On one side, this disposition can lead to greater fragility in the balance sheets. The impact of stock market reversals, after a speculative wave encouraging mergers and acquisitions, will be felt directly in balance sheets through goodwill depreciations and the correlative constitution of provisions. These provisions will cut profits. This will tend in turn to depreciate still further the market value of corporate equity capital in a vicious circle, the macro-economic consequences of which we study in Chapter 7. On the other side, two arguments suggest that the impacts of this valuation change may be mitigated for European companies. In the first place, most companies already make adjustments for capital gains when it is evident that depreciation has occurred.[14] In the second place, the fact that capital gain revaluation is done using an impairment test serves *de facto* to limit the adjustments. This is because the impairment test consists in comparing the accounting value of an asset with its recoverable value, defined as the higher of its market value and the actuarial value estimated using a model. If a company thinks that the adjustments introduced by taking into account the market value are too substantial, then it can always refer to an actuarial value calculated in such a way as to limit the losses (that is to say, greater than the market value). Here one sees that fair value is far from enjoying the objectivity that its defenders attribute to it: in particular, the introduction of 'marked-to-model' leaves huge opportunities in accounting. All in all, it seems to us that the obligation to revalue goodwill and to constitute provisions as a consequence, if it does not represent a radical change for European companies, is a factor that could weaken companies. The argument according to which companies, conscious of the danger that ill-considered acquisitions may cause, would be more prudent in their external growth strategies, appears mildly unconvincing. In periods of stock market euphoria, incentives to make acquisitions are such that it seems improbable that fear of future corrections would curtail this strategy.

An Abandonment of Sovereignty for Europe

The European Union's choice in favour of the IASB poses therefore a fundamental problem. It introduces principles that are both contrary to the European model (a shareholder-oriented rather than partnership-based vision of accounting) and contestable from a theoretical viewpoint (as regards fair value). The choice poses equally a problem of form, or more precisely a problem of governance: the regulation 1606/2002/EC marks a major abandonment of sovereignty by the Union. The accounting standards that will be applied to European companies will henceforth be produced by a private organization, headquartered in Delaware. The European Union possesses no direct representation within the IASB or within the IASC Foundation. If accounting standards were merely technical norms, there would be nothing to add. Yet we have underlined the deep issues encrypted in these standards, which contain a representation of the corporation. Hence, it is a real privatization of accounting, the public nature of which is evident, which has been ratified. The 'adoption mechanism' anticipated by regulation 1606/2002/EC changes nothing in this. According to this mechanism, an IFRS is first the object of an opinion given by a group of experts at the Commission, the European Financial Reporting Advisory Group (EFRAG). On the basis of this opinion, a committee composed of member state representatives, the Accounting Regulatory Committee (ARC), votes on the adoption of the standard. This is the process that led to the rejection of IAS 32 and IAS 39. Therefore, the Community can only accept or reject a standard. It can neither participate in the elaboration of the standard, nor modify it.

One could argue that since the European Union is the largest structure to have adopted the IASB system, it enjoys an informal but nevertheless significant influence on the elaboration of the IFRS (Crouzet and Véron, 2002; Véron, 2002). Yet recent events do not support this interpretation: on 29 October 2002, in signing the Norwalk agreement, the FASB (the US regulator) and the IASB committed themselves to making their two systems compatible, to coordinate their upcoming work programme, and even to adopt a 'short-term convergence programme'. Thus, and paradoxically, rather than orienting the IASB in a spirit closer to the continental European model, the adoption by the European Union of international standards seems to go hand in hand with an acceleration in the convergence of these standards, already largely inspired in spirit by the United States, towards the standards specific to the United States.

CONCLUSION

The systematization of fair value, even if it is not inscribed as such on the agenda, remains a plausible candidate. This project should be rejected at two levels.

From a technical viewpoint, it flattens out the diversity of balance sheet items. These items fall into three categories: (1) items for which the application of fair value contravenes accounting logic and the nature of entrepreneurial activity (non-disposable fixed assets, financial instruments used for hedging or pertaining to intermediation, and so on); (2) items for which fair value is legitimate and practicable (for example, financial instruments relating to market activities); and finally (3) items for which estimation according to fair value might make sense in theory but remains difficult in practice. This last category includes items for which accounting in terms of historical cost is deficient, but for which no liquid market capable of providing a market value exists (for example, stock options). Recourse to models in order to estimate this value, vaunted by the advocates of fair value, is problematic. It introduces a radically new language into accounting, that of theoretical models and their correlated forecasts. In its application of the principle of fair value indiscriminately to financial instruments, the full fair value project constitutes a first stage in the generalization of fair value: we have underlined the price that would be paid in terms of increased instability, destabilizing for financial and non-financial companies.

From a theoretical viewpoint, the extension of fair value goes in the opposite direction to a vision of accounting as an instituted convention of valuation. As such, accounting is profoundly ambivalent: it effects a synthesis, different according to each system, of a plurality of viewpoints (those of financial investors, management and workers, in particular). Presenting fair value as a simple advance in research boils down to a denial of this constitutive dimension of accounting language.

This chapter has enabled us to illuminate the underlying link which exists between a representation of a company which flattens out its specificity in economic coordination, the doctrine of shareholder value and the project of fair value.[15] That fair value has become the 'cornerstone', in the words of Mistral (2003), of the IASB is witness to the pro-shareholder orientation of that organization, which the European Union has just recognized as the sole standards agency. The abandonment by the European Union of the accounting harmonization process is a very clear factor of convergence of the European model towards the US model. In this respect, accounting today is part of the financialization of (listed) European companies.

In the same way as the Thirteenth Directive on takeovers was presented as a technical enactment aiming at facilitating the integration of European capital markets, so the international harmonization of accounting rules is presented today as a natural process, accompanying businesses and institutional investors in the globalization of their strategies. In both cases, the fundamental social and economic issues are relegated to the second level. It is then interesting to observe that if the Thirteenth Directive was the object of lively debate, accounting standards have hardly given rise to any controversy, at least in the European Parliament.

The grand manoeuvres of accounting confirm the importance of stock market dynamism in corporate governance, illustrated in the preceding chapters. Therefore it is now crucial to study in detail how financial markets operate. For, worst of all would be to justify the current workings of capitalist economies by pre-valorizing some totally irrelevant regulatory tendencies of financial markets.

NOTES

1. In a certain way, it thereby distances itself from the neo-classical representation of the firm, which squashes the enterprise's specific coordination in the production function. On the other hand, it returns to the institutionalist tradition which emphasizes the originality of the firm, since the work of Commons. For particularly interesting developments on the links between the dynamic conception of accounting and the institutional approach to the firm, consult Biondi (2003), pages 415 ff.
2. The costs of production when the assets are products, the price when they are purchased.
3. In the United States, unlike what happens in France, accounting standardization only involves quoted companies.
4. Generally Accepted Accounting Principles: US GAAP.
5. Even if the standards produced by the IASB are now called the IFRS, the term IAS is still current. We follow this usage in order to avoid any misunderstanding.
6. Thus it involves a less constraining process than that of accounting standardization.
7. The work directed by Casta and Colasse (2001) is an exception, like the special issue of the *Revue d'économie financière* (2003), entitled *Juste valeur et évaluation des actifs* (Fair value and asset valuation).
8. This is what in its own way the president of *Autorité des Marchés Financiers* articulated at the conclusion of a day organized by DELOITTE and the IASB on 3 December 2003: 'Accounting historians will analyse the revolution in value – and hail the aggiornamento of old Europe, which invented accounting, but which for too long has been supine under the tranquilising effect of its accounting certitudes and its sometimes debatable interpretation of the prudential principle' (our translation).
9. For developments on this point, see Bignon *et al.* (2004).
10. This, moreover, is the principle applied in France.
11. The Joint Working Group of Standard Setters (JWG-SS).
12. For more details, see Chapter 6.
13. Under a valuation regime entirely subject to the principle of historical cost, there are no fears of variations in value in the balance sheet. Fair value hedging has no reason to exist.
14. See for example the case of France Telecom, Chapter 8, Box 8.3.
15. See Biondi (2003) for more penetrating developments on the link between accounting theories and the economic nature of firms.

6. The logics of finance

The preceding chapters have shown how businesses have become dependent on finance. An obsession with stock market price has become a determining feature of capitalism in the last decade of the twentieth century. Financial liberalization has increased the depth and liquidity of capital markets. With the rise to power of institutional investors has come increased awareness of the shareholder.

Chapter 4 underlined the way in which the different actors of finance influence the objectives of corporate executives and the way in which they conduct strategy. These cross-influences tend to yield to shareholder value, which has multiple ingredients: threats of hostile takeovers, introduction of new management tools, mainstreaming of stock options, diffusion of a rhetoric associating business efficiency and shareholder well-being, and so on.

As yet, this analysis is incomplete: the 1990s were also a period of financial effervescence which accompanied serious distortions of corporate governance. External growth frenzy, hopes of immeasurable profits, and immoderate recourse to debt leverage, were very widespread. At the turn of the twenty-first century, these financial excesses came undone in a double crisis: a financial crisis unleashed by a stock market collapse, and a crisis of governance founded on shareholder value, initiated by the bankruptcy of Enron.

In this book, emphasis has been placed on the dual character of the crisis of the principle of shareholder value, which claims to govern contemporary capitalism. The quasi-totality of current explanations of these phenomena separates them completely. This enables one to reduce the financial crisis to simple market exuberance, and the governance crisis to conflicts of interest and defects in shareholder control of companies. The specific instability of the current growth regime is masked in this way. On the one hand, the belief is accepted that financial exuberance is due to exceptional events which have no reason to be repeated. On the other hand, one claims to treat the dysfunction of governance by an increase in regulation in order to strengthen shareholder control over companies.

Our conception is different. Chapter 2 showed that shareholder value does not rest on solid theory. A business is a collective structure which brings complementary skills together in accordance with purposes admitting a plurality of regimes. The theoretical model of Chapter 4 illustrated the dependence of these regimes relative to financial variables (level of debt, stock market price, sensitiveness of the stock market to proxy fights). We must explore more deeply these financial logics in order to show why and how the development of financial markets can cause cumulative disequilibria in company balance sheets.

The challenge of acquiring in-depth knowledge of the elementary functions of finance and of their transformation under the effect of the innovations borne by financial liberalization is considerable. We shall show that the assessment of credit risk by banks depends on the valuation of assets in the financial markets. This shared logic tends to erase the boundaries of banks and to hybridize the accepted categories of financial agents. The latter are linked through the tight interdependence of markets in which risks are transferred. Because the valuation of assets in financial markets is subject to very marked fluctuation, the close interdependence of debt markets and asset markets magnifies financial cycles considerably. Since company executives seek to exploit high valuations in the phases of financial expansion, balance sheets are strained to the utmost. The crisis of governance is grafted onto painful restructurings which become necessary in the phases of financial deflation.

Institutional investors bear a large share of responsibility for the instability of the markets governing organized financial systems. It is they who in effect drain individual and collective savings and who bring, in a structural way, liquidity to markets through the diversification of their investments. In addition, the herd behaviour of players, and the flight to quality when markets are under pressure, amplify the volatility during financial crises.

To study the logics of finance is therefore to establish the microeconomic foundations of the macroeconomic instability of financial markets. From an analysis of the principles of asset valuation, we proceed to an analysis of the principles of debt valuation, an examination of risk transfers and feedback loops between markets which these operations create, and finally to a study of observed asset management behaviour. First of all, however, it is useful to define what is meant by the hybridization of financial systems.

INFORMATION TECHNOLOGY AND THE HYBRIDIZATION OF BANKS AND MARKETS

Let us consider the usual way in which banking intermediation transforms balance sheet risks. Banks have clients with which they maintain continuous relationships. From these relationships, the banks draw informal and private information about their debtors. Through management of business accounts and loan portfolio monitoring, banks acquire empirical non-transmissible knowledge about the quality of their borrowers. They can classify them according to idiosyncratic risk categories. The degree of confidence established in this way, via the continuity of business relationships, is a preponderant determinant of these relationships. Risk premia, covering banks' perception of bundles of indecomposable risk factors, are applied to categories of borrowers, over and above the bank base rate. This stratification is too crude to avoid quantitative rationing within the marginal class of borrowers whose individual characteristics are indistinguishable (Stiglitz and Weiss, 1981).

The rationale or logic of risk valuation associated with client relationship banking might be called a logic of specificity. The process by which banks apprehend the quality of their loans is not observable from the outside. This sort of intermediation has the great merit of transforming risks. The collection of risks borne by the banks on the asset side is completely different from those risks they take on the liability side. It is in this way that the banks mediate between categories of agents whose risk profiles are completely different, for example 'entrepreneurs' and 'savers'.

Finance of this type has serious limits. Since banking expertise is invested in private non-externally observable knowledge concerning risk, banks cannot dispose of their loans. They must bear them until term. Further, the loans combine several risk factors: credit risk (non-performing loans), risk of volatility in market interest rate, risk of maturity mismatching between asset and liability sides of bank balance sheets, exchange rate risk, operational risk, and legal risk (when loans include contingent clauses relating to events whose interpretation is litigious). The value of loans recorded on the balance sheet in no way reflects the variation of their quality as a function of the variation in the risk factors. The original value is recorded right up to the term of the loans or until their non-performing character is clear. Correlatively, adequate provisions for loans are not made, since their economic value is not estimated on a continuous basis. Depositors, capital markets and often the supervisors themselves only become aware of the weakness of banks when the crisis has already happened.

The 1970s and 1980s in the Anglo-American countries and the first half of the 1990s in continental Europe witnessed repeated banking crises with enormous social cost. Bank intermediation is effective, it is true, when the banks know their clients well, when loan financing takes place in markets where interest rates are stable, and when bank weakness where it is manifested, is unconditionally covered by a lender of last resort.

Since the 1970s, the banking environment has altered profoundly. On the one hand, the general availability of banking services to the population brought considerable fixed costs, creating pressure to generate profits from fast-growing balance sheets. On the other hand, the search for new loan business and the opportunities to do this after the oil crises placed the banks in the presence of international borrowers whom they did not know. Arms-length loans were added to relationship loans and occupied an ever more important place in banks' balance sheets. With methods inadequate for the assessment of these new types of risk and balance sheets of huge dimension, the banks were submerged by risk monitoring problems over which they had no control. At the same time, loan financing conditions changed radically with high inflation followed by the shock of deflation. Extreme interest rate variation made risk transformation perilous. Banking crises sanctioned the inadequacy of a logic of risk intermediation exclusively through bank balance sheet risk transformation.

In such an adverse environment, banks began to adopt an entirely different approach, one supported by markets and enriched by financial engineering. This involves the capacity to unbundle complex risks into elementary risk factors. Once unbundled, risk factors can become an object of stochastic evaluation. The latter is formalized starting from hypotheses about parametric or non-parametric probability distributions. The postulation of these processes is born of analytic laws or inferred from historical databases. Because they are separate and formalized, giving rise to possible public evaluation in terms of reproducible models, risk factors can be negotiated on the markets. These markets are derivatives markets whose complexity stems from assembling three elementary categories: futures or forwards, swaps, and options. These elementary products can be recomposed into structured products in order to enable investors to decide what type and degree of risks they wish to bear.

The risk categories (interest rate, maturity, pure credit, exchange rate, etc.) cannot easily be homogenized. Certain risk categories can nevertheless be broken into elementary factors which are quantifiable separately and normalizable in the form of derivative contracts. Other risks (operational risk, legal risk, 'reputational' risk) have not yet received such rigorous treatment. *Ad hoc* hypotheses are still largely used in bank-internal models. Furthermore, the markets which disseminate risk factors are mainly over-the-counter derivative contracts. They are often not sufficiently liquid to determine reliable prices in every circumstance. The prices are thus model-based, which substantially understates the risks in stress conditions.

The quest for ever finer quanta of risk, contained in elementary factors, owes much to the digital revolution in information. Previously, few private assets could be traded on financial markets. The conditions of applicability of statistical methods were not satisfied in order to value the large part of private debt. The immense progress in data processing, computing power, mathematical modelling, and satellite and fibre-optic information transmission, have enlarged enormously the capacity of formal methods to determine price and to estimate risk. The concepts of valuation through marking to market and marking to model are closely linked (see Chapter 5). Computer-aided financial engineering can decompose complex risks into elements to which it has been possible to attribute probability distributions. For this reason, the risk characteristics of structured products (portfolios of securities and derivative contracts) can be calculated using computer networks. Professionals can negotiate these products on OTC markets.

The essential consequence of this logic of risk decomposition is the possibility of risk transfer. Risk transfer makes it possible to spread risks over the broadest population of financial investors. Here, the significance of hybridization within the structure of financial systems based on numerical risk valuation models becomes clear. This financial logic encounters serious problems in its turn, because risk spreading is only effective if the markets onto which the risks are transferred have the liquidity, that is to say, the depth and resiliency in every circumstance, to guarantee the continuity of public valuation of the transferred risk elements. This is far from always the case. The major advance in the division of labour in finance, which risk decomposition brings, offers to banks solutions to overcome intermediation dysfunction. However, the interdependences created by these processes render the financial system vulnerable to liquidity scares in certain segments of ever more complex chains of risk transfer.

In order to understand these two contradictory aspects of contemporary finance, it is necessary to analyse how corporate asset valuation on the stock markets and debt valuation are linked via market finance, in which banks are key players. This involves analysing the processes of risk transfer: why are they vulnerable to market liquidity evaporation? This question leads us to examine the behaviour of institutional investors, who are the main providers of liquidity in market finance. The logic of financial systems in their overhauling by the fundamental process of risk factor unbundling will thereby be made explicit.

ASSET VALUATION

The instability of financial markets is mostly clearly visible in stock markets. Stock price volatility is far greater than predicted by standard valuation models (Shiller, 1991 and 2000). Price variation has a marked cyclical profile, with prices signalling over-reactions over three-to-five-year periods. Imitative or herd behaviour is frequently observed (Banerjee, 1992;

Orléan, 1999). Do these anomalies call into question the hypothesis of informational efficiency, which is at the foundation of the academic theory of financial markets?

Informational Efficiency and Self-reference

According to theory, informational efficiency is the ability of the stock market to transmit unbiased information about the intrinsic value of companies to the actors of finance. The customary definition is the following: 'a stock market is efficient in terms of information if it disseminates all available information relevant to the determination of stock prices, so that these prices are unbiased estimators of the intrinsic value of companies'. Following Walter (2003), this proposition can be represented in the following schema (Figure 6.1).

The value of a company is assumed to be objective, completely exterior to the stock market. The latter is a public discloser, which has no influence on the intrinsic value itself. In the schema, the stock market is a mediator which produces information, the fundamental value of a stock, using information diffused by companies. The process which transforms the information is a valuation model. Market participants act independently of each other, yet they come to the same price from the same information disseminated by the stock market system. It all happens as if there were a single representative agent in the market. The price reached in this way is an equilibrium price, because there is no transaction at this price in the market.

The valuation model is supposed to select the relevant information from the flow of information emanating from firms. It is also supposed to set aside the endogenous information coming from inside the market: past prices, orders, transaction volumes, and so on. The representative agent

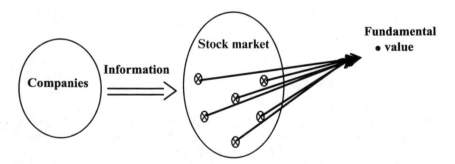

Figure 6.1   The stock market produces information through information

possesses a clairvoyance, an intelligence and a prescience of the future that are out of this world! According to the theoretical model, a rational individual acts like a super-human agent. What happens if new informa-tion reaches the market? All the market agents interpret it in the same way and without the slightest difficulty in a time interval which tends to zero. If the new information is not relevant, the price does not move; if it is relevant, then it jumps instantaneously to the new equilibrium.

According to this representation of the functioning of the market, specu-lation, understood as the incentive to discover good information, does not exist. No one at any moment over time, however small the time period, can make the least profit by obtaining information before others or by inter-preting it better than others. This leads to the paradox of informational efficiency, highlighted by Grossman and Stiglitz (1980). Unless information is manna from heaven, a market that is efficient in terms of information, in the sense defined above, cannot function. Whatever the price of informa-tion, no one will seek to acquire it if it yields no profit. It follows that the market price contains absolutely no exogenous information at all! This is the hypothesis of self-reference illustrated in Figure 6.2.

In order to understand properly the implications of Figures 6.1 and 6.2, we adopt the formalization introduced by Orléan (1999). Let s be (an item of) new information. The process P which transforms this information into a judgement about the market price p_s is private. Let $C_i[P(s)] = (p_s)_i$.

C_i is the belief of the agent i. It is specific to each participant. It is a belief in a valuation model enabling i to convert the information s into a view about the market price. The hypothesis of informational efficiency is then: $C_i[P(s)] = p_s$ for all i. All participants use the same valuation model, which is assumed to be the true model of the economy.

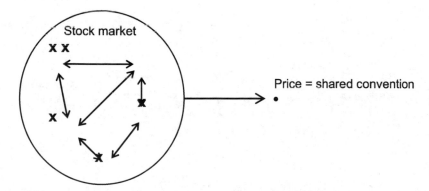

Figure 6.2   The stock market causes a shared convention to emerge through the interaction of market participants

The hypothesis of self-reference means that i believes the market's judgement overall about price, that is to say, the judgement of the community of all the participants. Let R be the belief of i about the market's belief: $C_i C_M(R)$. The convention of the market, as a product of self-reference, means that the view of each agent about the view of all agents converges to a common valuation: $C_i C_M(R) \to p_s$ for all i. R is true because it is self-validating.

These two ways of conceiving the formation of market prices are relevant since P or R can become common knowledge. Yet R has no relation to the determinants of price external to the stock market. R becomes common knowledge through the intersubjectivity of participants.

Can the two hypotheses be combined? The answer is positive if one accepts that information requires interpretation in order to be incorporated in the price. Interpretation is a subjective activity, which is personal and which demands time and effort. Participants' opinions about exogenous information s are diverse, and their transformation into a common view is the fruit of intersubjectivity. This leads to Figure 6.3.

Walter (2003) suggests that the more uncertain the interpretation of exogenous information, the greater the influence of intersubjectivity. For, in this case, the diversity of private views, resulting from individual interpretations, is broad. Because of the heterogeneity of viewpoints, participants are unsure of their interpretation. The notion of average value loses its meaning. Participants become more aware of the views of others. Imitation becomes a preponderant force in the market. Self-reference causes a market convention to emerge which is all the more detached from exogenous factors because these are subject to extreme variations, even to the extent that fundamental value becomes an illusory notion.

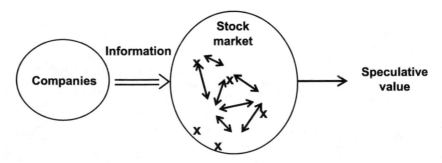

Figure 6.3   The stock market causes the interaction of the interpretations of participants

Determinacy or Indeterminacy of Fundamental Value?

Let P_t be the price of a collection of businesses compounding a stock market index and let D_t be the dividends payable by this collection of businesses. The variables P_t and D_t are governed by stochastic processes such that the ratio of the dividend to price $\Lambda_t = D_t/P_t$ is stationary. The rate of price variation is $g_t = (P_{t+1} - P_t)/P_t$.

Let r_{t+1} be the gross return *ex post* from holding the index over the time period t until $t+1$. Then:

$$1 + r_{t+1} = \frac{P_{t+1} + D_{t+1}}{P_t} = (1 + g_t)(1 + \Lambda_{t+1}).$$

Let us call r^*, g^*, Λ^* the average values of these stationary variables in the long term. Let $\rho = (1 + g^*)/(1 + r^*)$ with $r^* > g^*$, because $\Lambda^* = (r^* - g^*)/(1+g^*)$ is only defined if the above inequality holds. We take the logarithm of these variables:

$$p_t = \log P_t \quad d_t = \log D_t \quad \lambda_t = \log \Lambda_t \quad \lambda^* = \log \Lambda^*$$
$$\Delta d_{t+1} = d_{t+1} - d_t \quad \lambda_t = d_t - p_t.$$

Linearizing the equation defining gross return, doing forward iterations and taking rational forecasts of future values of dividends and rates of return, one obtains the following expression for the stock market price (the Campbell-Shiller decomposition (1988)):

$$p_t = d_t - \lambda^* + \sum_{\tau=0}^{\infty} \rho^\tau E_t(\Delta d_{t+\tau+1} - g^*) - \sum_{\tau=0}^{\infty} \rho^\tau E_t(r_{t+\tau+1} - r^*). \quad (6.1)$$

This equation shows that stock prices vary with current dividends (or current profit), shocks about expected dividend growth, and shocks about expected future discount rates. These last depend in turn on fluctuations in the interest rates of risk-free securities (the yield curve) and the equity risk premium which is non-observable.

The sources of uncertainty are multiple. This prevents the identification of the hypothesis of informational efficiency with any particular valuation model. 'Therefore informational efficiency leaves fundamental value undetermined' (Challe, 2002). There are infinitely many valuation models which are compatible with (6.1) according to the interpretation that one has of the equity risk premium. Since the latter does not result from the expectation of an observable exogenous factor, it is a shared market view resulting from self-reference. The equity risk premium, and consequently the expected future dividend discount rate, is a belief of market participants about the belief of others.

Thus stock market variations combine different sources of volatility. One is exogenous: uncertainty about the evolution of future profits and dividend distribution rates. The other is endogenous: uncertainty about discount rate fluctuations. This in turn is composed of uncertainty about the position and shape of the yield curve on the one hand, and uncertainty about the equity risk premium, which is influenced by the probability of corporate default, on the other hand.

Profit forecasting is the business of financial analysts. The performances of these intermediaries, who influence financial market participants, have been studied by Brender and Pisani (2001). Analysts seek to forecast profit streams. This is a rolling average of profits for the 12 coming months. In order to establish this valuation, analysts feed on information that they collect from companies. When one measures the quality of these predictions against historical data, one observes a gross and systematic over-valuation of future profits on all stock markets: these range from 30 per cent to 50 per cent in Europe, and from 20 per cent to 30 per cent in the United States.

Since the profit stream is the principal information which enters into determining stock market prices, errors which affect it act on the volatility of the indices. To these errors are added errors in expected growth rate of profits. Analysts are totally incapable of taking into account changes in rhythm of the macroeconomic environment. Profit forecasts are therefore readjusted with the discovery of macro-information about changes in business activity trends. For this reason, stock market prices amplify cyclical profiles noticeably. This amplification is minor compared with the exacerbation of stock market volatility caused by discount rate fluctuations.

Discount rate variations provoke extreme price movements when the components (the interest rate and the equity risk premium) of the discount rate are positively correlated (Zajdenweber, 2003). These variations are mediated by self-reference. Shocks about the expected interest rate depend on the market's view of monetary policy orientation which will determine the credit regime. As far as the variability of the equity risk premium is concerned, it expresses oscillations in the market's belief about the opportunity for exceptional profits on the one hand, and extreme losses flowing from a surge in the probability of corporate default on the other hand.

A brutal change in the market's view on the discount rate can provoke extreme stock market index movements above 5 per cent in a single day. This sort of change causes a movement in the opposite direction to supply and demand. Equilibrium is only established by a price leap because the market lacks liquidity. These extreme episodes indicate the close relations between self-reference and the creation of liquidity.

Financial Market Liquidity and the Interdependence of Participants

The liquidity of a financial market is by nature an interdependence of views, since, on such a market, each participant can pass from the position of a buyer to that of a seller and conversely. The market achieves equilibrium through the arbitrage of buyers and sellers comparing their price forecasts, mediated by the intersubjectivity which connects them to the current market price.

When a common convention is established, in the sense of a shared belief about the view of others, the information flows which criss-cross the market daily exercise only weak influence on prices. Since the split between buyer and seller is little affected, market makers can act as counterparties to endemic disequilibria and can establish continuous price equilibrium with small variations of the current price. Participants are thereby convinced that the market is liquid, because they can buy or sell at any moment without moving the market price in their direction.

For this reason, observable large fluctuations are concentrated in episodes of short duration, within a long time-series of trading days. Between 98 per cent and 99 per cent of trading days finish with little price variation. In 1 to 2 per cent of cases, they are extreme (greater than 5 per cent in a single day). These are the episodes when intersubjectivity is intense, because the belief of each trader about the common market view is changing. In these tense situations, liquidity is no longer taken for granted, a fact which causes polarized transaction attempts, creating a one-way selling pressure. A very large price movement is necessary to induce counter-parties to trade on the opposite side.

The questioning of belief stems from a shock of large magnitude or a succession of shocks. These events are interpreted as an accumulation of anomalies relative to the common view, which has hitherto functioned as a market convention. The erosion of the convention has its roots in the diversity of interpretations of the significance of the shocks: is this a transient perturbation and hence reversible? Is there a change in the movement of the exogenous factors of stock market prices expressed in equation (6.1)? Some participants fall into one or other of these categories. Others may yet be thrown into confusion by the loss of the point of reference that the preceding convention constituted; they choose to follow the nascent price movement. Others finally are pure speculators; they seek to anticipate the expectations of others. If, for example, a price fall begins and if the speculators think that participants believing in fundamental

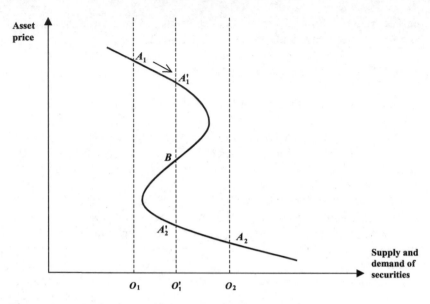

Figure 6.4   Multiple equilibria in financial markets

value are going to start thinking that fundamental value is changing, then they will sell short. They sell at the current price, hoping to buy back at a lower price. Therefore, they participate in the formation of a new belief directed towards a large price fall (Gennotte and Leland, 1990).

This market configuration leads to an aggregate demand function which is increasing relative to price over a range of variation (see Figure 6.4). If the initial shock causes the net supply of securities to exit the zone where the demand curve is normally decreasing, a discontinuous fall occurs. In the initial position, the supply of securities is O_1 and the equilibrium A_1 corresponds to a high price. When selling pressure appears, the equilibrium shifts continuously downwards with the price falling from A_1 to A'_1. Two other equilibria are nevertheless always possible. One, B, is unstable; the other A'_2 is stable. If the selling pressure is stronger (O_2), the equilibrium is A_2. The price plummets to a low equilibrium according to a schema which makes possible the existence of multiple equilibria. Using simulations, Gennotte and Leland (1990) show that this sudden collapse does not occur if the believers in fundamental value interpret the cause of the initial variation as a transient perturbation. They judge that the movement is a temporary deviation relative to an unchanged fundamental value. They buy securities and provide the required liquidity.

According to this theoretical interpretation, market instability flows from the possibility of multiple equilibria provoked by the erosion of the common view, under the effect of shocks which throw doubt on shared belief in this view. Deterioration of this belief causes an insufficiency of liquidity, which in turn provokes the price collapse to a low equilibrium.

This is not the only possible interpretation. In the model of Figure 6.4, there are two stable equilibria, one of which is virtual, in a zone of uncertainty about future price forecasts. The evaporation of liquidity in the presence of a falling price movement makes the previously virtual equilibrium into a price attractor. Models can be conceived where there is always only one equilibrium, but where common belief deterioration functions as a bifurcation threshold, above which the price is moved further and further in the same direction (Morris and Shin, 2000; Danielsson and Shin, 2003).

This category of models can be interpreted in the following way. Assume that the probability distribution of price is a normal random variable if the market is liquid:

$$\theta \approx N(u, \sigma(\theta)).$$

Let us call ζ the sensitivity of price to net excess supply:

> if the market is liquid, then $\zeta = 0$;
> if the market is stressed, then $\zeta > 0$.

Let θ^* be the threshold of bifurcation, and s = selling pressure = (net selling orders)/(transaction volume). Strategic interactions can be expressed through the following determination of price:

$p = \theta - \zeta s$;
$s = 0$ if $p > \theta^*$;
$s = f(\theta^* - p)$ if $p < \theta^*$, where f is an increasing function of its argument.

It follows that if a price shock at time t causes $p_t < \theta^*$, then $s_{t+1} = f(\theta^* - p_t) > 0$ and $p_{t+1} < p_t$. The price is sucked into a descending spiral.

Simulations of increasing values of ζ reveal the following result. For $\zeta = 0$, the probability density of the price has a normal (Gaussian) curve. As ζ increases, the tails of the curve become fatter and fatter. As one continues to increase ζ, a radical discontinuity occurs. The probability density has a bimodal curve, leading to a strong increase in volatility (Figure 6.5).

DEBT VALUATION

The hybridization of contemporary financial systems has already featured in the second part. The value of assets according to equation (6.1) depends in

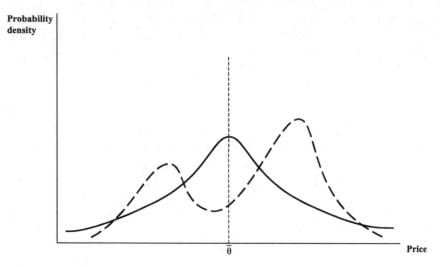

Figure 6.5   Shape of the price probability distribution under
*   liquidity change*

a crucial way on the discount rate and on expected future profits. The
discount rate is nevertheless linked in each future period to the interest
rate between the current date and the future period on the yield curve
and to the equity risk premium for the same time period. In effect, the
discount rate is the return on risky debt securities (private corporate bonds)
which constitute the alternative investment portfolio choice to holding
stocks.

The two components of the discount rate depend on the credit regime.
The yield curve, which serves as a benchmark for the structure of credit
interest rates, depends on the view formed in the market on the stance of
future monetary policy. It is a market belief. Any additional risk premia
come from estimates made in the debt markets of credit spreads, that is,
the spreads between risky credit rates and government debt which has no
default risk. Stock market valuation depends not only on the average
expectation of future profits, but on the market's judgement about corporate default risk which is found in these spreads. If future profits
become more uncertain for the same average expectation, and if this
uncertainty is perceived by the markets, then the credit spreads will widen
and raise the equity risk premium. Stock market prices will fall as a
consequence.

In this third part of this chapter on the logics of finance, we shall be concerned with the opposite relation: how do stock market prices influence
credit and corporate debt valuation?

The General Principle of the Economic Value of Loans

Above, we stressed the changes in the valuation methods of the banks deriving from their exposure to capital markets. Previously, they recorded the credit amounts at their original values. They carried out internal monitoring of their debtors. However, any possible deterioration in the quality of the commitments in the course of the life of the loans appeared neither on the balance sheet nor in the operating accounts, so long as the debtor had not defaulted on a payment. Therefore, there was no public economic valuation of loans in the course of the credit lifespan. Prudential requirements, financial return objectives set by shareholders and the intensity of competition nevertheless led banks to transfer their risks to other financial agents. As we have already remarked, this is only possible if risk is broken down into its elementary factors, and if each risk factor receives a valuation which can be transmitted to the financial markets.

The economic valuation of debt consists therefore in separating out the pure credit risk and in modelling the variations of this risk in order to arrive at an economic loan value which evolves in the course of the credit lifespan. The loan is thus treated like any other financial asset. Its economic value flows from the calculation of the discounted sum of expected future earnings flows. Thus it is the discounted value of future cash flows paid by the debtor according to the loan contract, adjusted for expected losses, which expresses the pure credit risk. The expected loss at a given date is the product of the probability of default and the loss given default. A loan is non-performing if the economic value thus defined becomes less than the accounting value of the loan recorded on the bank's balance sheet. When it is positive, the difference between the accounting value and the economic value must be covered by sufficient provision of capital.

The general formula for the economic value can be written in the following way. Let P_t be the economic value of a loan at the date t, and let $t+n$ be the payment date. Let C_τ be the cash flow resulting from servicing the loan if it is performing at $t+\tau$. Finally, let i_t^τ be the risk-free interest rate of credit at t for the period τ.

In the case where there is no credit risk, future cash flows drawn from loan servicing are certain. The economic value of the loan is given by the usual formula for the fundamental value of an asset.

$$P_t = \sum_{\tau=1}^{\tau=n} \frac{C_\tau}{(1 + i_t^\tau)^\tau}. \tag{6.2}$$

In the case where there is credit risk, we define the probability of expected default at time t in the period τ by π_t^τ and the cumulative probability of default between t and $t+\tau$ by Π_t^τ. If default occurs between t and $t+\tau$, the rate of the expected loss is α_t^τ. Finally, the risk premium demanded by lenders, over and above the risk-free rate, in order to cover expected losses, is λ_t^τ between t and $t+\tau$. Under these conditions, the economic value of the loan is determined by the following equation:

$$P_t = \sum_{\tau=1}^{\tau=n} \frac{\pi_t^\tau(1-\alpha_t^\tau)C_\tau + (1-\Pi_t^\tau)C_\tau}{(1+i_t^\tau+\lambda_t^\tau)^\tau}. \tag{6.3}$$

The numerator is the expected future cash flow on the servicing of the loan. It includes interest and principal payments during the lifespan of the loan (until possible default) and the amount of collateral collected by the bank after default, where these two possibilities are weighted according to the probabilities of their occurrence. Of course, if the probability of default is zero at every period during the contractual duration of the loan, then formula (6.3) reduces to formula (6.2).

Let us call the 'cost of credit risk for the bank at time t for $t+\tau$' the ratio φ_t^τ such that:

$$(1-\varphi_t^\tau)^\tau = \pi_t^\tau(1-\alpha_t^\tau) + 1 - \Pi_t^\tau.$$

The cost of credit risk is an increasing function of the probability of default and the loss amount in the case of default. The economic value of the loan is a decreasing function of the cost of credit risk.

$$P_t = \sum_{\tau=1}^{\tau=n} \frac{(1-\varphi_t^\tau)^\tau C_\tau}{(1+i_t^\tau+\lambda_t^\tau)^\tau}. \tag{6.4}$$

The economic value of loans, determined in this way by the method of discounted cash flow, uses the same concept as accounting does in using the market price in full fair value (see Chapter 5). Nevertheless, it differs in some essential points. If one calls 'fair value' the economic value defined by equation (6.4), it has the great advantage over full fair value accounting in that it does not consider all the price changes of an asset whatever their cause. Formula (6.3) focuses strictly on determining whether or not a loan is performing, as well as the economic capital to be constituted against loss in the case of default. Extracting the pure credit risk from market risks is the great advantage for bank risk control. This is why the discount rate in (6.3) is the original loan interest rate and not the market interest rate at the instant of calculation. In (6.3) therefore there is no change in economic value caused by fluctuations in the market interest rates.

In order to be able to apply this formula, it is necessary to have information on the future quality of credits, and thus on the probability of the default of borrowers. The estimation of these probabilities is the task of credit risk valuation models. These models have seen significant recent development (especially since 1998), although the theoretical basis is venerable. In effect, powerful computing capacity and sufficiently rich databases were necessary in order to gather enough credit events.

Credit risk models use two approaches. The first regroups models in reduced form. To apply formula (6.3), one must be able to determine the probability of default and the loss given default. Reduced form models achieve this by starting from the information contained in the risk premia of credit instruments observable in the debt markets. The second approach uses structural models, whose theoretical origins hail from the work of Merton (1974). These models feed on information drawn from the stock market value of companies.

Reduced Form Models and Value at Risk

To draw information from debt markets on the expected losses due to the possibility of a default, one must assume that the lenders operating in these markets are indifferent to risk, that is, they are risk-neutral. In the opposite case, there is indeterminacy, because there is no way to observe changes in lenders' risk aversion publicly. Risk neutrality allows one to postulate perfect arbitrage between risky debt markets and risk-free security markets of the same duration. Therefore, one can write that the expected return on an arbitrary risky asset is equal to the return on the risk-free asset. In any case, except for the absence of changes of risk aversion, this assumption is only valid if risky debt markets are sufficiently liquid so that the spread observable in these markets can be attributed to pure credit risk.

In the notation set out above, the assumption of risk-neutrality can be written:

$$1 + i_t^\tau = (1 - \alpha_t^\tau \pi_t^\tau)(1 + i_t^\tau + \lambda_t^\tau).$$

For a given level of the risk-free interest rate, there exists a monotonic relation between the risk premium and the expected loss due to default.

$$\lambda_t^\tau = \frac{\alpha_t^\tau \pi_t^\tau (1 + i_t^\tau)}{1 - \alpha_t^\tau \pi_t^\tau}. \tag{6.5}$$

Equation (6.5) encounters a problem of identification in calculating separately the probability of default and the loss in the case of default. Worse still, it has no empirical foundation. Observed credit spreads are very unstable and do not indicate the expected losses. There are solid reasons for this bad matching.

In the first place, the credit events that influence the risk premium are far more numerous and ambiguous than the simple opposition default/non-default. There are options hidden or embedded in the credits (early pre-payments, restructurings, debt for equity conversions, renegotiation clauses, etc.). Finally and above all, private debt markets have liquidity which is often very imperfect and very variable over time. These liquidity premia invalidate the assumption of risk-neutrality. Consequently, the attribution of all the risk premium to the expected loss from the possibility of default overestimates the probability of default. Finally, to complicate everything, the assumption of risk-neutrality does not take account of firm-specific risk and macroeconomic systemic risk. Risk premia fluctuate with the financial cycle, both as a whole and within their hierarchy.

In order to overcome these difficulties at least partially, reduced form models must have recourse to a source of evaluation of the probability of credit events occurring, from which the probabilities of default can be calculated. This source is provided by transition or migration matrices between risk classes, which the ratings agencies establish as a by-product of their activity. These agencies revise the ratings which they give to companies when they have knowledge of significant new information on their profitability and solvency. Migration is the name given to the shift of a company from one risk class to another. When one has a record of these migrations for a large sample of companies, it is possible to calculate the migration frequencies from one class to another. Summing all the migrations which lead to default, one can deduce an estimate of the probability of default. These matrices, and therefore the probabilities of default, are re-evaluated as new information is incorporated into databases. From the probability of default and from a separate estimate of the percentage of losses given default, banks can apply equation (6.5) to determine a risk premium for a class of risk. Otherwise, the existence of a risk premium based on market interest rates enables one to draw from equation (6.5) an estimate of the losses given default when an independent estimate of the probability of default is available.

Next, the multiplicity of factors influencing the probability of default, which it is impossible to predict, leads to the distinction between expected losses and unexpected losses. The concept which is incorporated into reduced form models to evaluate unexpected losses is called value at risk (VaR). Cover of unexpected losses is indispensable when extreme events have significant probabilities of occurring.

VaR is a concept that banks imported from the theory of insurance. It first inspired market risk valuation models (RiskMetrics in 1994), then credit risk valuation models (CreditMetrics in 1997). Constructed initially by J.P. Morgan, RiskMetrics and CreditMetrics were developed by a cluster of banks which created the RiskMetrics group in 1998. In the management of market risk, VaR claims to provide a common metric for the aggregation of the impact of a variety of risk factors (interest rate and exchange rate movements, shape shifts in the yield curve, variation in stock market prices, in derivative prices, etc.). VaR estimates the global effect of these factors on the potential losses of financial intermediaries.

More precisely, VaR is a probabilistic measure of the spot loss on a portfolio of given composition, resulting from future variations of the risk factors. VaR is defined as the probable maximal loss with a degree of confidence a per cent. It is thus a loss which will not be exceeded in more than $(100 - a)$ per cent of cases, when a position of constant proportions is maintained over a duration $[0, T]$. If V is the value of the position, then VaR is given by:

$$P_r\{V_0 - V_T \geq VaR\} \leq \frac{100 - a}{100}. \tag{6.5*}$$

The calculation of VaR according to equation (6.5*) takes into account the systematic risk which results from the variance–covariance matrix of risk factors, as well as the sensitivities of the portfolio holdings to these risk factors. It involves a measure of the unexpected component of market risk, since it stems from the extreme losses issuing from the tail of the probability distribution in conjunction with future variations of the risk factors. In the standard RiskMetrics model, the multivariate probability distribution is assumed to be normal and stationary. It formalizes an exogenous stochastic structure of risk (Figure 6.6).

The transposition of this method in order to evaluate extreme losses in the case of credit encounters serious difficulties. First of all, neither market price nor volatility is observable for the majority of loans. Credit events are not of the same nature as the daily variations of financial markets. In place of the variance–covariance matrix, one must have recourse to the probabilities of migration between credit risk classes, established by ratings agencies over much longer periods. The important point is that these matrices enable one to calculate the probabilities of transition separately from the losses linked to the transitions.

The asymmetric probability distribution of the return on credit constitutes a further difficulty, since a credit satisfies the contractual obligations except if default occurs. The tails of the probability distribution are

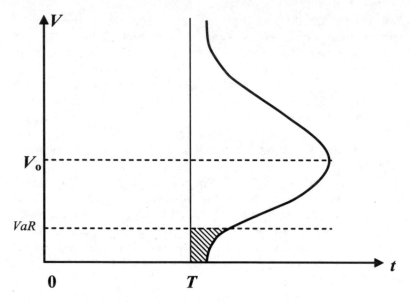

Figure 6.6   VaR *of a portfolio with normal probability distribution*

therefore fat on the loss side. Probability distributions of this kind must be estimated empirically rather than postulated as an analytic function. Certain models, however, use a generalized Pareto distribution which possesses a fat-tailed distribution. Let:

$$G_{\xi\beta}(x) = 1 - \left(1 + \frac{\xi x}{\beta}\right)^{-\frac{1}{\xi}} \quad \text{if } \xi \neq 0$$

$$= 1 - \exp\left(-\frac{x}{\beta}\right) \quad \text{if } \xi = 0.$$

ξ is the shape parameter and β is the scale parameter. For $\xi > 0$, the distribution has a fat tail on the loss side.

Finally, CreditMetrics draws term discount rates from sovereign securities extracted from the zero-coupon yield curve, to which are added risk premia calculated as averages of historical observations for the different risk classes.

From these elements, using the discounted cash flow method (equation (6.3)), one can calculate the discounted values of loans according to the different possible migrations between 0 and T. In this way, one can deduce the empirical probability distribution of the current economic value of

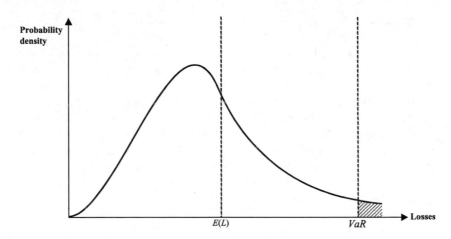

$E(L)$ = expected loss
$VaR - E(L)$ = unexpected loss = required capital

Figure 6.7   Expected losses and unexpected losses

credits. It is then possible to calculate the VaR over the time horizon T for a confidence threshold a per cent. From this, the expected loss and the unexpected loss per unit of risk exposure can be deduced (Figure 6.7).

Structural Models

On the reduced approach, stock market influence on debt is indirect. It is mediated by the use of information which the Stock Exchange gives on the values of corporate assets via the ratings agencies. The latter weighs this information with other strands of information in order to decide whether to downgrade or upgrade companies. It is from the frequencies of these migrations that the probability of default is determined. On the structural approach, on the contrary, stock market influence is far more direct.

The debts of a company are defined as put options, which creditors sell to shareholders, on the value of the company's assets. In effect, the return on a loan is defined contractually, if the company honours the servicing of its debt. On the other hand, if it defaults, shareholders are only responsible for losses up to but not exceeding their initial capital investment. If the company's losses exceed this amount, the creditors suffer the excess loss, the magnitude of which has no *a priori* bound. This is exactly the return profile of the seller of a put option.

Default occurs when the market value of assets is less than the face value of debts at the time of repayment. The latter value is the exercise price of the option. However, the value of a company's assets and their volatility are not directly observable. The essential idea that is exploited in the KMV model and Moody's model is that these variables can be deduced from the market value of the equities of a company and their volatility (observable variables) by inverting the option formula. The limited responsibility of shareholders allows one to consider them as holders of a call option on the value of the assets of the company. Unlike creditor losses, shareholder losses are limited to the amount of their capital investment but shareholder profits are not, if the company achieves exceptional results.

Since solvency is defined by a condition on asset value, in principle one can determine the probability of default if one knows the stochastic process which governs the evolution of the company's assets. Credit risk valuation models which use this method posit the assumption that asset values follow diffusion processes. It is then possible to estimate $E(V)$ and $\sigma(V)$, the expected value of the company's assets and the volatility, from stock markets data. Let V_t be the value of the company's assets at time t (the valuation date). We shall determine π_t^{t+1}, the probability of default at $t+1$.

The assumption of normality on the stochastic process yields the law of motion for V:

$$V_{t+1} = V_t \exp\left\{\left(\mu - \frac{\sigma^2}{2}\right)t + \sigma\sqrt{t}Z_t\right\},$$

where μ is the average of the stochastic drift, and Z is a standard normalized random variable.

Let B_{t+1} be the level of debt at time $t+1$. The probability of default at $t+1$ is such that:

$$\pi_t^{t+1} = P_r\{V_{t+1} \le B_{t+1}\}.$$

We calculate the normalized distance to default (that is to say, per unit of volatility):

$$DD = \frac{\log\dfrac{V_t}{B_{t+1}} + \left(\mu - \dfrac{\sigma^2}{2}\right)t}{\sigma\sqrt{t}} = \frac{\log\dfrac{E(V_{t+1})}{B_{t+1}}}{\sigma(V_t)}$$

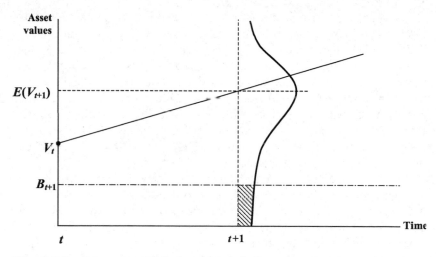

Figure 6.8   Distance to default at the end of one year

for which the asset volatility increases with the square root of time. *Ceteris paribus*, the more remote the payment date, the riskier the debt. This is reflected in a payment premium, incorporated in the interest rate, which increases with the maturity of the debt. In the above equation, the normalized distance to default diminishes with the square root of time for the same amount of debt and for the same expected future asset value. The probability of default measured by the shaded area in Figure 6.8 is evidently a decreasing function of the distance to default. It increases therefore when the volatility of the future return on assets grows and, of course, when debt leverage increases.

Formally, the probability of default is:

$$\pi_t^{t+1} = \phi(-DD)$$

where ϕ is the cumulative normal distribution function.

Banks can use other structural credit risk valuation models. A description of these models can be found in recent handbooks of financial management. We shall explore just two refinements.

The first consists in refining the stochastic process which governs the evolution of the value of the assets of the company. Since default is a discrete event, some models determine the probability of default in terms of a Poisson process, according to which the value of assets varies in jumps. Other models combine diffusion and jumps. The logic remains the same. The probability of default emerges from an analytic form deduced from the structure of the model.

The other type of refinement consists in endogenizing the bankruptcy threshold, which is the exogenous face value of the debts in Merton's definition. Debt contracts themselves become in effect more and more sophisticated. Some are contingent on credit events (for example, bank credit lines which insure companies against the risk of being unable to issue the desired amount of commercial paper). Others contain loan renegotiation clauses when market conditions change (for example, real estate credits). Finally, bankruptcy laws (for example, Chapter 11 of US law) become more favourable to companies. They aim, as far as is possible, to favour restructurings over liquidations.

These complications in the definition of debt contracts can render ambiguous the credit events which lead to default. Managers and shareholders of majority groups take advantage of this fact to adopt a strategic behaviour regarding creditors. They may have an interest in precipitating default in order to alleviate the burden of the debt. The bankruptcy threshold thereby becomes endogenous. It is determined in a manner that is optimal for the interests of those possessing the power to provoke a default.

Such behaviour assumes great importance when the corporate governance of companies obeys the principle of shareholder value. This is why in the next chapter we use a debt valuation model with an endogenous default threshold in order to demonstrate the instability of the interactions between credit and asset pricing.

The analysis of asset and debt valuation has given us a set of relations between stock market value, corporate debt leverage (the debt-to-asset ratio), the probability of default and credit spreads. One must remember that the interlinkage between stock markets and credit markets has become very deep. It concerns not only the behaviour of households through wealth effects and the behaviour of companies through the impact of the financial structure on investment, but is written into the very valuation of financial magnitudes and penetrates therefore into the balance sheets of the whole population of financial institutions. With the gigantic flourishing of credit risk transfers, these interdependencies are intensified.

CREDIT RISK TRANSFERS AND MARKET INSTABILITY

Credit risk transfers have boomed since 1998, spurred by the reform of the required capital provision (Basel II). They are a powerful accelerator of the bridging between banking intermediation and financial market intermediation. Two crucial questions spring to mind. Where does the transferred credit risk wind up? Does risk transfer reduce the vulnerability of financial systems to uncertainty?

Orthodox financial theory offers stereotypical answers. If new instruments of risk transfer are in strong demand, then that means risk is better dispersed. New markets appear, which allow one to establish prices for risk factors which previously had only been the object of internal valuations. Since markets become more complete and their liquidity improves, the financial system overall is more resilient.

Without doubt, this is largely true if one wishes to assume that risk factors are exogenous to the actions of financial agents. The answer is less clear if the interdependencies intensify the endogenous risk resulting from agents' reciprocal influences. This will be the case if risk transfers, while reducing the direct credit risk of banks, increase other risks which are far more difficult to detect and quantify. That is certainly the case for operational, legal and reputational risks which flow from conflicts of interpretation over the definition of credit events. It is also true for counterparty risk between the contracting parties and for the risk of correlation between the deterioration of the financial situation of the entity of reference (initial borrower) and that of the seller of protection (insurance). These risks complicate enormously the valuation of transfer instruments. Finally and above all, the endogenous risk accrues through the problems of liquidity encountered when obligations precipitated by credit events must be honoured.

A precise analysis of these questions necessitates the presentation of credit risk transfer techniques, which enables us to specify their characteristics (see Table 6.1).

Table 6.1 Credit risk transfer instruments

Instrument	Financed	Non-financed
Single name	Sale of loan	Bank guarantees Insurance policies CDS
Portfolio	CLN	Portfolio of CDS
Direct transfer	ABS, CDO	Synthetic CDO
Transfer via SPV		

CDS: credit default swap
CLN: credit-linked note
ABS: asset-backed security
CDO: collateralized debt obligation

Mechanisms of Risk Transfer

Risk transfers are divided into two categories, depending on whether or not the initial loans granted are written off the balance sheets of the loan-originating banks.

In the first category, the risk transfer is financed. The buyer of the credit risk (the seller of protection) purchases a single name loan or a basket of securitized loans. These securities can be transferred directly (credit-linked note) or via a special purpose vehicle (SPV)[1] in the form of homogeneous securities, backed by assets, or diversified (collateralized debt obligations). Asset-backed securities and collateralized debt obligations are recorded in the balance sheet of the investors (sellers of protection). The mediation of an SPV structures these by strata of risk, which allow different investors to choose their risk profile according to their own degree of risk aversion and the characteristics of their portfolio. The sale of asset-backed securities or slices of collateralized debt obligations provides liquidity which enables the SPV to acquire traded securities without credit risk. By putting these securities up as collateral, the SPV protects the upper strata of the CBOs or CDOs almost completely. Investors who buy the CBOs receive as remuneration the return on the collateral and the risk premium. The remuneration may be determined by using the method of discounted cash flow valuation, in which the probabilities of default for different annual periods up to the expiry of the securities, are extracted from the prices of *credit default swaps* (CDS), as we shall see below.

The second category of credit risk transfer instruments in Table 6.1 is a kind of insurance. The loans remain on the balance sheets of the lending banks. The risk is transferred via insurance contracts or credit derivatives without any obligation for the risk taker to finance the acquisition of the loans *ex ante*. The buyer of the risk (the seller of protection) only brings funds to the seller of the risk if a credit event occurs. However, contrary to bank guarantees and insurance policies, which are bilateral contracts depending on the nature of the insured party, credit derivatives are standardized products. They depend only on the definition, supposedly objective and codified, of credit events. This is why these derivative contracts are negotiable on the wholesale markets. Since they isolate the pure credit risk, they price this risk in the market. Market operators (large investment banks and securities houses) create liquidity by negotiating positions, even if they have no direct exposure to the entities of reference, that is to say, to the companies that borrowed initially.

The standard vehicle of credit risk transfer is the single name CDS. CDSs can be combined to form portfolios. The interposition of an SPV enables one to create a synthetic CDO which is issued in counterparty slices or tiers against a collection of diversified CDSs. Table 6.2 gives an example of a CDO structured as an SPV.

Figures 6.9 and 6.10 describe the mechanisms of direct transfer by CDS and of mediated transfer through an SPV in the form of a tiered CDO. The tiers are structured by increasing risk. In the case of SPVs holding diversified securities which include good quality securities issued in the securitization of good grade loans, it is possible to structure as liabilities

Table 6.2   Example of a CDO structured as an SPV

Assets (USD 100 million)	Liabilities = CDO (USD 100 million)
Bonds, loans extracted from bank balance sheets through securitization or purchased on secondary markets, CDS	*Super-senior* tranche: $70m *Senior* tranche: $20m *Mezzanine* tranche: $8m *Equity* tranche: $2m

Note: The tranches are differentiated by risk level: thus the *super-senior* tranche is riskless and the *equity* tranche is very risky.

No credit event occurs:

Premium $5m

Credit event occurs:

Payment $100m

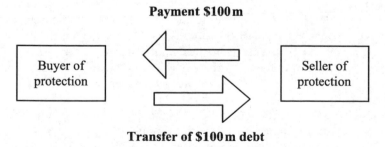

Transfer of $100m debt

Figure 6.9   Risk transfer mechanism via CDS

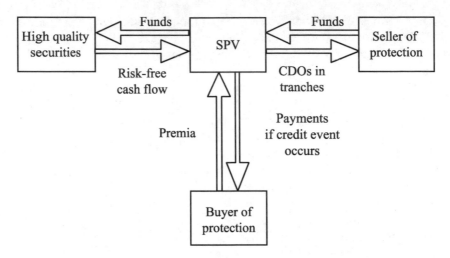

Figure 6.10   Interposition of an SPV in the structuring of a CDO

the super-senior and senior tranches which carry only very small credit risk. These tranches can therefore be sold to institutional investors who have guaranteed commitments. At the other end, the more risky upper tranches can be purchased by hedge funds. This is not the case if the CDOs are issued on synthetic portfolios of CDSs. Thus the SPVs created by Enron caused heavy losses for pension funds which thought they had guarantees.

Let us suppose that a company (the entity of reference) issues debt of $100 million over five years. The lending bank decides to buy insurance valued at 100 basis points (bps) per year. It pays therefore a premium of 100 bps per year for five years to a seller of protection. If the debt is honoured without hindrance by the entity of reference, then the seller of protection earns the premium taken from the interest paid by the borrower to the bank. If a credit event (specified in the contract) occurs, then the buyer of protection transfers the debt to the seller who pays the purchaser the value of the loan principal ($100 million), while the seller has the job of recovering what it can on the assets of the defaulting firm. In the case of an interposed SPV, the mechanism is the same for the buyer of protection. Investors who buy the upper tranches of the CDO benefit nevertheless from diminished risk.

It follows from the preceding that the CDS is the benchmark product for credit risk valuation. Therefore we must show how the prices of CDSs pertain to the valuation methods presented above. We saw under which hypotheses the risk premium of a risky security could be linked to the probability of default and the loss rates given default (equation (6.4)). The difficulties of empirical application stem from the fact that risk premia for risky bonds mix together many types of risk other than credit risk. On the contrary, the CDS is the most suitable instrument for isolating and expressing pure credit risk in the process of risk decomposition pursued by contemporary finance. This is why it is important to determine the price of CDSs in the structure of credit risk premia.

Let λ_s be the credit spread on a CDS issued on a loan of unit face value ($\$1$) and of one year duration. The current value of the loan of one dollar over one year is:

$$P = \frac{1}{1 + i + \lambda_s}.$$

Under the hypothesis of risk neutrality, the formula for discounted cash flow also gives:

$$P = \frac{(1 - \pi) + \pi(1 - \alpha)}{1 + i}.$$

Equating these two expressions for P, one obtains:

$$\pi = \frac{1 - \dfrac{1 + i}{1 + i + \lambda_s}}{\alpha} \quad \text{and} \quad \lambda_s = \frac{\pi\alpha(1 + i)}{1 - \pi\alpha}. \tag{6.6}$$

If therefore CDSs have liquid markets, equation (6.6) can be used to estimate the probabilities of default on the loans. This holds, however, only if the counterparty of the insurance purchaser does not default and if there is no correlation between the probability of default of the entity of reference and the probability of default of the seller of protection, when this last probability is non-zero. In the case of counterparty risk, the relationship is more complicated. The protection offered by the CDS has less value for the purchasing bank. A cost of counterparty risk must be deducted from the premium of the CDS determined by equation (6.6).

Let π_{rc} be the joint probability of default by the entity of reference and the counterparty (the seller of protection) from the origination date to the term of the CDS, and let χ be the probability that the counterparty defaults before the benchmark entity, thereby depriving the buyer of protection of the payment hoped for in the event of the counterparty's default.

The cost of counterparty risk is then: $\chi\pi_{rc}/\pi$ and the spread on the CDS becomes:

$$\lambda_s = \frac{\pi\alpha(1 + i)}{1 - \pi\alpha}\left(1 - \frac{\chi\pi_{rc}}{\pi}\right).$$

Conversely the seller of protection (for example, an insurance company) can suffer a replacement cost on the CDS if the bank which bought the protection fails before the expiry of the loan and before the entity of reference fails. In this case the seller of protection is deprived of the premium payment which it was supposed to receive according to the contract.

Let us call π_{rb} the joint probability of default by the benchmark entity and by the insurance purchasing bank from the origination date to the term of the CDS. Let ψ be the probability that the bank defaults before the benchmark entity. The price of the CDS is then given by the modified formula:

$$\lambda_s = \frac{\pi\alpha(1 + i)}{1 - \pi\alpha}\frac{\left(1 - \dfrac{\chi\pi_{rc}}{\pi}\right)}{\left(1 - \dfrac{\psi\pi_{rb}}{\pi}\right)}. \tag{6.7}$$

The valuation of risk transfer instruments then becomes extremely complex. Counterparty risk is quasi-impossible to estimate, given the very great insufficiency of obligations to disclose positions in derivative products. Still more illusory is the estimation of joint probabilities of default. Yet these risks vary greatly over the cycle. When the stock market suffers a profound fall, it has been shown that the probability of corporate default increases. The financial situation of insurance companies loaded with equities and credit derivatives also deteriorates. The result is a steep increase in the associated probabilities, at least for the credit derivatives whose underlyings are companies with mediocre or poor credit ratings. These movements are not generally taken into account in credit risk valuation models. They are therefore not included in the prices of CDSs. The distortion between the negotiated prices and the risk effectively borne by these instruments is the cause of unexpected losses and even often uncovered losses. For this reason, insurance companies, trapped with large portfolios of undervalued CDSs, rush to sell at any fall in the shares of the companies involved, in order to cover themselves, thereby feeding the downward movement.

Size of Markets and Types of Counterparties

One can get some insight into the expansion of credit risk since 1998 and into the relative importance of the instruments listed in Table 6.1 from the estimates presented in Tables 6.3 and 6.4.

Securitization using asset-backed securities (especially mortgage loans) has been overtaken by the rocketing development of CDSs. Table 6.4 shows that in terms of gross amounts, the banks are by far the most active players on both sides of the market. In net terms, a strong polarization is observable between banks and insurance companies. Banks, and to a lesser degree companies themselves, are the biggest buyers of CDSs, and insurance companies are the largest sellers.

Table 6.3 *Size of credit risk transfer markets in the United States (end-of-year amounts, billions of dollars)*

	1998	1999	2000	2001	2002
Sale of loans	78	79	102	118	123
CDS	350	586	850	1175	1726
ABS	684	816	947	1114	1230
CDO	48	85	125	167	191

Source: British Bankers' Association, Risk Magazine, ISDA.

Table 6.4 *Buyers and sellers of protection for credit derivatives (positions at the end of 2001)*

	Protection buyers (%)	Protection sellers (%)	Net positions (Billion $)
Banks	51	38	+210
Companies	10	5	+80
Brokers	15	16	−20
Hedge funds	4	5	−20
Insurers	11	26	−240
Others	9	10	−10
Total	100	100	0

Source: IMF, Financial Stability, September 2002.

Credit Risk Valuation Degradation and Self-reinforcing Feedbacks

It is probable that credit derivatives change the relationship between lenders and borrowers. Poorer quality credit risk valuation creates risks between buyers and sellers of protection. Because they benefit from internal information on companies, the banks that transfer credit risk may overestimate the quality of the transferred credits. Several expedients can palliate the dangerousness of this perverse selection: retention by the bank of part of the risk involving the entity of reference, independent valuation by ratings agencies, and multiple-period contracts between the buyer and the seller of protection. In the other direction, the uncertainty about the quality of transferred credits, and thus about the adequacy of the premia paid to the risk takers, is aggravated by the lessening of the banks' incentive to engage monitoring resources in order to obtain an intrinsic assessment of debtors. For this reason, risk takers, who have no relationship with the borrowing companies, prefer to buy the risks of companies rated by the most prominent ratings agencies, or those risks which are backed by portfolios of securitized loans. In any case, credit derivatives, by breaking the long-term relationships on which reciprocal trust between borrowers and lenders is built, promote market intermediation.

Furthermore, credit derivatives are highly incomplete contracts. Credit events are all the more difficult to define because the banks selling the risks can influence them. Definition is also difficult because of the fact that assertion of the occurrence of these events may be ambiguous. In both cases, the way is open to opportunistic behaviour creating endogenous risk. If one wished to codify rigorously all the rights and obligations, then the suppleness of OTC instruments would suffer. Credit derivative growth would brake or go into reverse. Yet if one does not codify, then risk transfers must leave residual risks in the banks to limit opportunistic behaviour. In situations of tension, risks that one thought had been transferred may return to their departure point, especially if the credit risk on the borrowing companies and the counterparty risk become closely correlated. If therefore credit risk transfer raises the level of risk taken, for example by reducing the economic capital required by the banks for unexpected losses, then insurers and reinsurers may well withdraw from the credit protection markets when losses pile up.

To honour the obligations resulting from the simultaneous occurrence of credit events, sellers of protection, who are essentially insurers, need liquidity in order to effect payments falling due immediately. Since, given the nature of their liabilities, they are not liquid agents, they must liquidate loan commitments. The danger lies in those situations where the correlation between the increase in the credit risk of the entities of reference and the illiquidity of the risk takers grows quickly. Precipitous liquidation of assets reinforces the fall in financial markets. We have shown that the evaluation of the probability of default, which is reflected in credit spreads, depends on the stock market prices of companies. Therefore, the consequent induced raising of the probability of default increases the risk premia of CDSs.

These risk premia are the benchmark of the spreads across the universe of corporate debt instruments. Thus a vicious circle is self-generating, constantly boosted by the attempts to hedge the protection takers, unwilling to bear the risk. The outcome is represented in Figure 6.11, which is a destabilizing process akin to portfolio insurance. Selling into falling markets worsens market liquidity.

The preponderance of endogenous risk in this environment of tension re-enters the banking system, which is the ultimate source of liquidity in extreme circumstances. The lesson is that risks are not reduced by a broader distribution among financial institutions if the transfer creates interdependencies that lead all risk takers to hedge their positions. Hedging loops contribute to the increase in market price volatility and, thereby, provide microeconomic foundations for non-diversifiable macroeconomic risk.

This interdependence of risks may be internalized within financial conglomerates. In this case, it gives rise to conflicts of interest. Many markets are dominated by financial conglomerates, for example, the bancassurance groups. When the markets in which the conglomerate offers its services are imperfectly liquid, the entities which operate in that market may price their

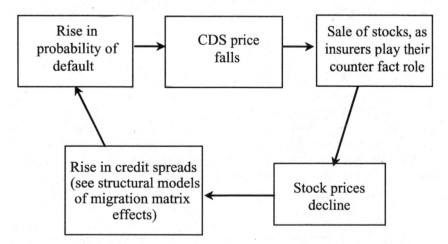

Figure 6.11   Risk interdependence through protection taker hedging

products at levels that serve the interests of a particular stakeholder group to the detriment of others. The management of the conglomerate and of its constitutive elements is then weakened by conflicts of interest.

For example, let us consider a conglomerate formed of a bank and a life insurance company. The underwriters of life insurance contracts have an interest in keeping any profits in the short term in order to compensate for possible falls in the value of the insurance company's assets. Shareholders, on the contrary, have an interest in the distribution of profits. The situation may become inextricable if the insurance company is a mutual partner company which limits profit distribution, whereas the conglomerate is a capitalist company. In financial groups of this type, it is in the interests of shareholders that the credit risk transfers which the insurance company takes are over-valued according to equation (6.6), in order to shift the profits of the insurance company over to the bank.

To counter such practices, significant advances in financial regulation are necessary: harmonization of the economic capital required between banks and non-banks, as well as an integrated supervisory agency along the lines of the British model of the Financial Services Authority (FSA). Far more precise procedures are needed to regulate the consolidation and 'decon-solidation' of assets within diversified financial groups, but also in order to disclose the financial situations of sellers of protection in real time. Because protection takers are institutional investors, these problems lead us to examine the behaviour of financial asset managers.

THE VAGARIES OF ASSET MANAGEMENT AND THEIR EFFECT ON FINANCIAL INSTABILITY

The asset management industry has acquired great importance in the hybrid financial systems which have issued from financial liberalization. It is a complex industry nourished from several sources of savings, the weight of which is very different from one country to another.

Retirement savings and salary savings, in the form of collective savings promoted by large companies or unions, are savings plans which create commitments for the plan sponsors.

Most notably, this is the case for defined benefit pension funds. Funded by the contribution of employers and beneficiaries, these funds are close to insurance products, in that they are guaranteed by the sponsors. The beneficiary risk is thus limited to the default or provision failings of the sponsor. In any event, the nature of the corporate revenue (deferred salary) paid to the beneficiaries, which the benefits of these plans represent, creates pressure to install a safety net guaranteed by the state. Just as the availability of banking facilities to the entire population led to public deposit insurance in the last resort, so the ageing of the population must inevitably lead to public insurance of retirement benefits in the last resort.

As insurance products, these collective savings plans are related to life insurance, which represent the commitments of insurance companies. The difference lies in the investment horizons and in the composition of the invested assets: more stocks in the portfolios of pension funds, more bonds in the portfolios of insurance companies whose commitments are actuarial with fixed payments. In any case, the differences between defined benefit pension funds and insurance products depend on the legislation above all else. Thus these differences are disappearing in the UK, where the complementary public capitalized regime on the one hand, and personal or corporate retirement plans on the other hand, must pay a rent of a certain minimum amount at the time of retirement. This actuarial component has favoured the management of retirement savings by life insurance companies. In France, the bulk of retirement benefits come from pay-as-you-go schemes.

Alongside the forms of saving defined above, there has been an enormous development of the pooling of individual savings in collective investment vehicles: defined contribution pension funds, mutual funds, private investment partnerships, hedge funds. These vehicles seek a risk/return profile that individuals cannot achieve directly. This is because the asset management industry is one of increasing returns: indivisibilities to be overcome through diversification, fixed costs of collection and treatment of information, fixed operating costs for index funds, use of size to obtain better commission pricing and better ranges of negotiation with outsourced management and brokers.

The savings managed by these investment companies have risk characteristics similar to those of defined contribution pension funds. In both cases, savers are placed in front of a menu of investment choices. Risk is borne entirely by the beneficiaries, with revenues being determined by cumulative investment performance.

Table 6.5 gives some indication of the power of the asset management industry and the respective weight of its different components in the principal countries with ageing populations. The numbers are comparable with those presented in Table 1.3 in Chapter 1. Noteworthy is the formidable development of institutional savings in the 1990s. Its importance (as a percentage of GDP) is certainly large in countries with funded retirement provision (the United States, the Netherlands, the UK), but it is also very high in France, under the growth surge of mutual funds in the 1980s and life insurance in the 1990s. The structures are converging in France and Germany. Moreover, insurance companies in both countries, as well as in the UK, have played a great role in stock markets and in credit risk

Table 6.5   Financial assets of institutional investors

Country	1992					2000				
	Total assets (% GDP)	Investment companies	Pension funds	Insurance	Other	Total assets (% GDP)	Investment companies	Pension funds	Insurance	Other
		(% of total financial assets)					(% of total financial assets)			
France	60.6	58.9	–	41.1	–	133.8	46.5	–	53.5	–
Germany	33.8	26.0	8.5	65.5	–	80.8	47.5	4.1	48.4	–
Italy	18.5	18.3	17.0	32.7	32.0	98.2	39.7	4.6	21.1	34.6
Netherlands	132.8	8.5	57.3	32.5	1.7	211.4	12.8	54.5	31.9	0.8
United Kingdom	115.2	11.4	45.8	42.8	–	226.5	13.8	37.6	48.6	–
Japan	103.7	8.8	41.8	49.3	–	141.1	8.0	43.9	48.1	–
United States	133.3	20.2	37.5	27.2	15.1	197.7	33.0	35.4	20.6	11.1

Source: Committee on the Global Financial System. Report of a Working Group on the incentive structures in institutional asset management and their implications for financial markets. **BIS**, March 2003.

transfers. An explosion of collective saving is observable too in Italy in the period of convergence to EMU. Ultra-restrictive budgetary policy, followed by the vertiginous interest rate fall, boosted the mutual funds (OPCVM) created by the banks.

In order to understand better the influence of asset management on the financial markets, it is necessary to analyse the behaviour of the players in this industry, and then to deduce the effects on the volatility and liquidity of financial markets.

The Problem of Delegated Management

Asset management flows from the separation between the property and the control of the financial wealth of households. In a world of perfect financial markets and rational economic agents, there would be no need of any intermediary, whether banks or institutional investors.

All the previous material on asset valuation, risk management and market liquidity has shown the extent to which financial systems are foreign to the concept of a perfect market. This concept is not a useful intellectual benchmark of which concrete systems are approximations. That is certainly why insolvency valuations founded on the hypothesis of risk neutrality and the perfect liquidity of debt markets cause wide undervaluation of risk, which leads to weakness in financial institutions.

In the field of asset management, it is the hypothesis of perfect rationality that is erroneous. Behavioural finance research on the actions of individual shareholders concludes with devastating observations on the way in which individuals make their financial decisions. They overestimate greatly their capacity to make choices. Overly influenced by immediate performance and obsessed by instant enrichment, they always over-react to good news in an optimistic climate and to bad news in a pessimistic climate. They are trapped in a cycle of greed and fear. In rising markets, their greed drives them to want to get more than others. In falling markets, they are overwhelmed by the fear that the markets will never come back and stabilize. In these conditions, it seems sure that delegating financial decisions to professionals can only improve the rationality of choice. Alas, this is far from always being the case!

In the UK, the Myners Report on pension funds showed that the vast majority of pension fund trustees possess utterly insufficient asset allocation skills. Hence, just like individual savers, they delegate to fund managers. To play their role as guarantors for savers, and thus to monitor the decisions taken by the fund managers, trustees hand themselves over to consultants. These multi-tiered, principal–agent relationships dilute responsibilities and surrender the real decision-making power to advisers in the shadows with neither mandate nor obligation. Consultants and fund managers toss back and forth between them the responsibility for the over-weighting of equities in pension fund portfolios, which fuelled rising speculation in the years 1998–2000.

As remarked above, the relevant distinction in the institutional management of savings lies in risk allocation. All forms of contractual saving to which guarantees of return are attached for the underwriters are a kind of insurance product. Asset management is in principle subject to prudential rules, either imposed by the regulator, or tacitly recognized by the profession. These rules limit the weighting of risky assets in the portfolio holdings. However, the disorders of financial markets have forced a number of insurance companies to exit the prudential schemas supposed to characterize the profession.

In the years following the reversal of financial markets, life insurance has particularly suffered because of the dependence of insurance companies on equities and credit derivatives, and because of the fall in interest rates. The result has been a disconnection between the values of assets and liabilities. On the liability side, the revenue guarantees given to the insured parties are hidden options whose risks are borne by the insurers. When the return on their assets falls below the guaranteed revenue on the liability side, the policyholder's requirements trigger the exercise of the option. Insurance companies then seek to take more risk in their investments in order to achieve the required return. Hence, they throw themselves at the credit risks which the banks wish to jettison. They have all the more incentive because they are subject to less stringent regulation than the banks. Thus they can accept credit risks at prices that the banks cannot bear.

Earlier in the chapter it was shown that credit risk materialization provokes sudden variations in liquidity, which cause the price of credit derivatives (CDSs and CDOs) to fluctuate wildly. These sources of instability are disastrous for asset managers who must provide contractual revenue to the insured parties. This perverse logic can only be aggravated by the introduction of the International Accounting Standards (IAS), which generalize market price valuation. Net results could become extremely volatile, though the management of assets which are counterparties to long-term commitments should not be the same as the asset management for liquid commitments. Caught up in this dissonance, insurance companies sold stocks when the risks borne by CDSs became exacerbated. They thereby contributed to the vicious circle described in Figure 6.11 presented above. It involves one of the channels through which asset management fuels financial instability.

The other big category of institutional management is that of investment companies, of which mutual investment funds constitute the largest part.

In these types of investments, savers bear the risks without making any savings allocation decisions other than the choice of funds in which they place their resources. The result is a highly asymmetrical informational situation, which causes cross-relations of principal–agent type. The individual saver invests his or her savings in a collective plan (retirement plan, savings plan) or in a pool proffered by a financial company. To this first agency relation a second is added, because the administrators of the mutual funds and the savings plan sponsors are rarely the managers of the portfolios built by investing the resources collected by the funds. The management is delegated. This gives rise to a second level of agency relation. The asset managers that are delegated are investment banks, investment boutiques and specialized subsidiaries of bank groups or insurance companies. The criteria according to which delegation contracts are constructed have a profound effect on the dynamic of financial markets.

The responsibility of this second agency relation is crucial because the decision to allocate the portfolio between the major asset classes (equities, bonds, short-term securities) is far more important for the level of risk borne by the fund than the decisions concerning the structure of investments within each asset class. Let us suppose, for example, that a manager receives from the administrator of a pooled fund a mandate to invest in equities in a period where the stock market benchmark index falls 40 per cent. If the manager runs the portfolio in such a way that its value falls by 33 per cent, he has delivered an excellent performance. After all, he is not responsible for the bad idea of investing in equities. If, on the contrary, the manager has responsibility for the portfolio allocation to the principal asset classes and if the portfolio falls 35 per cent, he has delivered a dreadful performance (Bossaert, 2003).

This distinction is important, because there are no asset allocation specialists capable of detecting the risks linked to the choices of the asset structure among the larger categories, that is, at the asset class level. What is necessary in this area is to fine-tune a dynamic hedging method adapted to the client risk/return profile. Discovering the risk/return profile of individual or institutional clients is particularly difficult for reasons which research in behavioural finance illuminates. Clients in general do not have a coherent view: they want a large quantity of equities in their portfolios, but say that they cannot suffer losses! Have they an absolute return goal, or are they obsessed by markets? Is their benchmark cash or the market?

Determining risk tolerance in order to optimize client preferences is therefore the most important and least codified task of the manager. It is all the more delicate because clients' risk aversion changes a great deal with the collective psychology of the market: the opportunity losses that one may suffer in a rising market are felt far less painfully (or not at all) than the real losses which impact the capital base of clients in a falling market. If managers deploy dynamic portfolio insurance to prevent downside risk, they restrain massively the proportion of equities in the portfolios of institutional clients during the phases of stock market depression. Restriction on diversification maintains the downward pressure on prices.

In addition, the principal–agent relation implied in the delegation mandate encourages similitude in principal asset class allocation. This similitude is caused by the portfolio insurance constraint flowing from the bias of clients in their risk aversion relative to the market trend. The relation also brings with it uniform reactions at the second level, namely, the management of the equity portfolio. At this level, herd behaviour is codified in the performance criteria on which the incentives of the appointed professional managers depend.

Delegated management for stock markets is subject to the valuation problems which rule these markets and which were analysed in the second part of the present chapter. There is no true valuation model that is also common to all participants. There are multiple models in which confidence is limited. This uncertainty is the cause of self-reference, that is to say, the interdependence of participants' viewpoints in search of a common view.

When the intervening parties are themselves delegates, self-reference is reinforced by the asymmetry of information from which managers benefit *vis-à-vis* their appointers. To incentivize managers to get the most out of the portfolios which are entrusted to them, the appointers put them in competition and monitor their performance according to predefined criteria. This is only possible if the assessment period is short (three to six months at the maximum) and if it is as objective as possible. For this purpose, nothing beats measuring performance relative to the same benchmarks (Davis and Steil, 2001).

It is therefore essential to understand that market uncertainty and misapprehension of the risk profiles of investors cause the greatest incompleteness in delegation contracts. To surmount this problem as far as possible, contracts are marked according to short-term performance relative to benchmarks. This is the functional norm of delegated management.

Performance Criteria and Incentives

Benchmarks are indispensable for the evaluation and relative comparison of the individual performances of the managers appointed by fund administrators. A benchmark is an index linked to a notion of risk–return equilibrium. The effective individual performances are calculated relative to this index, are classified as a result and are published in the specialist trade press every quarter. Three performance measures are used (Committee on the Global Financial System, 2003): the Sharpe ratio, the Treynor index, and the Jensen alpha. The Sharpe ratio (S) relates the return to the variability of the portfolio: $S = (R - R_f)/\sigma$ where R and σ are the return and the standard deviation of the return of the fund over the period being considered, and R_j is the risk-free interest rate. The manager outperforms if S is greater than the return on a portfolio constructed by selecting securities at random.

The Treynor index relates the return to the risk of the portfolio: $T = (R - R_f)/\beta$, where β is the systematic risk of the fund (the risk that cannot be diminished by adding more securities to the portfolio). If the market is in equilibrium, then T is the same for all funds. If the market is not in equilibrium, then performances can be classified according to T. This classification is highly correlated with that obtained according to S, because σ and β are themselves correlated.

The Jensen alpha is the difference between the observed average return of the fund and the equilibrium return that the portfolio could have achieved. It is calculated as the difference between the return on the fund and the theoretical return that it would have earned according to the capital asset pricing model (CAPM, see Chapter 1, Box 1.1):

$$R - R_f = \alpha + \beta(R_M - R_f) + e$$

A fund is outperforming if α is positive.

Performances relative to a benchmark serve to define performance targets incorporated in the appointment mandates. To make allowance for random variations in return, a tracking error around the benchmark is permitted; the tracking error is the standard deviation of the variation of return spreads relative to an equilibrium over an historical period:

$$TE = \sqrt{\frac{1}{T-1}\sum_{t=1}^{t=T}\left(\alpha_t - \frac{1}{T}\sum_{\tau=1}^{\tau=T}\alpha_\tau\right)^2}.$$

TE is therefore a statistical summary of the degree of dispersion of return deviations. It increases with the risk of the portfolio. For this reason, the correct performance measure associated with α is the information ratio α/TE. Like S and T, it is a risk-adjusted measure of manager performance.

How should investment management contracts be defined that incentivize performance? Relative performance-related remuneration is one possible contractual element. The manager's remuneration increases with his or her own performance and decreases with the benchmark's performance. This nudges one towards self-reference again, since the manager must do better than the average.

Investment management delegation has perverse effects. Managers' remuneration is drawn from commissions that the management companies charge their clients. These commissions depend on the size of the funds under management, which grow with the new saving that the funds may attract to the detriment of their competitors. These net funds, however, are strictly correlated with relative past performances. Investment mandates therefore push funds to grow at the same time as pushing them to seek relative returns. Since the latter are systematically incompatible with an equilibrium situation, fund managers are encouraged to make risky bets in order to avoid at all costs underperforming and losing clients. Managers who have had the luck to outperform in a given year have an interest in locking in their gain by hugging the benchmark the year following. Asymmetrical, excessive risk taking is the result, because it is possible to attract new savings flows in order to make the industry of mutual fund management grow. The proliferation of funds has gathered extraordinary pace in the United States, where retirement plans are evolving in the direction of a risk transfer onto the savers. From 1990 to 2002, assets managed by mutual funds multiplied by seven. Ninety-five million savers put their resources into 8300 funds, of which half are invested in equities. Their strategy has become ever more aggressive, as the cardinal objective has been to amass more and more assets to manage. Besides excessive risk, the consequence of this perverse form of competition has been the explosion of costs charged to savers. The remuneration of fund managers has started to rival that of executives of large companies. In 2002, the operating costs of this industry reached the vertiginous amount of 123 billion dollars with the sole vain goal of beating the indices.

To recoup these costs, the management companies charge ever more fanciful commissions: management charges, administration charges, custodian and transfer charges, shareholder (nominee) charges, auditing charges and judicial advice. On top of all that come the commissions for buying and selling fund units (entry and exit charges), which can reach 4.5 to 5 per cent of the saver's initial money.

Thus the end result is a bundle of stark contradictions. The enormous amounts of savings to be managed transform asset management into an industry standardized by investment mandate contracts. At the same time, these contracts lead to an explosion of inefficient costs for an activity the rationality of which is simply to follow average return. To bring some ethics into this profession and render it more efficient, its staffing must be drastically reduced. A small number of very large passively managed funds with very reduced commissions should provide a quasi-public service for the vast mass of savings. Alongside this industry, there could exist specialized management companies of hedge-fund type targeting absolute performance (Baudru *et al.*, 2001).

The Effects of Asset Management on Financial Markets

Through their capacity to attract new savings flows, mutual funds are the outstanding structural providers of liquidity in the financial markets. However, the informational asymmetries inherent in delegated management bring into being investment management contracts that cause strong strategic interaction between managers. This is because relative performance is preponderant in this industry.

In circumstances of uncertainty about market price movements, we showed in the second part of this chapter that self-reference becomes preponderant and can cause strong instability. This results from one-way selling or buying pressure caused by the self-reinforcing dynamics occasioned by portfolio insurance and sheep-like behaviour. When these conditions are present, bringing market prices in one direction, there is no guarantee that professional managers will take any contrarian positions motivated by restabilizing arbitrages.

If the appointed managers are overwhelmingly subject to evaluation by short-term relative performance, they have no interest in taking heavy contrarian positions with the money of their clients who will judge their performance on a short-term basis. Others, who operate according to criteria of absolute return, can do that. They will be submerged by those, far more numerous, who seek to stick to their benchmark (Shleifer and Vishny, 1997b). When this configuration occurs, market liquidity is lacking and prices undergo great variation, as we showed earlier. Investors validate this behaviour: a good relative performance brings in new money to the fund, a bad one causes withdrawals through unit sales. Consequently, the more that delegated management is structured by relative performance, the more funds will constitute a homogeneous group vulnerable to sheep-like behaviour (Riley, 2003). Liquidity distortions of this type are more likely to happen in narrow markets, where the volume of available exchangeable securities is weak.

In this chapter, microeconomic efficiency conditions for financial systems founded on the hybridization of bank intermediation and financial markets have been illuminated. This efficiency rests on the decomposition of risk which makes economic valuation of assets and debts possible. Asset and debt valuation is the basis of the transfer of economic risks, which are spread over a universe of financial agents much broader than the risk-initiating agents.

The process by which this financial logic develops creates interdependencies between markets of a kind and intensity unknown hitherto. These interdependencies create problems of stability which depend on the liquidity of markets. Liquidity is essentially a matter of strategic interactions between market participants. In situations of uncertainty about the bases of asset and debt valuation, the agents who play a determining role in the provision of liquidity are linked by behaviour which leads to high instability of financial markets. The macroeconomic consequences of these facts must now be drawn.

NOTE

1.   The term 'special purpose entity' (SPE) is also used; see Chapter 7.

7. Financial crises and the economic cycle

From spring 2000 to mid-autumn 2002, Western stock markets fell by between 50 per cent and 80 per cent. Business investment declined everywhere. Debts mounted dangerously. Those businesses most in debt were caught in the noose of an increase in credit spreads, drying up debt financing, and the reticence of banks to lend. The fall of stock market prices brought about vertiginous capital losses on business assets which had been acquired at exorbitant prices. The annihilation of billions of dollars of artificially inflated wealth shook the credulity of savers to the core.

Our position is markedly different from the claim that the financial crisis that swept the Western world is an accident flowing from a cocktail of fortuitous events, clandestine frauds and passing failures to adapt to financial liberalization. The preceding chapter established the relations which we now tie together in order to reach an understanding of the economic cycle generated by finance. The interlinking of the financial logic of markets and of a regime of corporate governance controlled by the stock market is a dynamic system that oozes instability. In the present chapter, we show that the financial cycle is endogenous in economies where stock market valuation is the pivot of business strategies.

A fruitful way to treat the problem is to take a certain historical distance, which economists almost always neglect. Yet the history of financial crises overlaps that of capitalism. Kindleberger (1996), who has spent a lifetime studying these problems, provides a magnificent synthesis. Financial crises can have the most diverse origins. All are unique depending on sector, factor, scope or channels of propagation. Nevertheless, the financial logic which imprints its form on the macroeconomic cycle is common throughout history.

Kindleberger distinguishes five phases in the financial cycle. The first is expansion. Fed by a wave of innovations, business investment gives support to vigorous growth. The rewarding profitability of investments justifies the expansion of credit and causes the stock market to rise progressively. The second phase is euphoria. Under the stimulus of ever more optimistic market forecasts, a self-reinforcing interaction develops between credit and the rise in the prices of financial assets. The enthusiasm for credit and stock market appreciation generalizes from innovative sectors to the whole economy. The latter becomes possessed by speculative frenzy. In this phase, the underestimation of risk, which is the driver of overinvestment, spreads unknown to economic agents. The third phase is paroxysm and crash. Enthusiasm explodes in a short speculative spike. An unforeseeable catalytic event precipitates the crash, which takes the form of a stock market panic. The fourth phase is regression and the beginning of pessimism. Financial investors, who thought risk had disappeared in the euphoric phase, now overestimate risk. Herd-like, they fly to securities of the surest quality. The lending banks worry about the deterioration in the quality of the loans with which they had stuffed themselves. An obsession with liquidity is general in the debt markets. Getting rid of debt becomes a survival imperative. It provokes recession in the real economy. The fifth phase is debt deflation and balance sheet restructuring. Numerous businesses are trapped, like Alstom in the summer of 2003. The profits cut by the fall in sales cannot absorb the losses stemming from the capital depreciation of past acquisitions. Since it is very difficult to renegotiate debt in order to undo debt constraints, companies resign themselves to more or less drastic balance sheet restructuring. Numerous businesses go bankrupt, others benefit from public rescue plans. This very painful phase must however be sufficiently far advanced in order for investment to restart.

This five-phase characterization of the financial dynamic is applicable equally to the great crisis at the turn of the twentieth century, the Depression of the 1930s, and the prolonged stagnation of the beginning of the twenty-first century. Of course, the five phases should be understood as logical processes and not as a chronological succession. For example, the fourth and fifth phases overlap and interact in calendar time. Further, the relative magnitude and duration of the phases depend on overall economic regulation, notably on the existence or otherwise of stabilizing forces deployed by the economic institutions of the state.

This foray in retrospect suffices to reject the peremptory cheers of the ultra-liberal propagandists of the 'new economy' at the end of the twentieth century. The *Wall Street Journal* was at that time the principal echo chamber for an ideology that wiped clean the slate of economic laws. The cycle had been abolished once and for all, growth was perpetual, and the market was expanding towards infinity. Forecasts of 100 000 for the Dow Jones in the year 2005 flew about.

Contrary to these extravagances, it is notable that events since 1997 have matched closely the phases of the financial cycle identified by Kindleberger. Beyond mere description, however, arduous theoretical problems exist. Why the sudden enthusiasm? Why does financial weakness develop in the midst of full growth? Why is it concealed from both the markets and monetary authorities? Why was post-war growth followed by an inflation-ary cycle and effective demand, and not by a financial cycle? What are the consequences of the return of financial instability for twenty-first-century capitalism? For this chapter, these questions are fused into a discourse on two levels: the main text follows a set of arguments expressed largely in non-technical language; technical boxes, the reading of which is not essen-tial for understanding the logic of the main exposition, support the proofs at crucial junctures.

INNOVATION AND THE VALUATION OF BUSINESSES

The valuation of stocks, presented in the first part of the preceding chapter, showed that two sources of uncertainty exist. One stems from future profits (and the rates of dividend distribution); the other comes from the discount rate of these profits which is the sum of the long-term risk-free interest rate and the equity risk premium, which in turn is a function of the financial situation of firms.

Statistical study of stock prices according to these two sources of uncer-tainty rests on the decomposition of price movements (the Beveridge-Nelson decomposition). Empirical estimates of price variability in terms of this decomposition of US (Shiller, 1981) and British (Challe, 2002) data, for which very long statistical series exist, yield evidence for a remarkable result. The stochastic trend of prices is entirely governed by that of profits. Cyclical fluctuations are almost entirely determined by the stationary vari-ation of the discount rate. They result from the endogenous risk originat-ing in the intersubjectivity of stock market participants in their judgements on liquidity.

In this chapter, we make use of these two sources of uncertainty in order to show the macroeconomic instability of the dynamics which link credit and stock market prices. First, we concentrate our attention on the uncer-tainty stemming from future profits. This uncertainty is particularly large for the profitability of innovations. It is in the nature of innovation that the accu-mulated knowledge of the past is insufficient to predict its future impact. Innovation cannot be enclosed within a precise identification of possible states of the world, on which a rigorous probabilistic calculus depends. The more an innovation is generic and the more its diffusion is a matter of sup-position, the bigger is the set of stocks affected by that uncertainty. Efficient use of innovation, by firms which introduce it, is mediated by organizational changes (see Chapter 1). However, the success or failure of these changes in terms of their impact on future profits is very difficult to gauge.

It follows that the probability distribution of future profits for this type of investment is very dispersed. High profits or losses have probabilities that are non-negligible, yet very hard to estimate. Under these conditions, the notion of an average expected value loses all meaning. The current valuation model, which sums the average expectation of discounted future profits, does not apply. In the case of major innovations, which create new economic activities and which modify old economic activities profoundly, a supplementary difficulty is the absence of data on past profits. Huge diversity of opinion about the returns on investment is therefore possible. Furthermore, the confidence that one can attribute to one's own view is at best mediocre. In the preceding chapter, we saw how this environment is propitious to the self-referential formation of market prices, in which a collective belief emerges from the interdependence of operators. This collective belief fabricates a scenario which takes on the irresistible force of a convention in the choice of stock market investment. In the years 1998–2000, it was the convention of the 'new economy' that swept market movements along. Therefore, the wave of innovation of the 'new economy' raises the following question: what sort of uncertainty ended in the massive overvaluation of future profits?

The first chapter showed that the 'new economy' is a source of uncertainty. Two features are particularly relevant for stock market valuation schemes: the preponderance of intangible elements in the products supplied to consumers and network effects. The latter can be divided into two categories. Network effects on the demand side mean that a product is increasingly useful to each consumer as the number of user-consumers increases. Network effects on the supply side are economies of scale. They occur when there are fixed costs of production independent of the number of product units sold. They appear as a reduction in the average cost of production as the sales total grows.

When financial markets (that is to say, the consensus view of market participants) postulate that innovation is characterized by network effects, the consequences are spectacular. Markets place the highest valuations on the strategies of those businesses aiming to grab the market before others, in order to acquire dominant positions enabling them to expand market share. That means that to lose money in the hope of winning future sales is valued as a highly profitable investment. Clearly, in this environment it is the valuation models themselves that have been caught up in the turmoil of innovation and entered the world of illusion. Financial analysts rejected models of discounted expected future profits rationally informed by past profits. The boomerang effect on the corporate governance of those businesses strongly dependent on the stock market was dramatic: 'first mover in new markets at any cost' has become the fashionable slogan.

Network effects where the first entrant wins all do exist in the case of software (Microsoft) and microprocessor integrated networks (Intel). The reason is that these technological businesses produce standards. There are strong network effects. Clients captured by the higher market share of the first entrant do not change providers when competitors attempt to penetrate the market. There is a lock-in effect. Therefore, a defect in coordination supports this market structure. Even if a competitor proposes a superior product subsequently, each user believes that the other users will continue to use the inferior product already in service. Because the first provider has already acquired a high market share, the switching cost depends on the expectation of each user concerning the expectations of other users about the respective sizes of competing networks. When the product is a common good, compatibility with other users is the first characteristic. Conversion to a different standard involves changing simultaneously the stock of existing products, not simply the flow of new products.

It is not so difficult therefore to understand the real basis for the overvaluation of stocks and overinvestment of businesses. If all economic agents are convinced that the 'new economy' is different from the old because of network effects, then all businesses that seek to invest in these technologies must be the first entrants in order for those investments to be profitable. Since not everyone can be the first entrant, overinvestment is guaranteed. Stock markets are absolutely uncertain about the outcome of the race. Gigantic expenditure, vertiginous indebtedness and abyss-like losses are interpreted as signs of the capture of irreversible market share.

The convention of the Internet was far worse (Liebowitz, 2002). The 'Web' seems to have exercised a quasi-magical attraction on financial markets. It is true that investment banks, advisers, and the financial press all added to the mystification of savers. The persuasion was so strong that network use *ipso facto* has given birth to the presumption of network effects. Of course, AOL and Yahoo benefited from strong network effects, but no network effect should reasonably be expected from the sale of tomatoes or books over the Internet. Certainly, the creation of an Internet site has a fixed cost. It is derisory relative to all the more prosaic costs of trade. This enormous mystification contributed to the creation of an avalanche of start-ups which attracted torrents of investment funds. Their shares soared on introduction to the Stock Exchange, only to collapse when economic reality began to dispel the ideological mist.

Alongside the uncertainty that provoked poor assessment of network effects, stock markets were shaken by another source of mystification: virtual goods. These are linked to expected changes in consumer habits. Ordering a pizza on-line rather than by telephone has no more effect on the preparation and delivery of pizzas than on consumer taste for Italian food.

However, there may exist products whose purchase in virtual stores could change consumer choice. That is the case for digital entertainment products, booking services and financial services.

Virtual goods are at one extreme of the scale of products for which the ratio of weight to price is low. Electronic networks can be the most efficient means of delivery. In most cases, the assessment of the advantages and disadvantages of retail purchases over the Internet relative to the usual trade channels is far from simple. The good old determination of the price by the cost of production and a constant mark-up tends to disappear. It is the immaterial elements of valorization linked to consumer psychology that are becoming preponderant. How can markets estimate the profitability of e-businesses in competition with the forms of traditional trade? There again, uncertainty about market equilibria provoked enormous overinvestment. It induced stock market overvaluation, expecting a consumer rush for a form of trade based on fallacious interpretations of consumer psychology.

From this analysis, it emerges that the 'new economy' was at the heart of a speculative bubble on stock markets. The bubble comes from innovation in a capitalist economy (Kaplan, 2003). It took root in the business strategies that led to the overinvestment and the uncertainty concerning the size, duration and allocation of gains from innovation. The bubble comes from the absence of an 'objective' valuation model, and hence, from the lack of a fundamental value pre-existing the public valuation of financial markets.

It follows that stock market price valuation can effectively govern the economy. For business executives, it can give the illusion of benchmarks which pull them into overinvestment. For credit risk valuation models, it can give signals which push them towards the undervaluation of risk. Thus the unstable financial dynamic that we shall now outline is profoundly written into the rationales, powers and strategies which have been studied up to this point.

THE DYNAMIC OF CREDIT AND STOCK PRICES

Uncertainty about the forecasting of future profits nourishes a speculative bubble in the sectors of innovation. A bubble incorporates hopes of profit that cannot be realized. Nevertheless, these hopes foster the demands of high financial returns, which are the imperative of a corporate governance exclusively oriented towards shareholder value. As was shown in Chapter 4, financial return is amplified by leverage effects. For this reason, the stock market bubble was financed by a progression of credit much more rapid than increases in production and in demand for goods and services.

Lenders also postulated the realization of profits without incorporating the risk of non-realization in high-risk premia. Had they done so, the equity risk premium would have increased strongly and the bubble could not have developed. The speculative bubble on the stock market was therefore accompanied by an undervaluation of risk in the credit markets. This dual process provoked an unstable financial dynamic (Allen and Gale, 2000). The interactive process of credit and asset prices thus makes up the fabric of the financial cycle, the phases of which have been identified by Kindleberger (1996) and given a theoretical analysis by Minsky (1982). We deepen these lessons and apply them to the financial debacle of the 'new economy', appealing to contemporary theories of credit risk valuation (presented in the preceding chapter), which show the close interaction between corporate credit risk and the stock market.

Stock Market Valuation: Real Options and Corporate Default Risk

An illuminating way to formalize the speculative bubble of the 'new economy' is to interpret it as the stock market valuation of real options on innovation-linked growth. Box 7.1 in the next section describes this formalization and shows that, conditional on the non-occurrence of the default of businesses engaged in first mover competition, the greater the probability of corporate default, the higher the stock market investment return.

Real options reflect the uncertainty about opportunities offered by network technologies. The value of the option is an increasing function of the variability of profits produced by the investments designed to capture those opportunities. When businesses are created (like young shoots), acquire other businesses (through external growth), or buy at exorbitant prices licences for the potential exploitation of future technologies, they are buying options. In effect, they are investing in order to position themselves to exploit opportunities which may appear in the future, but which are not known at the moment when the decision to invest is made. Since future states of the world cannot be identified precisely at the decision-making moment, the standard valuation models are inoperative, because they are undetermined.

Consider the index of the stock market as a whole. It includes 'old economy' stocks which are valued according to the discounted profit model and 'new economy' stocks which incorporate real options. This partition is not fixed. As innovation spreads, the sphere of influence of the 'new economy' expands. The importance of speculative valuations grows. In this way, the growth phase moves into the phase of euphoria.

Of course, the weighting of the speculative component depends on the index. For example, in its rise and fall, the NASDAQ experienced a range of variation much wider than that of the S&P 500. European 'new markets' had an even wider range of variation than the NASDAQ due to their lack of liquidity.

The stock market combines therefore 'orthodox' valuation models and real option models. The more the process of diffusion of the 'new economy' convention spreads throughout the financial community, the more the stock market rise accelerates. Stock market investors might consider that the very high valuation of the bubble compensates the risk that the options expire worthless, that is to say, with the default of businesses engaged in the race to capture markets. Globally the population of holders of stocks should not suffer loss after the bubble deflates, even if, of course, enormous reallocation effects can be observed in this population. The debts underwritten to finance overinvestment were always underwritten with risk premia that were far too low to cover default risk. Since credit risk valuation models incorporate observed stock market prices, the very high valuation brings with it an apparently low probability of default during the phase of speculative euphoria. The perversity of full fair value can be grasped here (see Chapter 5). When the market turns down, the probability of default soars and the quality of credits agreed in the euphoric phase deteriorates drastically. Therefore, when the speculative bubble explodes, it is the credit market and borrowers' balance sheets that are ravaged.

Enter Debt Constraints

The increase in the probability of default, which lenders perceive after the stock market reversal, results from the debt valuation models presented in Chapter 6.

Using the notation for valuing investment opportunities, let W be a random variable representing the value of the assets of innovative businesses and K the level of debt which finances these businesses. The indebtedness in the next period is:

$$K_{t+1} = K_t + \Delta K_t$$

We can define the normalized default distance, that is to say, the distance-to-default per unit of volatility of the asset value variable:

$$DD = \frac{E(W_{t+1}) - K_{t+1}}{\sigma(W)}$$

The probability of default in one year is:

$$\Pi = P_r\{W_{t+1} \leq K_{t+1}\}$$

As was shown in Chapter 6, this is a decreasing function of the distance-to-default.

After the stock market reversal, asset values decline with stock values and asset volatility increases with stock volatility. Therefore, the distance-to-default decreases sharply, and the probability of default grows. Furthermore, loss-making businesses must resort to supplementary short-term debt in order to finance their current capital (ΔK_t). Thus stock market price fluctuations in the retrenchment phase of the speculative bubble and the increase in short-term debt are the principal factors in the rise in the probability of default.

The rise in the probability of default has repercussions on credit risk premia. It follows that the quality of debts underwritten in the euphoric period is downgraded and translates into a fall in the value of the balance sheets of lenders in market value. In all cases, they require provisions designed to cover potential losses, which cut bank income. The deterioration in the net income of banks, coupled with the downgrade in corporate ratings and the rise in the cost of credit, bring a diminution of new credit.

From this, there results a financial dynamic in which credit and asset price movements form a strictly co-cyclical process (Borio *et al.*, 2001). On the slope of the fall in stock market prices, the devaluation of the market value of assets is accompanied by a hardening of constraints due to indebtedness. Financial deflation occurs which forces business balance sheet restructuring. The macroeconomic peril lies in the systemic risk that builds up in this phase (Aglietta and Orléan, 2002). (See Box 7.1.)

BOX 7.1 SPECULATIVE BUBBLES AND THE PROBABILITY OF DEFAULT WITH REAL OPTIONS

Suppose that an economy is composed of an 'old economy' sector of businesses for which the stock market value is defined by a discounted dividend valuation model (with D the dividend and R the discount rate):

$$V_t = \sum_{\tau=1}^{\infty} \frac{D_{t+\tau}}{(1 + R_{t\tau})^{\tau}}$$

and another 'new economy' sector of businesses which commit at time t to a process of innovation which may possibly open up very high profit opportunities at time $t+\tau$. This innovation requires financing at a cost K_t, which is the strike price of the exercise of the real option. The random variable of the opportunity resulting from the innovation is $W_{t+\tau}$. The value of the option at time $t+\tau$ is its intrinsic value:

$$Max\{W_{t+\tau} - K_t, 0\}.$$

Its value at t is the sum of the intrinsic value and the time value of the option for this collection of businesses. This is a function which is increasing in $W_{t+\tau}$, decreasing in K_t, increasing in the volatility of the underlying asset $\sigma(W_{t+\tau})$, decreasing in the discount rate $R_{t\tau}$ and increasing in the time variable. Let B_t be the value of the option. Then the value of the stock market index can be written:

$$S_t = V_t + B_t.$$

Let us calculate the stock market return associated with the valuation schemas above:

$$\frac{S_{t+1} - S_t + D_{t+1}}{S_t} = \frac{(V_{t+1} - V_t + D_{t+1}) + (B_{t+1} - B_t)}{V_t + B_t}.$$

The discount rate is the sum of the risk-free interest rate and the risk premium: $R = i + \lambda$, so that the non-speculative component is expressed by the formula:

$$V_t = \sum_{\tau=1}^{\infty} \frac{D_{t+\tau}}{(1 + i + \lambda)^\tau}.$$

Let us assume that market belief about the growth of the bubble is a rate g and that the probability of corporate default obtained from the credit risk valuation models is Π. B_t/V_t is the relative value of the speculative component. The expected return incorporating the probability of default is then:

$$\tilde{E}\left[\frac{S_{t+1} - S_t + D_{t+1}}{S_t}\right] = \frac{i + \lambda}{1 + B_t/V_t} + \frac{(1 - \Pi)gB_t/V_t}{1 + B_t/V_t}. \quad (7.1)$$

This return equals $i + \lambda$ under the assumption of risk neutrality. Thus the expected return can be expressed as follows:

$$\tilde{E}\left[\frac{S_{t+1} - S_t + D_{t+1}}{S_t}\right] = \tilde{E}\left[\frac{V_{t+1} - V_t + D_{t+1}}{V_t}\right]$$

$$+ \tilde{E}\left[\frac{B_{t+1} - B_t}{B_t}\right]\frac{B_t}{B_t + V_t}.$$

The expected return of the component which does not involve the options is $i+\lambda$ by definition. The expected return of the speculative component under the condition that the bubble explodes is the same return. The total return is therefore also $i+\lambda$.

The expected return conditional on the absence of default is:

$$E\left[\frac{S_{t+1}-S_t+D_{t+1}}{S_t}\right] = \frac{i+\lambda}{1+B_t/V_t} + \frac{gB_t/V_t}{1+B_t/V_t}$$

$$= i+\lambda+\Pi g\frac{B_t/V_t}{1+B_t/V_t}. \qquad (7.2)$$

From (7.2), equating the expected return with its equilibrium value, one can deduce the following equation:

$$\frac{i+\lambda}{1+B_t/V_t} = i+\lambda-\frac{(1-\Pi)gB_t/V_t}{1+B_t/V_t}. \qquad (7.3)$$

Substituting in the formula for the expected return conditional on the absence of default, one obtains:

$$i+\lambda-\frac{(1-\Pi)gB_t/V_t}{1+B_t/V_t}+\frac{gB_t/V_t}{1+B_t/V_t} = i+\lambda+\frac{\Pi gB_t/V_t}{1+B_t/V_t}.$$

The return calculated by equation (7.3) is therefore greater than the expected return which incorporates the probability of default in the risk premium on the debt financing the investment in the option. The excess is an increasing function of the expectation of the growth of the bubble, the probability of default and the relative value of the speculative component. This excess return is what shareholder value rewards over and above the opportunity cost of equity capital $i+\lambda$ (see Chapter 1).

FINANCIAL DEFLATION
AND BALANCE SHEET RESTRUCTURING

The fall in stock prices has several malign effects on the financial situation of businesses. Ratings are downgraded and credit spreads widen. The cost of equity capital and the cost of debt rise simultaneously. Hence, there is an increase in the cost of capital. The acquisitions of assets, made at exorbitant prices in the euphoric phase, suffer severe capital losses. Defined benefit pension funds reveal a yawning gulf of undercapitalization. Provision for losses must be made, which absorbs current profits. New stock issuance is tarnished. Only some prestigious signatures can reconstitute their equity capital by appealing to the stock market. Institutional investors run for shelter in bond markets, either in sovereign debt, or in the highest grade bond classes.

The profile and duration of the descending phase of the financial cycle depend on the vigour with which businesses react to the deterioration of their balance sheets and on how these efforts are interpreted in the financial markets. The sensitive variable in this phase is the debt-to-asset market value, because it influences the debt quality underwritten previously. The financial constraints which businesses experience during this phase depend therefore on the evolution of this ratio. Moreover, this ratio is not at the discretion of businesses, since asset values depend on the valuation by financial markets. If the ratio increases in the course of financial deflation, while stock market prices decrease at first, the situation of businesses worsens, despite attempts to improve balance sheet structure. In this case, balance sheet restructuring is a long and painful process. That is why when financial disequilibria imprint their mark on the global economic cycle, the phase of recession is far more protected than if the cycle were the result of variations in inflation with the fluctuations in global demand. The disappearance of inflation, as a means of devaluing debt and thereby regulating the ratio of debt to asset value, is of decisive importance in the mode of regulation of global capitalism. Financial constraints have replaced wage/profit sharing in the concerns of executives. The following section shows that financial constraints are active in regimes of governance placed under the preponderant influence of financial markets.

The Frustrated Efforts of Businesses

Businesses are condemned to restructure their balance sheets out of current profits, which have been curtailed by 'provisions' for losses. Thus the fundamental feature of this phase which makes it both dangerous and of uncertain duration appears: debt leverage grows at the same time as asset values fall, despite efforts of businesses to reduce their indebtedness.

The rise of the leverage effect in the full recession phase is the crucial characteristic of financial deflation. It distinguishes the financial cycle from a macroeconomic cycle modulated by effective demand fluctuations. In this last case, excess effective demand accelerates inflation in the goods markets. Inflation devalues the debts of businesses. To revive growth, all that is needed is a short period of slowdown in production and destocking, accompanied by a temporary fall in interest rates. Inflation regulates the financial situation of businesses.

On the contrary, when balance sheet distortions stem from the joint rise in stock prices and debt, the stock market reversal with perceived probability of corporate default increases debt leverage expressed in market values. The financial situation worsens. Balance sheet restructuring is all the longer and sown with pitfalls (Fisher, 1933).

This result is demonstrated in Box 7.2, later in this section, in terms of a model which determines debt valuation as a function of asset valuation (Leland, 1994). It is shown that the ratio of debt to asset value $(D(V)/V)$ is a decreasing function of the asset value (V) when the latter is high. It increases therefore when stock prices fall, as long as the probability of default remains lower than a given threshold. The higher the asset volatility and debt interest rates, the lower the threshold. Beneath this threshold, the financial situation continues to worsen. Above the threshold, financial constraints bite effectively: the ratio of debt to asset value varies in the same direction as the asset value (Figure 7.1).

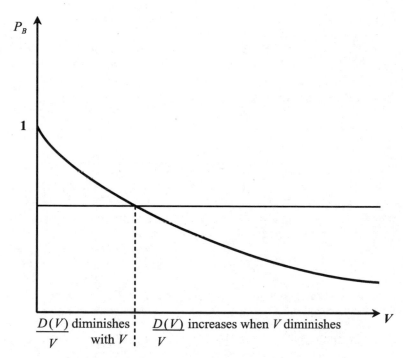

Figure 7.1   Probability of default, debt leverage and asset prices

In the phase of speculative euphoria, however, the variable V increases strongly, since asset value is pumped up by the real options incorporated in the stock market valuation. It follows that debt leverage falls with the perceived probability of default. This explains how the destabilizing dynamic of growth in indebtedness and asset prices kicks in: knock-down risk premia, strong credit growth, but still more rapid progression of asset prices, which causes debt leverage to fall. This cumulative process does not engineer a countervailing force. It can lead only to the bursting of the speculative bubble.

When the evolution of stock market prices reverses, the diminution of V causes an increase in debt leverage with the probability of default, because the reversal of V occurs at a high level where the probability of default is low. As V falls, debt constraints become more onerous with the increase in the probability of default (see Figure 7.1). As this probability rises continuously during this phase, there comes a moment when it crosses the threshold calculated in Box 7.2. Debt constraints harden to the point where businesses must reduce their expenditure in a sufficiently drastic way to soften the debt constraints. The phase of balance sheet restructurings properly speaking now begins, where debt leverage varies in the same direction as corporate asset values. In this last phase of financial deflation, debt repayment results from stock flow adjustment. If the deterioration of the financial situation is too severe, debt repayment is not possible through the progressive reconstitution of profits. Businesses become insolvent. They may then throw themselves into a drive for resurrection, possibly mixed with fraudulent transactions, as we will show in the next chapter.

BOX 7.2   ASSET VALUATION, DEBT LEVERAGE AND PROBABILITY OF DEFAULT

We start from a model conceived by Leland (1994). It assumes that corporate assets evolve according to a general diffusion process (with W a standard normalized random variable).

$$\frac{dV}{V} = \mu(V,t)dt + \sigma dW.$$

It can be shown that the debt of a firm $D(V,t)$ must satisfy the following partial differential equation:

$$(1/2)\sigma^2 V^2 D_{VV}(V,t) + iVD_V(V,t) - iD(V,t) + D_t(V,t) + C = 0,$$

where i is the risk-free interest rate.

This equation has no analytical solution in the general case. However, if one assumes that the process is stationary over time, then it has an analytical solution which can be written in the form:

$$D(V) = A_0 + A_1 V + A_2 V^{-x}$$

with $x = 2i/\sigma^2$. The constants are determined by the boundary conditions. For simplicity's sake, we shall assume that the debt is perpetual and yields a constant coupon c as long as it is not in default. Let B be the level of V that triggers default and α the rate of loss in the case of default. For a given level of B, the constants are determined as follows:

$$A_0 = \frac{c}{i} \quad A_1 = 0 \quad A_2 = \left[(1 - \alpha)B - \frac{c}{i} \right] B^x.$$

The value of the debt as a function of the asset value is expressed as follows:

$$D(V) = \frac{c}{i} + \left[(1 - \alpha)B - \frac{c}{i} \right] \left(\frac{V}{B} \right)^{-x} = \frac{C(1 - p_B)}{i} + B(1 - \alpha)p_B.$$

$p_B = (V/B)^{-x}$ can be interpreted as the current value of one monetary unit of debt contingent on a future default when V tends towards B. It is thus the probability of default. c is the coupon, i the risk-free interest rate, α the rate of loss in the event of default, and B the default threshold. The optimal value of this last variable is obtained by maximizing the value of the equity capital:

$$F = V - p_B \alpha B - D(V) = V - (1 - p_B)\frac{c}{i} - p_B B.$$

Expressing the first-order condition, one finds:

$$B = \frac{x}{1 + x}\frac{c}{i} = \frac{c}{i + \frac{\sigma^2}{2}}.$$

Note that the default threshold depends neither on V, nor on α. The probability of default itself is therefore independent of the rate of loss in the event of default. Finally, the default threshold is, unsurprisingly, all the lower when the interest rate and asset volatility are high.

The debt leverage can be calculated: $D(V)/V = 1/i\,(C/V) - [(C/i) - B(1 - \alpha)]p_B/V.$

Let us study the variation of debt leverage with asset value.

$$V^2 \frac{\partial}{\partial V}\left[\frac{D(V)}{V}\right] = -\frac{C}{i} - \left[\frac{C}{i} - B(1-\alpha)\right]\left[V\frac{\partial p_B}{\partial V} - p_B\right]$$

$$p_B - V\frac{\partial p_B}{\partial V} = (1+x)\left(\frac{V}{B}\right)^{-x}$$

$$V^2 \frac{\partial}{\partial V}\left[\frac{D(V)}{V}\right] = -\frac{C}{i} + \left[\frac{C}{i} - B(1-\alpha)\right](1+x)\left(\frac{V}{B}\right)^{-x}.$$

This expression is negative if:

$$\left[\frac{C}{i} - B(1-\alpha)\right](1+x)\left(\frac{V}{B}\right)^{-x} < \frac{C}{i}.$$

Let (7.4′) be the condition: $p_B < (C/i)/[C/i - B(1-\alpha)]\,(1/(1+x))$.

This condition does not hold for all values of V, because the second term of the inequality is constant relative to V which is <1 when $\alpha > 0$, taking into account the optimal value of B obtained above. On the other hand, p_B is a decreasing function of V which equals 1 when $V = B$ and which tends to 0 when V tends to infinity. Debt leverage is therefore an increasing function of V when the probability of default is greater than the threshold, and decreasing when it is less than the threshold. This result is represented in Figure 7.1.

Financial Deflation and the Low Pressure Macroeconomic Equilibrium

This stock flow adjustment is particularly difficult, first for each business in particular and especially for the entire population of businesses. To reduce debt leverage in the balance sheets (the current ratio), it is necessary to reverse in a lasting way the flow gap between investment and non-distributed profit. However, this last variable decreases under shareholder pressure and loss provisions. The pressure of shareholders, frustrated by the devaluation of their wealth, translates into a demand for higher dividend distribution rates. The proportion of dividends in net operational surpluses has increased in the United States and in Europe since 2000, thus reducing non-distributed profits (see Figure 2.1, Chapter 2). The increase in provisions results from capital losses, which are the remnants of external growth. To this is added the depreciation of overinvestment, which causes a rise in provisions for the depreciation of capital, relative to the gross operational surplus. As a result, not just the balance sheet structure, but also the structure of the operational and income accounts is distorted. The result is clearly a strong fall in net non-distributed profit. There is therefore only one way to reverse the gap between investment and non-distributed profit in each of the businesses where debt leverage has increased. This is the collapse of net investment. This path amplifies or prolongs, at the very least, the financial difficulties that occur when numerous businesses adopt it simultaneously (Koo, 2003).

Under a passive political economy and unchanging household behaviour, the fall in corporate investment reduces production, and hence the primary income of private agents and corporate profits. If the debt constraint is still in effect because of the deterioration of the financial situation (the probability of default is above the threshold determined in Box 7.2), expenditure must be cut still further to prevent the ratio of debt to income from continuing to increase. In Box 7.3, later in this section, it is shown that if the growth rate of nominal private income is lower than the average interest rate on existing debt, then aggregate demand from the private sector grows even slower than income. This is because the private sector, that is to say, businesses when the financial constraints weigh on the sector, must increase savings in order to cope with debt servicing. However, the aggregate demand in a given period determines the income for that period which will be spent in the following period. It follows that the nominal growth rate falls continuously while debt constraints are in effect. The fall in growth leads to deflationary pressures. These depend on the structure of the debt and its contractual conditions.

In the period of financial deflation, the constraint depends on the debt servicing (interest and repayment) with account taken of nominal income. If the debt is long-term, the repayment expense is extended and thus diminished at each payment date. If it is at a fixed rate, however, and if it has been contracted during the phase of enthusiasm for credit (at high rates), and if renegotiation is expensive, then the interest change is rigid. Flexible monetary policy cannot help reduce corporate debt directly. It can only do so indirectly by encouraging private agents to spend or by lowering the foreign exchange rate. Budgetary policy is more efficient, because it enables the state, as borrower of last resort, to spend so as to compensate for the wavering of private expenditure (see Box 7.3). Political economy in this phase is thus more effective when the financial system is hybrid. It unleashes large risk transfers: from banks towards non-banks, from businesses towards other agents (households, the state, or non-residents).

Thus one can understand why the three largest countries in the Euro-zone (Germany, France, Italy) have fallen into stagnation since 2001

(Bordo *et al.*, 2001). Credit in the zone is essentially long-term and fixed-rate. Businesses contracted debt at high interest rates at the end of the 1990s, in large part in order to acquire assets in the United States during the enthusiasm for the 'new economy'. They suffered the effect of the depreciation of these assets after the stock market crisis, but did not benefit from an expanding monetary policy. In the end, the budget was padlocked by the Stability Pact at the moment when declining private sector demand required support. Under these conditions, the economies of the Euro-zone slipped gently into stagnation and businesses were unable to free themselves of debt. On the contrary, Canada, the UK and the United States use either variable interest rates, or active renegotiation of debt when market rates fall. A very active monetary policy has transferred corporate debt to households in a massive way. Businesses therefore have been able to free themselves of debt rapidly. In addition, budgetary policy in the United States has been very expansive. The two faces of political economy have had to be combined in an expansive effort to pull the economy out of recession, where financial deflation had been leading it irremediably.

There still remains a question concerning the public management of financial deflation. Can the excess of debt contracted in the euphoric phase be depreciated? Should one favour risk transfers that would shift the problem of debt onto other agents and credit risk onto non-banks? Does the stretching of balance sheet adjustments over longer periods of time avoid the social costs of a financial crisis which devalues corporate assets brutally, in order to make investment take off again more quickly? Such are the major problems of the regulation of a capitalism founded on corporate governance oriented towards shareholders and market finance.

BOX 7.3   DEBT DEFLATION
AND NOMINAL EXPENDITURE GROWTH

We adapt the model used by Brender and Pisani (2003). Let D be the nominal amount of private sector debt, R the nominal private sector income excluding interest, and i the effective interest rate on the debt. The solvency constraint is then:

$$\frac{iD}{R} \leq \bar{i}.$$

Let $\bar{d} = \bar{i}/i$ be the upper bound of the debt-to-income ratio. The total income is: $R + iD$ since interest is paid to the private sector. Private sector spending is: $C = \lambda(R + iD)$, where λ is the average propensity to spend. The increase in the level of debt includes debt servicing and new borrowings: $\dot{D} = iD + \Delta D$, subject to the solvency condition: $\Delta D = (\bar{l}/i)\dot{R} - iD = \bar{d}\dot{R} - iD$.

Consequently, debt cannot increase more quickly than nominal income:

$$\frac{\dot{D}}{D} = \frac{\dot{R}}{R} = g.$$

The private sector budget constraint is: $C + \dot{C} = \lambda(R + \dot{R}) + \lambda i(D + \dot{D}) + \Delta D$. From this, the private expenditure growth rate can be deduced:

$$\hat{C} = \frac{\dot{C}}{C} = \frac{\lambda[\dot{R} + i(iD)]}{\lambda(R + iD)} + \frac{(1 + \lambda i)\Delta D}{\lambda(R + iD)}.$$

Dividing the right-hand side by R so as to introduce g and to use the solvency condition, the following expression for private expenditure growth can be deduced:

$$\hat{C} = g + \frac{\bar{d}(g - i)}{\lambda(1 + \bar{l})}.$$

Expenditure grows even less quickly than income, because income increases less than the rate of interest.

Let H be net public expenditure and $C + H$ be the total expenditure. The growth rate of $C + H$ required so that total income grows at the rate of debt is:

$$\frac{\dot{C} + \dot{H}}{C + H} = \gamma \hat{C} + (1 - \gamma)\hat{H} = i$$

where γ is the weight of private expenditure in GDP.

From this, the required amount of the budget deficit can be deduced:

$$\hat{H} = \frac{i - \gamma g}{1 - \gamma} + \frac{\gamma \bar{d}(i - g)}{\lambda(1 + \bar{l})(1 - \gamma)}.$$

The required deficit is all the higher the wider the gap between the interest rate on the debt and the rate of nominal income growth and the larger the weight of private expenditure.

PRUDENTIAL REGULATION AND MONETARY POLICY

Subjecting the entire economy to the financial cycle increases considerably the responsibilities of public authorities to master financial instability. The reason is that a capitalism open to the globalization of markets is less sensitive to inflation risk and more sensitive to debt fragility. Systemic risk is no longer confined to the banking sector. It extends to the whole of finance, which is interconnected by a dense network of risk transfer markets. As shown above in this chapter, the dynamic interdependence between credit and asset prices renders finance vulnerable to cumulative disequilibria. They provoke economic distortions in real investments, as the recent experience of the 'new economy' illustrates. These distortions are long and difficult to absorb in the financial deflation which follows the speculative excesses of market enthusiasm.

This financial environment cannot limit the social costs of financial deflation, which may be transformed into an open crisis unless public authorities enact renewed regulation to cope with it. The first pillar is prudential. This prudential policy, which has reached the international level, is a long-term effort (Mishkin, 2000). For many years it has been pursued for banks, but it has hardly been begun for the other financial institutions. It is a task loaded with pitfalls, since conflicts of interest and perverse effects loom in front of attempts to establish harmonized standards and coordinated inspections. The second pillar is monetary. It is effected through the renewal of the principles of monetary policy. The latter must incorporate the consequences of financial fragility on the demand for liquidity of the financial system in situations of stress. Therefore it involves transforming monetary policy. Targeting inflation, a legacy of monetarism, must incorporate the capacity to respond to all the global risks which stem from the new financial environment.

The Unfinished Business of Prudential Regulation

Prudential regulation influences corporate governance, since the latter depends closely on financial rationales. The spearhead of reform in this field is the process undertaken in Basel, under the auspices of the Committee of Central Bank Governors, in order to take better account of changes introduced by banks into risk monitoring due to their hybridization with capital markets. Contrary to the first agreement, called 'Basel I', which established in 1988 a very rough capital ratio required for assets bearing credit risk, the new agreement, 'Basel II', under development since 1995, introduces reforms in several directions (Basel Committee on Banking Supervision,

2001). It considers market risk, refines the credit risk measure, pushes banks to analyse and quantify operational and legal risks, suggests steps forward to render the supervision of banks more efficient, and finally seeks to improve the release of information.

The progress and aporias of Basel II
The approach of Basel II seeks to cover the losses of banks stemming from the variation in the specific risks of their borrowers. Its first pillar is a minimum amount of capital calculated as a regulatory percentage of the amount of assets weighted for risk. The great advance of Basel II is to distinguish risks finely and to bring together the regulatory capital and the measure of the economic capital of a bank. For credit risk, the formula for weighting risk makes regulatory provision into an increasing function of the probability of default and of the loss rate given default. Thus deterioration in the quality of corporate bank debt causes a supplement of prudential requirements which banks must put up with. After lengthy exchanges between banking lobbies and the Basel Committee, the two sides reached a compromise on the slope of the curve linking the required capital surplus to the increase in expected losses on loans (Thoraval and Duchateau, 2003). Nevertheless, the hypothesis remains that risk is a game against nature. Risk factors are assumed to be exogenous to banking behaviour. While this may be an acceptable approximation during peaceful periods, the hypothesis is erroneous in periods of stress. One might even defend the view that the uniformization induced by the use of the same statistical model for credit risk valuation (aggravated by recourse to the market ratings provided by three agencies copying each other) might aggravate considerably the phases of expansion and contraction of credit.

The most pertinent criticisms of Basel II highlight the insufficient attention given to endogenous risks. Among these, the procyclicity of the required capital ratio is the most widely discussed (Goodhart, 2002). The amplifying effect of the cycle due to prudential requirements is mediated through the positive relation, mentioned above, between surplus capital required and the increase in the probability of default. If, therefore, the estimate of the probability of default is a decreasing function of a cyclical factor, then a procyclical effect will certainly occur. The provision to constitute capital will be low and the credit supply high in the ascending phase of the cycle, but it will be high and the credit supply low in the descending phase.

Dietsch and Garabiol (2003) have examined several empirical studies seeking to measure the procyclicity of ratings. There is no ambiguity for banking models which use scoring methods: these models are blatantly procyclical. What happens when banks use the sub-products of ratings agencies, which claim to calculate credit quality with the help of variables observed over long periods? Even in this case, empirical studies show that ratings changes go in the direction of the economy. Bank reaction to a deterioration in ratings manifests itself in a flight to quality. Banks reduce their credit offers in the worst risk classes. They redeploy them to the best classes at the moment when the number of candidate-borrowers in these classes is diminishing. There is a simultaneous reduction in the overall supply of credit and a greater selectivity in the descending phase of the cycle.

As regards structural models (see Chapter 6), these are founded on the distance-to-default, that is to say, on the value of assets relative to the face value of debts. Since these models deduce corporate asset values from their equity prices, the procyclical amplification of the integral use of internal models in banks is hardly in doubt.

If procyclicity is an evident characteristic of the Basel II reforms, the distortions of competition are more insidious. First, they will take effect to the detriment of European banks that will be subject to the new legislation, contrary to the rest of the world where it will only hit the so-called international banks. These distortions are thus inscribed in the very capital ratio philosophy, which favours the US model of bank risk transfer. The clearest distortion is the disadvantageous treatment of SME credit relative to retail consumer credit. It attacks head-on the German model of risk sharing by the banks in the *Länder*. At the heart of retail consumer credit, the Basel Committee favours systematically the US method of securitization, especially in the field of housing and 'revolving credit', in opposition to the European method of physical guarantees for housing credit and operating leases. Yet these guarantees reduce loss in the case of default. If the US model becomes preponderant, it will owe nothing to improved efficiency and everything to uniformizing rules which reflect the inability of the Basel regulators to take account of the diversity of financial systems (Garabiol *et al.*, 2002). Nevertheless, other choices are possible for surmounting the defects of Basel II.

Alternative solutions
One proposition consists in amending the risk weightings and in taking specific account of the endogenous risk in order to combat the procyclical orientation of the capital ratio. Arguments in favour of a more ambitious approach might be drawn from the response of the United States to the banking crises of the 1980s of promulgating prudential legislation (the Federal Deposit Insurance Corporation Improvement Act or FDICIA). This approach would reverse the relation between regulation and supervision in the direction of a preponderance of supervision. The capital ratio

required would eliminate all risk weighting and would be covered by issuing subordinate debt.

The proposition to combat the procyclical danger of the endogenous risk comes from the London School of Economics, under the impetus of Charles Goodhart. According to this proposition, the capital required would be composed of three tiers (Danielsson *et al.*, 2001). The first tier keeps the method of risk weighting, starting from banks' internal estimates. These estimates must be approved by the regulators on the basis of a rigorous inspection of the internal models. Supervision must concentrate particularly on leverage effects and the risks of inconsistencies or discrepancies of payment dates and of currencies. The second tier would be founded on the adequacy of banks' estimates relative to the effectively observable risks. Banks which invest in more risky assets, but which have proved their competence in valuing these assets, would have to hold less capital than banks which invest in less risky assets, but which have poor risk estimation capacity. The second tier aims therefore to provide an incentive to excellence in risk management. Finally, the third tier would be deliberately counter-cyclical. Meeting systemic risk, it would be uniform for all banks: *capital provision during the ascending phase of the cycle in order to provide a shock absorber in the descending phase.* The position in the cycle, by which this supplementary provision would be indexed, would be measured by the usual economic indicators, or by the gap between the evolution of the ratio of credit to GDP relative to a long-term average (an indicator researched and advocated by the Bank for International Settlements).

The US proposition emanates from a group of reformers led by the promoters of the federal law for the improvement of deposit insurance (FDICIA), George Benston and George Kaufman. This law, adopted in 1991, provides a general framework and strengthened legitimacy for supervision (Bentson and Kaufman, 1997). Unlike the tolerance that was so costly in Europe in the 1990s and in the United States in the 1980s, the FDICIA has as its crucial characteristic the obligation to take prompt corrective action. The degree of rigour in the intervention of the regulators depends on the amount of capital provision by the banks. The thinner the capital relative to the risk exposure, the more strictly the regulators are bound to impose on the banks concerned conditions aiming to reduce risk and increase capital. The constraint is therefore progressive and not funded on a single minimum ratio threshold. It is accompanied by a restructured deposit insurance with a restrictive sense for institutional investors who are encouraged to monitor the banks themselves.

The extensions of the FDICIA envisaged by the group have the following orientation: maximum recourse to market value to calculate economic capital; bank responsibility in the definition of the amount of capital desirable under the constraint of early corrective action; encouragement of banks (obligation for the large banks) to finance this required capital by issuing subordinate debt; and complete and regular disclosure of the financial situation in order to give the holders of subordinate debt the means to monitor the banks. This schema abolishes risk weighting. Assets at risk are ideally the market value of all the securities and loans on the balance sheet and all off-balance-sheet contracts. Regulation is the combination of three dispositions: a capital ratio adequate for the style of governance and risk management capacity specific to each bank; a public watchdog equipped to enforce the early corrective action demanded by law; and a market discipline induced by the existence of subordinate debt instruments.

The thorny question of the chain of financial professions

The disparity in the treatment of the capital required for banks and non-banks is a thorny problem. This disparity was justified when non-banks engaged in activities very different from those of banks. It becomes perverse when banks offload their credit risk onto non-banks in massive amounts. In the preceding chapter, it was shown that insurance companies had recently been the counterparties of banks in buying credit derivatives in order to enable the banks to reduce their regulatory capital. This risk transfer was done on the CDS market in the United States, at the core of financial conglomerates in Europe.

However, the financial situation of insurance companies is complex. They take on banking-type risks in which they have no expertise. Nevertheless, on the liability side, they have contractual obligations which are very different from those of banks. The determination of risk-adjusted regulatory capital must therefore take into account simultaneously the risks on both sides of the balance sheet. The correlation of risks and vulnerability to extreme losses requires an integrated approach to risk. The international association of insurance company supervisors undertakes this task.

Repeated corporate financial frauds at previously prestigious firms have brought to light the deficiencies of audit firms in the certification of accounts (see Chapter 8). On their side, big institutional investors and private shareholder associations have risen in rebellion against the systematic bias of financial analysts.

Overoptimistic profit forecasting bias has been particularly accentuated in the rising stock market phase. Analysts consider companies one by one. In the 'new economy' particularly, it was impossible for all the forecasts to be realized, since the hyperbolic profit expectations were founded on the assumption of the first mover in markets with strong demand externalities. No one did the overall sum in order to warn stock market investors of the impossibility of the simultaneous realization of all the forecasts. Financial analysts, whether employed by brokers or investment banks, whether forecasting from a corporate perspective or from an investment perspective, almost all gave the recommendation to buy. Analysts nevertheless introduce detailed documentation on businesses into equity prices. The influence of analysts can earn a great deal of money for their employers.

It is on the investment banks that attention should focus. Different reforms might be suggested to moderate the conflicts of interest which the financial analysts employed by these banks embody. One idea is to forbid investment banks from holding shares in firms with which they have a business relationship. Another idea is to force analysts to invest in their own account, in conformity with the advice they give to savers, specifying a holding period of sufficient length not to be able to derive advantage by anticipating their clients' operations. There again, it is another matter to enforce the rules. Thus, in the United States, it was not until 2000 that the SEC forbade investment banks to reveal information to privileged clients before the general market. Yet the SEC has hardly sought to enforce application of the rule. So true is it that transparency was far more a propaganda argument than a concern for regulation, at least until the corporate governance scandals broke out.

More serious is the systematic discrimination practised by investment banks in the initial distributions of shares in stock market flotations. To participate in a flotation, ordinary savers had to buy shares in the secondary market, when they were resold to their primary beneficiaries at an exorbitant margin relative to their flotation price. This practice, which consists in the systematic undervaluation of prices, encourages investment banks to provoke the maximum of mergers and acquisitions, thus stimulating the market for control. Yet the SEC, the AMF, and every other market watchdog could have ordered the investment banks to have recourse exclusively to auctions in order to allocate shares in IPOs and prohibit reserved shares. If procedures were transparent, it would be difficult to justify commissions of 7 per cent on the funds raised, which the investment banks cream off. The amounts at stake, and hence the interest in preventing transparency, are enormous at the height of speculative bubbles that these operations help to maintain. Thus it is estimated that the undervaluation of IPOs was in the order of $66 billion on Wall Street in 2000. It is easy to understand investment banks' interest in this price distortion.

Finally, the Basel II approach confers a disproportionate importance to ratings agencies, yet these are outside all control. They are accountable to no one; their performance is never evaluated; and even worse, three agencies are supposed to rate the borrowers of the entire world. Their catastrophic performance during the Asian and Russian crises is admitted, with the effects of over-reaction resulting from their failure to perceive the signs of financial fragility. In the prudential role that they are supposed to play, they will also be actors in discrimination against European businesses. The agencies have accumulated long and detailed information only on businesses in the United States and a small number of multinationals. The quality of the evaluation of the credit risk of European businesses can only be inferior to that of businesses in the United States.

The ratings agencies, which so far have remained at a distance from the propositions to improve the monitoring of corporate governance, are in reality key. This matter of fact that neither governments nor prudential authorities seem to wish to modify poses a question of principle. If prudential monitoring of the financial system is a relay so that market discipline contributes to improving corporate governance, then institutions capable of turning information into a public good must be created. In this regard, ratings agencies are unavoidable institutions. The fact that they are oligopolistic, remunerated by the economic agents that they evaluate and free of all public monitoring, negates the role that is claimed for them to play.

It is important to accept that ratings agencies provide a public service and to confer on them the status and responsibility that result from this (Aglietta *et al.*, 2000). The agencies should therefore be accredited and supervised by the prudential regulators. Also, they should be financed by a uniform tax on the population of financial agents, since the latter all benefit from the public good they provide. The European Commission and the Committee for Banking Supervision, which networks national bank supervisors, should encourage the creation and accreditation of public European ratings agencies.

Flexible Inflation Targeting and Global Financial Stability

Since financial globalization and technological innovation have disconnected the financial cycle from inflationary tensions, monetarism has been shipwrecked as a guide for monetary policy. It has been necessary to define a line of operational behaviour, prior to any theoretical elaboration, in order to regulate the liquidity of the economy. This has been called 'inflation targeting', so as not to appear to break verbally with the old monetarist credo (Svensson, 1999). In fact, inflation targeting is a broad doctrine which carries disparate operating procedures. Some purist practitioners of monetarism, in the sense of obedience to rigid rules, think it is best represented in the antipodean monetary practices of New Zealand. At the other extreme, the Federal Reserve operates according to an institutional rule that has been labelled 'constrained discretion' (Bernanke *et al.*, 1999)!

Confidence in currency is a behavioural rule. It imposes no pre-announced numerical target *a priori*. Nevertheless, it constrains monetary policy to adapt to sufficiently low inflation expectations of private agents, so that the latter set their individual prices without feeling the need to have recourse to indexation formulae. This behavioural rule is a medium-term commitment (two to three years) by the central bank. In this framework, the central bank must contribute to realizing sustainable full employment, and therefore master the financial cycle as much as this can be done (Borio *et al.*, 2003). It implies a discretionary policy in the development phases of the cycle. It follows that the rule and the discretion are not on the same logical level. To set oneself a rule is to choose an implicit range of inflation in the medium term, coherent with explicit expectations of stability, since they do not unleash conflicts of indexation. To practise a discretionary policy is to interact in the short term with the dynamic of credit and financial asset prices in order to moderate financial instability, in such a way as to avoid, or at least to absorb, situations of liquidity stress (Bordo and Jeanne, 2002).

The monetary doctrine compatible with contemporary finance is clearly the two-level schema of discretionary constraint. It leads one to take into account the advantages of inflation, the costs of inflation and the costs of financial weakness from the viewpoint of the central bank. Determining an optimal policy in this enlarged framework is modelled in Box 7.4, later in this section.

The advantage of inflation in the short term is well known. It is the movement along the Phillips's curve: the possibility of increasing economic activity when the central bank judges it insufficient by accepting a rise in inflation. It is known that this relation can be established for given inflation expectations. The economic advantage of inflation is proportional to the observed rate of inflation, but its level is all the more reduced when inflation expectations are stronger.

The cost of inflation is the cost of the uncertainty about the allocation of income and wealth which results from the variability of inflation. This uncertainty unleashes conflicts, which private agents seek to exploit by attempting to impose private indexation formulae. Indexation chains then form, which can cause inflationary spirals. These allocation conflicts have real effects when the indexation bases are disparate. As inflation accelerates, it becomes more uncertain. The disparities are then greater and are perceived as unfair by its victims. By seeking to catch up their lag in the allocation, they revive the inflation process. High inflation is also very variable inflation, relative to which everyone feels threatened. It is in this way that loss of confidence in the currency is expressed. The central bank suffers a loss of reputation because of the defiance of private agents. To take account of the snowballing of the process as inflation accelerates, we assume in Box 7.4 that the cost for the central bank is an exponential function of the volatility of inflation.

The importance of financial weakness: the degree of dissonance

The cost of financial weakness requires greater attention. The global risk that the disequilibria accumulated within the financial system entail for the central bank must be formalized. To do this, we introduce a variable called the 'degree of dissonance' between the central bank's commitment to a range of inflation rates in the medium term and the credit regime.

To give some intuition of this concept, consider two opposing situations. The first might be called a creditor regime. Savings are strong; there is weak incentive for businesses to contract debt, and there is weak growth. In this regime, there is no tolerance for inflation. The central bank must have a very firm attitude in order to be compatible with private expectations (absence of dissonance). If, on the contrary, it seeks to reduce the real yield of savings, it unleashes a reaction on the part of households seeking to protect their financial wealth (through disintermediation, for example). There is dissonance. The second situation concerns the debtor regime. Strong investment growth, financed through high rates of indebtedness, can only be sustained if the real interest rate on debt is lower than the growth rate of profits. This requires tolerance for inflation, without there being slippage. If, on the contrary, the central bank chooses a very restrict-ive policy to thwart inflation expectations, the real cost of indebtedness precipitates financial weakness (rise in the probability of default). There is dissonance again.

To systematize rigorously this intuition, the concept of a neutral real interest rate, issuing from the Wicksellian theory of endogenous money, can be used. The neutral real interest rate is the rate which finances balanced growth of full employment at a constant rate of indebtedness. The market for loanable funds expresses no tension that might cause the interest rate to move, neither favouring excessive savings desires, nor favouring excessive investment incentives. Therefore, we say that the credit regime is a debtor regime if the real interest rate is lower than the neutral rate; it is a creditor regime if the real interest rate is above the neutral rate. The state of a financial system can be calibrated by an index S ranging from 0 to 1. This index normalizes the gaps between the real interest rate on bonds and the neutral real interest rate from the extreme creditor case ($S = 0$) to the extreme debtor case ($S = 1$).

The commitment of the central bank to a definition of price stability wins acceptance of money as a collective good. It leads to the acceptance of the nominal unit of account as the common basis for the setting of individual

Table 7.1   Institutional framework of monetary policy (determinants of the degree of dissonance for polar regimes)

		Credit regime	
		Creditor	Debtor
Degree of commitment of the central bank	Strict	0 0	1 0
	Relaxed	0 1	1 1

prices. In any event, preservation of the unit of account over time in an endogenous money framework is the outcome of implicit coordination between the intentions of the central bank and the expectations of private agents. It does not rest on any exogenous reference that would predetermine price stability. Moreover, central banks which announce inflation targets explicitly are far from making the same choices. Hence, one can define a commitment index (E) normalized from 0 to 1, that is to say, from the strictest attitude to the most relaxed attitude. By combining the extreme situations of credit regimes (S) and central bank commitments (E), one arrives at Table 7.1.

Now the degree of dissonance can be defined by the expression: $x = |E - S|$. It is thus logical to assume that deterioration in confidence due to financial weakness is a decreasing function of the degree of dissonance. If the degree of dissonance is at its maximum, then confidence is at its lowest. If it is zero, then any increase in dissonance downgrades confidence. In Box 7.4 we give a simple analytic expression for this function (a hyperbolic function).

Optimal monetary policy with two hierarchical levels
The discretionary level of central bank action consists in maximizing its net advantage (the advantage of inflation relative to given expectations, less the cost of the variability of inflation, less the cost of the loss of confidence due to dissonance). This occurs for a given environment which is institutional (degree of commitment to price stability) and structural (credit regime and inflation expectations of the private sector).

In Box 7.4 it is shown that the optimization of the central bank programme determines an unambiguous optimal monetary policy, that is to say, a unique inflation target. This result can easily be translated into instrumental form, since for the given structural institutional environment, the target inflation rate is a decreasing function of the interest rate.

BOX 7.4   AN INFLATION-TARGETING MODEL TAKING FINANCIAL WEAKNESS INTO ACCOUNT

The utility function of the central bank is: (inflation surprise advantage) − (inflation volatility cost) − (cost of financial weakness). To express these three components, we use a function of exponential form. It allows one to determine the optimal rate of inflation directly, when one takes the logarithm of the first-order condition. The economic meaning of each component is discussed in the main text.

Inflation surprise advantage: $\hat{p} \exp(-\gamma \hat{p}_a)$, where $\hat{p}$ is the rate of inflation and $\hat{p}_a$ the inflation expected by the private sector.

Inflation volatility cost: $- \exp(\hat{p})^2$

Cost of financial weakness: $- \exp((1 - x)/(1 + x))$, where $x = |E - S|$ is the degree of dissonance defined in the main text.

The central bank's programme in the short term can then be described. It consists in determining $\hat{p}$ so as to maximize its utility function U, given the institutional environment (E) and the structural environment (S, $\hat{p}_a$), and hence x.

$$\underset{\hat{p}}{\text{Max }} U = \hat{p} \exp(- \gamma \hat{p}_a) - \exp\left(\hat{p}^2 + \frac{1 - x}{1 + x} \right).$$

In the utility function, the interest rate (the instrument of monetary policy) does not appear explicitly. In any event, it is easy to accept that for a given environment, i is a decreasing function of $\hat{p}$. Therefore, one may consider the optimal value of $\hat{p}$ as the guiding interest rate or the operational goal of monetary policy.

The first-order condition expressed as a logarithm yields:

$$-\gamma \hat{p}_a - \frac{1 - x}{1 + x} = \hat{p}^2 + \log(2\hat{p}).$$

Let us denote $f(\hat{p})$ by the expression on the right-hand side. This is an increasing function of $\hat{p}$, which is intersected by the horizontal line representing the expression on the left-hand side (Figure 7.2).

The first-order condition determines a monetary policy and a unique $\hat{\rho}*$. It is easy to see that this policy is a decreasing function (and the interest rate is an increasing function) of the inflation expectation of the private sector. It is an increasing function (and the interest rate is a decreasing function) of the degree of dissonance.

In any case, monetary policy is credible if, in the medium term, the following condition is respected: $\hat{\rho}* = \hat{p}_a$. Combining the credibility condition and the optimality condition, one obtains:

$$-\frac{1-x}{1+x} = (\hat{p}_a)^2 + \gamma\hat{p}_a + \log(2\hat{p}_a) = h(\hat{p}_a).$$

For given inflation expectations and credit regime, this equation determines the degree of commitment which supports these expectations. Expectations cannot be deemed exogenous, since they depend on private sector trust in the commitment of the central bank. The latter can therefore determine a credible inflation range corresponding to the two extreme values of the degree of dissonance 0 and 1. The inflation range bounds within which trust in monetary policy is self-reinforcing are:

$$(\hat{p}_a)_{min} \quad \text{and} \quad (\hat{p}_a)_{max}, \text{ such that:}$$

$$-1 = h(\hat{p}_a) \quad \text{and} \quad 0 = h(\hat{p}_a).$$

The important lesson for monetary doctrine relative to inflation-target models drawing inspiration from monetarism is that the output of the model includes the standard precept, but modulates it as a function of financial weakness. The inflation target must be all the lower (and the interest rate higher), because private sector expectation is higher. That is the anti-inflationary posture of the central bank. The rate of inflation must, however, be all the higher (and the interest rate lower), because the degree of dissonance is higher. That is the posture of responsibility of the central bank against systemic risk. This explains why a modern central bank operating in a liberalized financial system must constantly diagnose the balance of risk and define the orientation of monetary policy on the basis of the most threatening risk in the given situation.

This involves just the first level of the strategy for fostering confidence in the currency that legitimates the status of the central bank at the summit of the financial hierarchy. In order for monetary policy to be credible in the

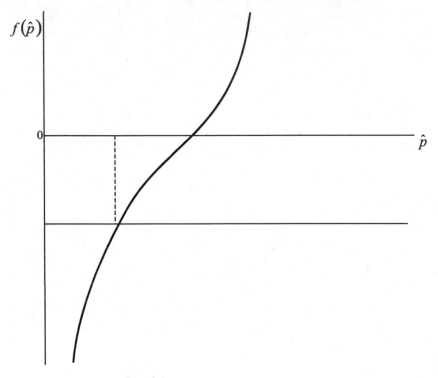

Figure 7.2   Optimal monetary policy

medium and long terms, it must be able to force the convergence of private
sector inflation expectations to the target it chooses. Satisfying this condition depends on the behavioural rule of monetary policy. It concerns
the upper level of decision-making in the two-tier schema. The decision
variable of the central bank, in providing an anchorage for inflation expectations, is its degree of commitment E. By fixing its degree of commitment,
the central bank determines the degree of dissonance for a given credit
regime S, since $x = |E - S|$.

By writing the convergence condition in Box 7.4, it can be shown that for
a given credit regime and inflation expectation, the degree of commitment
which supports this expectation is well-determined. In any case, expectations cannot be held to be exogenous, since they depend on private sector
confidence in central bank commitment. The latter can therefore determine
a credible inflation range corresponding to the two extreme values, 0 and 1,
of the degree of dissonance.

Monetary Policy versus Financial Deflation and Low Inflation

This formal explanation of inflation targeting gives the sense of the constrained discretion disposition. The analysis has been developed assuming that the credit regime was constant and represented by its inclination in favour of creditors or debtors; however, as earlier sections of the present chapter have shown, the financial cycle is deployed according to phases where the credit regime is subject to endogenous transformation.

In the euphoric phase of stock market speculation, profit expectations are high; the probability of corporate bankruptcy is perceived as low; investment and external growth drive indebtedness. The financing gap between the demand for funds and current savings is positive and increasing. It is a debtor regime. In the phase of financial deflation, the probability of bankruptcy grows strongly. Interest rates on credit increase, and the need to unwind debt is demanding. It is a creditor regime, in which, as we have seen, the debt constraint brings the nominal growth rate of the economy down, as soon as the latter is lower than the nominal interest rate on the debt. A continuous decline in the nominal growth rate causes inflation expectations to fall nevertheless. The threat of price deflation acquires a non-negligible probability. The balance of risks for the central bank is therefore modified. The main peril becomes the combination of the debt constraint and too low inflation. This creates the fear that the economy may slide into deflation, rendering it difficult to unwind debt. This is what happened in Japan and has threatened Western economies since summer 2002.

If the rate of inflation is persistently low, the presumption is that the nominal rate is also persistently low. Because the nominal rate cannot descend below zero, its response to shocks in a neighbourhood of zero is asymmetric. This characteristic is not without impact on the response of monetary policy to the wilting of income growth caused by private sector efforts to diminish its debt.

Hitting the zero bound

Consider a standard macroeconomic model in which the global supply function is given by a Phillips's curve (an increasing relation between the output gap and the variation in the inflation rate) and where global demand is a decreasing function of the gap between the real interest rate and a neutral rate (the rate for which the output gap is zero). Monetary policy acts on global demand by varying the real interest rate. To do this, it follows Taylor's rule: the nominal rate is determined in such a way that the real rate varies in an upward direction around the neutral rate, this upward variation being greater the higher the output gap and the distance from the rate of inflation to a fixed target. This rule is effective in stabilizing the economy around potential GDP. However, it is only applicable if the resulting nominal rate is positive. Otherwise, the nominal rate is zero; the rate of inflation is negative; and the real rate equals the opposite (absolute value) of the rate of inflation.

In this model, a stable equilibrium exists in which GDP achieves its potential (the output gap is zero) and the rate of inflation equals the target. There exists a second equilibrium of deflation, in which the inflation rate (which is negative) is the opposite of the real neutral rate. This equilibrium is not stable however. A recession shock will cause the economy to fall into a deflationary spiral (Reifschneider and Williams, 2000).

Simulations using this model, carried out by the authors, make it possible to estimate the frequency of falls into a deflationary trap and the average duration of such episodes, when these occur as a function of the level of the inflation target (Table 7.2).

The frequency of hitting the zero bound grows rapidly and the duration of deflationary episodes lengthens steadily when the inflation target set is lower. The volatility of production increases markedly without gaining on the volatility of inflation. From these simulations, the results show that too low a level of inflation is inefficient. For the United States, at least, an inflation target above 2 per cent is recommended. It is better still not to set an explicit target, but to pay attention to that risk which has the highest probability. In the Euro-zone, the European Central Bank has come to recognize that its target (0–2%) was too low, and it wants to announce a target as close as possible to 2 per cent.

To understand the reason for the rapid deterioration of monetary policy performances when inflation becomes too low, one should examine the formation of nominal interest rates under such conditions. Since future inflation rates are uncertain, the lower the inflation target, the higher the probability of the inflation rate becoming negative. However, the probability of deflation is reflected in the expectation of future interest rates.

Table 7.2   Frequency of the zero-rate barrier, duration of deflation episodes and economic volatility

Inflation target (%)	0	1	2	3
Zero-rate hit frequency (%)	14.0	9.0	5.0	1.0
Average duration of deflation (quarters)	6.0	5.0	4.0	3.0
Output gap volatility (standard deviation)	3.6	3.2	3.0	2.9
Inflation volatility (standard deviation)	2.0	1.9	1.9	1.9

Source: Reifschneider and Williams (2000, p. 952).

These are virtual rates when they become negative, since the nominal rate is bounded below by zero.

The reason for this state of affairs is profound. It is not due to some rigidity or other possible market imperfection; it has to do with the very nature of money. Because fiat money is absolute liquidity, private agents have the option of converting risk-free securities into cash, without cost and without limit. It follows that there is an option embedded in the nominal rate (Black, 1995). In order to make it explicit, let us write out the zero-rate floor constraint in the definition of the nominal rate:

$$\text{nominal rate} = \max\{0; \text{virtual rate}\}.$$

This equation can also be written:

$$\text{nominal rate} = \text{virtual rate} + \max\{0; -\text{virtual rate}\}.$$

The virtual rate is the rate that would be determined by monetary policy if it were following any well-known standard rule (for example, Taylor's rule). From the second equation, one sees that the nominal rate is the return on a synthetic financial product. It includes a security that returns the virtual interest rate combined with the purchase of a put option whose exercise price is zero. This option guarantees the floor 0 when the virtual rate becomes negative (Figure 7.3). It is implicitly sold by the central bank on the opposite of the virtual rate.

When the intrinsic value of the option is positive, the observed nominal rate is too high relative to the virtual rate, which the central bank should fix in order to move the economy back towards optimal production (output gap 0). The economy is stuck in a liquidity trap for a reason which has to do with the nature of money, and which has nothing to do with capital market imperfections, nor with price rigidity in goods markets. On the contrary, the more flexible prices are, the more the risk of deflation is manifest (for example, in Hong Kong, where price reduction reached 15 per cent).

For this reason, the effect of the interest rate floor spreads over the entire interest rate curve. Options have time values. When low inflation is expected to be sustained, expected future short rates have a non-negligible probability of turning negative, hence virtual. The term rates (for example, the three-month rates) observable on the yield curve incorporate the option value for the term considered, in conformity with the following equation:

$$\text{Three-month rate in one year} = \text{expected virtual rate}$$
$$+ \text{term premium} + \text{option value}.$$

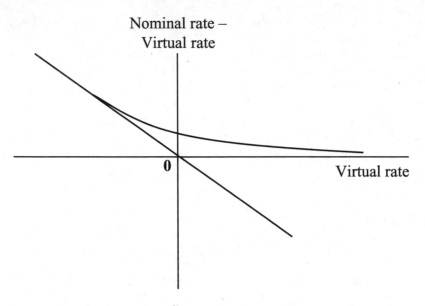

Figure 7.3   The future short rate as an option on the expected virtual rate

The option value impacts on the long rate:

$$T\text{-year rate} = \text{average of expected future short-term rates} + \text{risk premium} + \text{option value.}$$

The risk premium expresses the effect of the volatility of future short-term rates. The last term is the hitting of the zero-rate barrier if the volatility of future rates causes the virtual rate to fall below zero. Since the time value of the option increases with the volatility of future short-term rates that grows with time, the yield curve is deformed relative to its shape in the normal situation. The informational content of the yield curve is therefore altered (Figure 7.4).

Assume that the virtual yield curve is decreasing. It indicates a fall in future interest rates, hence an economic slowdown. However, this yield curve is not observable. An increasing curve is observed, because the volatility of future rates can bring them to levels which would be negative, a situation in which agents would exercise their option to convert their securities into cash. The gap between the two curves is the time value of the option. It increases with time, because the value of the option grows with the time lapse over which it can be exercised (Saunders, 2000). In this circumstance, it would be a dramatic error to infer from the positive slope

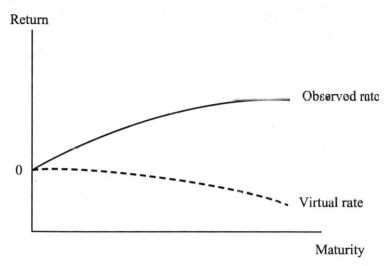

Figure 7.4   Yield curve distortion in a neighbourhood of a zero nominal rate

of the yield curve that economic activity would improve in the future. On the contrary, it heralds prolonged stagnation.

Lessons for monetary policy

From the preceding analysis, it follows that the customary rules of monetary policy, which accompany the inflation targeting, are at best inoperative and at worst dangerous when inflation is low. If the macroeconomic situation is such that a stabilizing policy should lead to a negative real rate and that the constraint on the nominal rate prevents this being achieved, then an equilibrium of underutilization of production capacity may persist. Productive investment is discouraged. If the economy has inherited a high level of debt, then debt unwinding is hindered by insufficient income growth.

The central bank must attempt to diminish the time value of the option in order to lower the slope of the yield curve and thereby to reduce long-term real rates, even if it no longer has any degree of freedom concerning current short rates. The right policy consists in exiting its customary behavioural line by committing itself to maintain the short-term rate at a very low level as long as the virtual nominal rate has not returned to its normal level. This normal level is the sum of the real neutral rate (the rate for which the output gap is zero) and the inflation target. If this commitment of the central bank influences bond market expectations, it can be embodied in long rates immediately. The real long rate will become lower than the neutral rate, contributing to the recovery.

It is preferable that the central bank adopt a pre-emptive attitude. In diagnosing the risk of a scenario which might lead to short-term interest rates dangerously close to zero in the near future, the central bank could decide to lower rates immediately, and simultaneously announce that it will maintain this policy as long as the risk of deflation has not disappeared. This is the attitude chosen by the Federal Reserve (Bernanke, 2002). In this way, it has been led to deviate significantly and lastingly from Taylor's rule in order to take out any risk of a deflationary spiral. Nevertheless, this involves a profound change in the doctrine of monetary policy. Instead of building credibility through an immutable rule, this credibility is sought through the management of macroeconomic risks.

If the central bank has not been able to foresee the slide into deflation, exceptional action must be taken in order to cause the rate of inflation to climb. The central bank can intervene directly on the secondary market for Treasury bonds. It can also buy a large range of private loans from commercial banks. If banks are handicapped by a poor quality of credit, so that they will not lend even on liquid securities, the central bank can buy loans from non-banking intermediaries on the private debt markets (such as, for example, the mortgage market regulatory agencies in the United States or the building societies in the UK) in order to influence bond market expectations.

Such prescriptions, widely implemented by the Federal Reserve, underline the extent to which the conduct of monetary policy under uncertainty has distanced itself from the mechanical rules that were advocated at the time of high inflation. In a speech given at Jackson Hole on 29 August 2003, Alan Greenspan emphasized that in order to achieve his objective of monetary stability, the central bank must adopt an attitude of macroeconomic risk management. It is not enough to equip oneself with the means to guide the economy along a desired trajectory, even if this is the most probable path. One must worry about the probability distribution of other possible evolutions and estimate their costs and advantages. If there exist scenarios of low probability, but whose costs are very high, the central bank would do well to take these into account, even if this leads to suboptimal actions relative to the most probable trajectory. These kinds of considerations led the Federal Reserve to worry about the risk of deflation, although average forecasts did not envisage it.

The US Federal Reserve Board versus Deflation

The above analysis of the theoretical foundations of monetary policy shows that the central bank should adapt its behaviour to the shocks which are preponderant in the global economy. The problems that monetary policy is called on to resolve are not the same if the source of instability is an inflation snowball on goods and services markets or speculation on financial markets. In the former case, the systemic risk is the loss of confidence in the value of the currency as purchasing power over goods and services. In the latter case, it is financial deflation that can cause an economic depression. Up until now, the Federal Reserve has been the central bank which has adapted its behaviour most explicitly to the new financial environment.

According to the theory presented above, the central bank should be attentive to the dissonance which can occur between its commitment to price stability and the degree of fragility which is present in the financial system after a phase of euphoria in the financial and real estate asset markets. In order to avoid the transformation of financial deflation in the corporate sector into a generalized crisis, asset prices must not all plunge at the same time. In the third section of this chapter, we showed that equities and the majority of corporate debts are devalued in this phase. To counter the impact of debt deflation, the central bank must therefore act so that sovereign bonds and real estate assets increase in value, that is to say, so that sovereign bond interest rates and mortgage rates fall. Certainly, its customary means of action lies in short rates. Yet the markets in public securities are unified by futures and swaps. By making known its determination to pursue an expansive direction since the beginning of January 2001, the Federal Reserve was able both to influence the slope of the yield curve and at the same time to make the entire curve slide downwards. It thus supported bank interest margins and global demand by making the financing of the public deficit attractive.

The impact of monetary policy on the residential real estate sector has been even more important in combating financial deflation. Above, we observed that real estate credit had accelerated constantly. Now, mortgage loans alone account for 30 per cent of all debt issued by non-financial agents and 50 per cent of total debt value negotiated on the financial markets.

How does monetary policy act on mortgage rates? It cannot act directly since mortgage credit is extremely fragmented in the United States. The transformation of a scattered primary market into a unified secondary market is mediated by large-scale securitization and the guarantee of the two federal agencies Fannie Mae and Freddie Mac, which regulate the secondary market in residential mortgages.

The role played by these agencies in the US financial system is enormous, as is the credit risk that is concentrated in them. In buying securitized mortgage loans in the form of Mortgage Backed Securities (MBS) and in issuing bond debt themselves, Fannie Mae and Freddie Mac enable acquirers of housing to benefit indirectly from capital market liquidity.

At the end of 2001, these agencies had bought 43 per cent of the total of housing loans, of which 24 per cent was invested in securitization funds and resold to institutional investors in the form of MBS, and 19 per cent was securitized and held directly on the balance sheets of the two agencies. In total they bore assets of $1400 billion, financed by a debt of $1330 billion, in other words a capitalization far lower than the standards that banking regulation imposes on banks.

The agencies cover the credit risk by the collateral of mortgages and by the purchase of tranches of MBS, which benefit from clauses enhancing the quality of the underlying loans (credit enhancement). They are exposed to the market risks which arise from differences between the market value of their assets (the MBS held and the guarantees on the MBS resold) and their liabilities (the bond debt issued). These risks stem from the variation in interest rates and the mismatching of asset and liability maturities caused by early repayments of the underlying loans. In order to counter these risks, the agencies use dynamic portfolio rebalancing and option hedging. The former consists in modifying the composition of liabilities by renewing debts or by contracting swaps with counterparties to adjust the expected asset and liability payment schedules when interest rates vary. The latter stems from the fact that the assets of the agency are themselves optional, since their maturity depends on the option that borrowers have of early repayment. That is why the agencies buy swaptions (options on interest rate swaps). Combined with the debt instruments on the liability side, swaps and swaptions create synthetic debts of variable duration. They seek to marry changes provoked by fluctuations of accelerated mortgage loan repayments as a function of variation in interest rates.

These linkages form a unique relay of monetary policy because falls in bond rates have repercussions on mortgage credit rates via MBS prices. Households rush to make early repayments. The effective maturity of fixed rate mortgage loans, and thus also of the assets of the agencies, diminishes. The latter seek therefore to rebalance their liabilities. To this end, they buy swaps (receiving a fixed rate, paying a variable rate). Their counterparties, who are paying the fixed rate, must buy bond debt. This amplifies the downward movement of rates.

Figure 7.5 shows the extraordinary reactivity of households to the stimuli given to mortgage credit rates by the Federal Reserve. Households proceeded to 'liquefy' their real estate holdings. Instead of profiting from the fall in interest rates in order to reduce their indebtedness, they contracted new loans on the basis of their mortgage collateral. Thus, in addition to the acquisition of new housing by households attracted by the fall in the cost of mortgage credit, the new loans helped consumer spending. The macroeconomic result was the spectacular rise in real estate prices, the collapse of

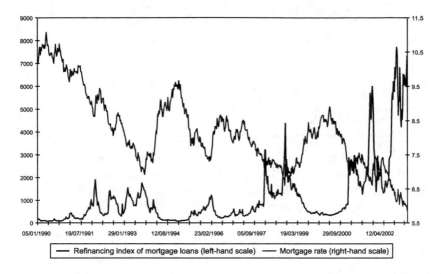

Source: Datastream.

Figure 7.5 Mortgage loan refinancing

the household savings rate and sustained global demand despite depressed corporate investment.

One should not forget the extent to which the type of capitalism founded on the preponderance of stock markets and shareholder value depends on the regulation of liquidity by the central bank in order to contain the instability which this capitalism oozes. The Federal Reserve caused interest rates to move from 6.5 per cent at the beginning of 2001 to 1 per cent at the end of 2002, and all through 2003 and the first half of 2004 maintained this exceptionally low rate, as measured by the criteria of the last 50 years. It is in this atypical macroeconomic environment that the crisis in corporate governance exploded with the disaster of Enron.

8. Reinterpreting the financial scandals of the Enron era

On 16 October 2001, Enron announced an exceptional expense of $500 million for hedging with LJMs 1 and 2, companies managed by Enron's own Chief Financial Officer (CFO). The result was a loss of $638 million in the third quarter, after a profit of more than $400 million the quarter before. On 17 October, the personal enrichment of the CFO, to the sound of $30 million, was made public by the *Wall Street Journal*. On 22 October, the Securities Exchange Commission (SEC) launched an investigation. From that point on, nothing could break the fall. The stock price collapsed, and ratings agencies lowered their assessments. On 2 December, Enron was placed under bankruptcy protection according to Chapter 11 of the Bankruptcy Code.

At $63 billion in assets, this has been the largest bankruptcy in US history. In terms of stock market capital that vanished, the loss inflicted on share-holders was considerable: at the end of November, the stock traded at 26 cents. For Enron's 27 000 employees in 40 different countries, the damage was just as heavy. They lost their jobs, and their retirement fund evaporated. The in-house pension fund, based on the 401(k) Plan and thus exempted from the ERISA law imposing diversification, had been 60 per cent invested in Enron shares (Bratton, 2002).

Enron's bankruptcy was remarkable not only for the sheer magnitude and extent of the disaster, but also because it hit such a model corporation, one which had adopted all of the management norms in vogue at the time: the creation of shareholder value, permanent re-engineering, e-business, derivatives trading, and so on. Behind this facade, the industrial, commercial and accounting practices brought to light by various investigations[1] would prove to be astounding in their ingenuity and dishonesty, to say nothing of the political lobbying activities uncovered. Heavyweights of the US financial industry numbered among the actors compromised by this bankruptcy: the audit company Arthur Andersen, which would pay for its part in the scandal by its disappearance and the investment banks J.P. Morgan Chase & Co. and Citigroup, sentenced by the SEC to pay $255 million in an out-of-court settlement.

Even though WorldCom's June 2002 bankruptcy surpassed Enron's in scale ($104 billion in assets, $41 billion in liabilities), the latter remains symbolic of how adrift capitalism had become at the end of the twentieth century. It would be mistaken to see nothing but the hand of corrupt company executives at work in these spectacular bankruptcies. Enron and WorldCom were the tip of the iceberg, the most visible symptoms of a larger structural crisis. The crisis is all the more notable for two reasons: first, it hit the US economy, which was presented as a model up until the moment the first problems appeared; second, it concerned elements that were sources of pride – transparency of financial markets and reliability of corporate accounting.

Discussion of these excesses invariably points the finger at corporate governance, but any consensus ends there. Identifying the precise nature of the aberrations and diagnosing the extent to which structures have been adversely affected by repeated financial scandals, remain objects of debate. Why did the executives of companies like Enron engage in such manipulative operations? Why did external and internal safeguards fail so easily? How can such things be avoided in the future?

This chapter proposes to answer these questions, analysing in detail the reasons behind the crisis. The first section concentrates on the Enron example to the extent that it is characteristic of the financial excesses that have taken place since 2001. The second section presents the standard explanation, at least in the United States, of these aberrations, which points out the culpability of those charged with monitoring listed companies. The third section puts forward a different argument, highlighting the responsibility of shareholder sovereignty. Finally, the fourth section looks at legislative measures taken in reaction to the crisis, the pertinence of which we will try to assess.

EXAMINING THE US CRISIS: THE ENRON CASE

One of the most troubling aspects of the Enron affair is the huge contrast between the corporation's public image before October 2001, an image confirmed by its stock market price, and the reality of the practices at work internally.

A Model Company: The Enron Success Story

For the vast majority of observers, Enron distinguished itself by a complex, yet particularly attractive, business model and a very close application of managerial standards emblematic of the 1990s.

At its creation in 1985, Enron was simply a pipeline management company based in Houston, Texas. It quickly oriented itself toward market intermediary activities on deregulated markets, facilitating supply and demand coordination in the area of energy products – first gas and later electricity. Enron played a part in the liberalization of the latter through powerful lobbies. In order to make itself more attractive to clients and increase its competitiveness as an intermediary, Enron specialized in derivatives trading, managing risks associated with the sector's high cash flow volatility. Market actors were able to hedge transactions where Enron acted as the intermediary. Over the years, this area of Enron's activity expanded more and more, effectively transforming the company into a speculative hedge fund. Enron began to feel threatened when legislation was introduced to regulate the trading of these financial products. Using its influence with a senator, Enron obtained a special 'Enron clause' in the Commodity Futures Modernization Act 2000. The senator's wife was a member of Enron's board of directors. The clause exempted derivatives trading companies in the energy sector from regulations concerning financial disclosure requirements. In 2000, Enron could thus boast of being an unregulated investment fund. The final touch was when Enron decided to invest heavily in e-business. The company made a $1.2 billion investment in high-speed fibre-optics networks, which would later prove disastrous. *Enron On Line* was created as a platform for online commodities trading. In spite of all this, Enron's dominant business activity at the end of the 1990s was neither risk management in the energy sector nor investment in new information and communication technologies, as we will see.

Associated with this business model, unfurling at the forefront of finance and new technologies, were the rhetoric and practice of shareholder value creation and constant re-engineering. For this reason, Enron developed a structure that was not hierarchical, but flat, and organized around profit centres. It was accompanied by the recruitment of young, highly skilled employees and a very strict, extremely individualized style of personnel management. Employee autonomy and responsibility were established as management principles, the goal being sustained growth of the value created for shareholders.

Enron's development was remarkable in all respects. Arthur Andersen, one of the 'big five' of the audit industry, certified Enron's financial statements regularly; almost every securities analyst recommended its shares; and ratings agencies gave it an excellent credit rating. From 1990 to 2000, turnover increased tenfold; it doubled between 1999 and 2000, reaching $100 billion, and making Enron the seventh largest US company. In August 2000, Enron shares were trading at a record $81.

Manipulations and Accounting Fraud

It is surprising that such astounding economic growth did not raise more questions at the time. Apparently, the source of profits matters little as long as they continue to arrive quarter after quarter. In the frenzy of the 'new economy', which some claimed emancipated from the classical laws of economics (see Chapter 1), Enron's penetration into derivatives trading and e-business was perceived as a guarantee of sustained profits. Behind the mask of success, however, were hidden fraudulent accounting policies. In terms of solvency and liquidity, it was the only way for the Texan company to maintain its extraordinary growth. The policy took three forms: heavy recourse to off-balance-sheet accounting, the hijacking of fair value, and creative accounting on the income statement, as discussed in the next three sub-sections.

The asset light strategy, or the systematization of off-balance-sheet accounting

Enron's success at risk management in the energy sector is indisputable, so the reasons behind both its rapid expansion and its collapse must be sought elsewhere. In the second half of the 1990s, asset reduction became the dominant strategy of Enron's management. Economizing capital was established as a fundamental guiding principle for the company. In so doing, Enron was obeying the commandments of shareholder value, which made the asset light strategy its mantra (see Chapter 1) by developing appropriate management tools (EVA and MVA). The goal was to increase to the highest degree returns on capital assets. One of Enron's particularities was to have instituted this as a *permanent* (recurring) strategy for ensuring long-term profit (Chatterjee, 2003). If financial markets do not fully address the paradoxical nature of this principle (constant asset reduction), its concrete application leads to a policy of asset repurchasing and large-scale investment, for the simple reason that to sell, one must control assets in one way or another. This was so much the case that Enron, in its last years, was much less an energy sector corporation than a firm specialized in the trading of very diverse assets, from which it derived more than two-thirds of its profit. Enron's inordinate profit growth was due less to its choice of investments than to its policy of covering up the inevitable losses inherent in this type of activity. Its policy essentially consisted of transferring the most devalued assets, *a priori* unmarketable, to companies which appeared at first glance to be autonomous, but which were in fact controlled by Enron. Heavy use of off-balance-sheet accounting and deconsolidations, allowing Enron to undervalue its debt and to dispose of troublesome assets, became the company's trademark. In fact,

Enron used a galaxy of almost 3000 small companies it controlled indirectly. It would transfer the most downgraded elements of its balance sheet to these companies, avoiding consolidation by respecting certain conditions fixed by the SEC.

There are two types of structures commonly used in the United States. The first is equity affiliates. The parent company (in this case Enron) is not liable for the debt of these affiliates providing it holds less than 50 per cent of the equity capital. However, transactions between the parent company and its affiliates cannot be registered in the accounts. This second point leads to another type of structure Enron used – Special Purpose Entities (SPE). Like equity affiliates, SPEs enabled Enron to lighten the balance sheet while simultaneously engaging in completely legal operations equivalent to those made between two fully independent companies. There are multiple possibilities for creative accounting: increased revenues through virtual transactions, disclosure of an asset's 'real' price by applying the fair value principle, and so on. Unofficial SPE regulations state that an external investor must control more than 50 per cent of the SPE's common stock, which must itself represent more than 3 per cent of the SPE's total capital. SPEs are common in the United States. They are used to avoid paying taxes on foreign transactions, to make risk transfers (see Chapter 6), and, of course, to make off-balance-sheet deconsolidations. In Enron's case, there are three particularities:

1. the number of SPEs: 3000, of which almost 700 were set up in fiscal paradises, most notably the Cayman Islands;
2. the extent of deconsolidation: in April 2000, 50 per cent of assets were non-consolidated;
3. the misuse of company property: these structures would allow for substantial personal enrichment.

The LJM companies and the Raptor transactions have come to symbolize these fraudulent practices, all the more because they were the direct cause of Enron's collapse (see Box 8.1).

**BOX 8.1   LJM AND THE RAPTORS: THE DEALS
THAT BROUGHT DOWN ENRON**

Between 1999 and 2000, two private investment funds, in the form of limited partnership companies, were created at the instigation of Enron's executives. LJM1 and LJM2 were named using the initials of the wife and children of Enron's CFO, who was also the majority shareholder and director of the two funds. External investors, such as Merrill Lynch for LJM2, participated in the financing of these funds. The purpose of these funds, clearly explained to the directors of Enron, was to support Enron's policy of asset disposal: in addition to transactions made directly with Enron, the two investment funds regularly played the role of external investor for Enron's SPEs. This was flagrant circumvention of the SEC's implicit rule. A company controlled by one of Enron's executives could hardly be considered as an 'external' investor. What is more, the conflicts of interest are so evident that the silence of Enron's board of directors is astonishing: for each transaction, the general manager of the LJMs was negotiating with a company whose financial state he knew better than anyone else, as he was its CFO.

LJM1's first transaction was a taste of what was to come. Enron's stake in Rhythms NetConnections, acquired in a takeover for $10 million, was valued at over $300 million at the time of LJM1's creation. Having recorded these capital gains in its income statements, Enron carried out what appeared to be a classic hedging operation with LJM1 in order to guard against a loss of value. However, the cost of this operation was not charged to Enron. Instead, the deal ended in a payment of $50 million from LJM1.

Transactions with LJM2 were even more spectacular: the fund's first six months of business brought Enron a profit of $200 million. The board of directors was informed of all these transactions. As the US Senate Report notes, '[no] Directors asked how LJM was able to produce such huge funds flow with such minimal effort by [Enron's CFO]' (Permanent Subcommittee, 2002, p. 105). In fact, what Enron's board did not realize is that, in the end, it was the LJMs which were benefiting from these transactions. Thanks to them, the LJM general manager pocketed a total of $45 million ($23 million from LJM1, $22 million from LJM2).

The objective of the four Raptor operations, carried out beginning in June 2000, was to hide losses related to depreciated investments. Approximately $1 billion in losses was transferred in this way. An SPE, intended to receive the assets that Enron wanted to hedge, was created for each operation (Raptors I, II, III and IV). Each time funding came from two sources (see Figure 8.1): a contribution from Enron in the form of pledges of Enron stock and call options, and $30 million in liquid assets from LJM2. LJM2's investment was nevertheless accompanied by a commitment to repay within six months with a premium of $11 million (to make a total reimbursement of $41 million). Consequently, Enron stock was the only tangible capital that Raptor had for hedging Enron assets. In short, Enron 'hedged' itself, counter to all financial logic. The gatekeepers' reactions were varied: from Arthur Andersen, worry, but no action taken; from the board of directors, enthusiasm. Thus it was that one of the board members suggested that Enron's CFO file a patent on the accounting techniques used in the Raptor operations. This director would later qualify the Raptor operation as 'leading hedge accounting' in his hearing with the Senate committee.

The stock market turnaround of March 2000 was to deal a fatal blow to these hedge operations: Enron's shares lost 40 per cent of their value in the first half of 2001. Raptor solvency declined as a consequence of being wholly dependent on Enron's stock price, while hedged assets continued to depreciate. In order to counter this downward motion, Enron staged complex financial operations with the help of Arthur Andersen, which seemed not to have realized the gravity of the situation. In August 2001, one of Enron's employees broke the silence and informed one of Andersen's agents. In September, Andersen made a 180° turnabout and told Enron to cancel all hedging made with the Raptors, forcing Enron to announce an exceptional expense of $500 million on 16 October 2001. Revelations about the personal enrichment of the CFO, followed by the deterioration of Enron's rating in October and November 2001, finished the company off. Enron found itself obliged to repay, finance or provide cash of $4 billion, just as the financial community was waking up to the scale of Enron's manipulations.

Abusing fair value

Besides resorting to large scale off-balance-sheet accounting within the framework of an 'asset light' strategy, Enron's management turned the fair value principle to its own benefit. As outlined in Chapter 5, the principle consists of evaluating a corporation's balance sheet items according to their market value as estimated by liquid markets (marked-to-market). Where no such market exists, reference to models is encouraged (marked-to-model). This approach is in line with the doctrine of shareholder value: the fair value principle holds that financial markets produce the most accurate valuation of a company's activity. Besides using shareholder value as the ultimate justification, promoters of fair value insist that it limits internal manipulations that the historical cost method allows. The Enron case,

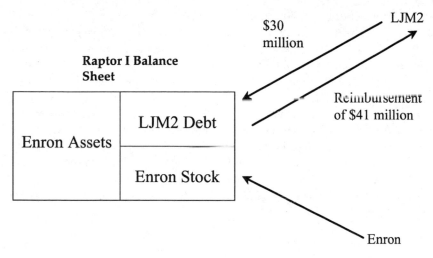

Figure 8.1 Example of a Raptor hedging operation

however, runs counter to this conventional representation of the effectiveness of fair value as a guarantee against managerial misconduct.

The 'dark fibres' example is particularly illustrative (see Mistral, 2003). Enron invested in an enormous network of high-speed fibre-optics cable of which a large part had not been activated. Internally valued at $33 million, this embarrassing asset was sold to LJM2 for $100 million. Enron saw a $67 million profit on the transaction. It was a classic example of Enron's practices, making a fictitious capital gain by passing off depreciated assets onto affiliates at arbitrarily fixed prices. The story does not end there. Not content with making a profit on a poorly performing asset – the result of a disastrous investment – Enron took the opportunity to re-evaluate all of its assets that were similar to the 'dark fibres'. Shrewdly arguing that this operation revealed the 'fair value' of its assets, in other words their market price, Enron's management had but to apply 'marked-to-market' in order to increase the value.

Marked-to-model was also an opportunity to inflate asset values artificially. In particular, evaluating energy trading contracts using fantastical discount rates, in an updated classical cash flow model, allowed for a much improved presentation of financial statements, even if it is difficult to determine to what extent (Bentson and Hartgraves, 2002, p. 115).

In the end, Enron seems to have exercised the fair value principle capriciously, using it when convenient (when market prices rose), but omitting lower balance-sheet values when market prices fell. An internal document of July 2001 thus recognized a $2.3 billion overvaluation of international assets resulting from this unconventional use of fair value.

Creative accounting, or how to improve results
The last form of accounting manipulation Enron employed was at the
limits of 'creative accounting'; it affected income statements directly and
aimed at improving profits. First of all, revenue was artificially increased.
In the area of intermediation, it sufficed to register the total value of transactions in the accounts, and not the true value of the commissions Enron
received. The endless exchange of goods with other companies (especially
SPEs), exchanges that had no economic motivation, was used in the same
fashion. Next, expenses were minimized as much as possible through pro-
longing capital depreciation and underfunding risks. Finally, the accounts
were presented in an obscure fashion, systematically using *pro forma*
accounting as permitted by the SEC. This allowed Enron to avoid registering exceptional charges.

Beyond Enron: A Systemic Crisis

For all that Enron's bankruptcy was exceptional in scale and for the huge
contrast between its image (its business model) and the reality of its practices, it still showed the fragility of the US model. It was not an isolated
case. In the months that followed Enron's collapse, massive bankruptcies
of listed companies in the United States followed one after the other. The
telecommunications sector was hit especially hard by the bankruptcies
of Qwest, Global Crossing, and WorldCom, all three audited by Arthur
Andersen. In each case, accounting fraud and manipulation became
systematic, to guarantee favourable stock market valuations. For example,
Global Crossing, created in 1997, used its inordinate market capitalization (more than $40 billion at the end of 1998, just months after being
listed) to pursue a particularly aggressive acquisition policy. This was
accompanied by extensive use of *pro forma* accounting. All sectors were
involved: in 1998, 158 listed companies were the objects of earnings
restatements; in 2000, this number rose to 223, a 43 per cent increase at
the height of the 'new economy'. According to a report published by the
General Accounting Office in October 2002, between January 1997 and
June 2002, nearly 10 per cent of listed companies in the United States
restated their earnings at least once due to accounting irregularities.

Very few experts attribute scandals like Enron solely to the dishonesty of
a few executives. One would be hard-pressed to explain the recrudescence
of dishonesty in the second half of the 1990s on the basis of psychological
factors alone. The vast majority of US commentators on the Enron affair
are not mistaken: Enron is regarded as the clearest symptom of the crisis
suffered by the US model, characterized by the decisive role given to financial markets. Dormant until 2001, all the crisis needed to produce its effects

was the bursting of the economic bubble that came in March 2000, and the end of the new economy. Enron was the first tremor.

Even though the diagnosis of a structural crisis (revealed by Enron's bankruptcy) is largely shared, the precise identification of the affected zone and the assessment of the seriousness of the crisis remain matters for debate in the United States. First of all, it is entirely possible to consider that it was simply the chain of information which failed (see Chapter 2), by which we mean all the actors and procedures, whether formal or informal, which together produce information on a company's activities. This chain leads from the production of accounting data, to the verification and interpretation of this data by professionals charged with the social construction of this information. It is equally possible to consider that it was not so much information about the behaviour of corporations that is to blame, but the behaviour itself. More than the chain of information, it is the mode of governance, that is, the corporation's goals which pose the problem (see Chapter 3). This is the argument defended here.

THE CHAIN OF INFORMATION IN QUESTION

The chain of information can be broken down into two stages involving distinct actors.

Rule-based or Principle-based Accounting Regulations?

The first stage begins with the codification and formatting of company activity into numbers. Therefore, it concerns the quality of accounting standards. From this comes a first interpretation of the crisis: the financial scandals reveal the weak points of US accounting standards, and thus of the accounting system put in place by the SEC and the FASB (see Chapter 5). By going into greater detail, we can indeed pick out certain defective standards. For example, allowing firms to present their accounts *pro forma* poses numerous problems. More than half the S&P 500 companies now use the technique, invented within the telecommunications sector at the beginning of the 1990s. In a more general sense, it is the detailed, rule-based character of accounting in the United States that is called into question. Compared to the IASB or European systems, the number of rules to follow is considerable. The FASB offers a conceptual framework containing a huge spectrum of standards aimed at anticipating every possible situation. If these rules are respected, that is the end of the matter. Enron is a perfect case in point; it got around the regulations by systematically respecting the 3 per cent rule (respectively the less than 50 per cent rule) for incorporating an SPE (respectively equity affiliate). The construction of an off-balance-sheet galaxy and the proliferation of deconsolidations escaped reproach despite the patently problematic nature of these operations. In the event of infraction, retrospective verification by a judge is largely facilitated by the system's precision, and is in fact characteristic of US regulation. In contrast, European and IASB systems are less detailed and thus more flexible. The spirit of the law counts more than strict adherence to a standard fixed *ex ante* in a necessarily arbitrary manner (why 3 per cent and not 2.98 or 3.03 per cent?). Paradoxically, the large number and the inflexibility of the rules in the United States make them easier to circumvent. We will see later in this chapter that the advantages of a principle-based, less legalistic approach to accounting are currently being considered in the United States.

The Gatekeepers' Failures: The Standard Argument

The second stage of the chain of information is the verification and the synthesis of the information given on the company's business. An ensemble of actors, theoretically independent, intervenes once these activities have been registered in the accounts according to accepted accounting principles. These actors, the 'gatekeepers', are responsible for verifying the honesty and the relevance of the registered items and for using the information to give the best advice possible to investors. Their purpose is to reduce informational asymmetries between investors and insiders (agents in the company) so as to ensure the proper working of financial markets. This intermediary function, codified in part by financial market regulation, rests largely on the worth of the actors' reputations. There are five actors:

1. auditors, who verify and certify companies' accounts;
2. securities analysts, who compile information in order to make buy-and-sell recommendations on securities;
3. ratings agencies, which assess companies' solvency;
4. investment banks, which manage mergers and acquisitions, Initial Public Offerings, or share issues;
5. attorneys, who handle the legality of transactions.

The failure of the gatekeepers in the Enron affair is so evident that it is now common to characterize the US crisis as a gatekeeper crisis. This explanation, strongly defended by the legal expert Coffee (2002), is in fact the most widely accepted in the United States.

Calling auditing into question

Among the five types of gatekeepers, audit firms were the most affected by the Enron affair. Arthur Andersen, responsible for auditing Enron and WorldCom, blindly and systematically endorsed the accounts handed over by Enron's management. This blindness was surprising considering the extent of the fraud, as well as Andersen's prestigious reputation. Nevertheless, the punishment fitted the crime: after being convicted for destroying documents, the company ceased to exist. The Big Five (Andersen, Deloitte-Touche-Tohmatsu, Ernst & Young, KPMG and Pricewaterhouse-Coopers) were now only four. This increased the already high concentration of the audit industry. Nonetheless, Andersen was not the only guilty party, just the most unlucky. The Enron affair condemned it more certainly than any other firm. In relation to its revenues, the number of frauds endorsed by Andersen was the same, even less, than the other four firms; Andersen verified the accounts of 21 per cent of the Big Five clients, but was only involved in 15 per cent of the earnings restatements involving these clients. The reputation of the entire audit profession was tarnished by the scandals.

How can this blindness, this failure to fulfil their mission, be explained? According to Coffee (2002), the economic reasoning is simple. If audit firms were led so far astray in the second half of the 1990s, it was because the cost of error was relatively low historically and the related profits much higher. Naturally, this led to laxer surveillance. In fact, in the 1990s, a series of legal decisions made legislation on auditors' responsibilities more flexible. During the same period, conflicts of interest in these firms were taking on growing significance. The conflicts arose as firms began to provide consulting services to their clients (beyond auditing). Certifying a company's accounts provided audit firms with a certain expertise on its activities and allowed them to charge for their consulting services. The consequences were immediate: not wanting to lose this lucrative consulting activity, audit firms tended to be more indulgent toward the accounts presented, because it was highly unlikely that a company would be inclined to maintain a business relationship with an audit firm quick to denounce its accounting practices. The independence necessary to an auditor's effectiveness was thus undermined by providing consulting services. These conflicts of interest were nothing new, but they became particularly widespread over the course of the 1990s: according to the Panel on Audit Effectiveness, from 1990 to 1999, earnings from consulting rose from 17 per cent to 67 per cent of total fee income. The panel was put into place in 1999, at the request of the SEC, which was already beginning to worry about auditing practices. Regarding Enron and Andersen, the numbers speak for themselves: in 2001, audit fees were $25 million; consulting fees were $27 million. It was for fear of losing this financial windfall that Andersen turned a blind eye to Enron's accounting practices. It proved to be a disastrous decision. At the same time as Enron revealed the vicissitudes of the audit industry, the weakness of its system of self-regulation came to light. Indeed, if the process of setting accounting standards has been independent of the auditing profession since 1973 in the United States, this is not the case for audit supervision, which is regulated at the federal level by a national, professional auditors' organization (the American Institute of Certified Public Accountants, or AICPA), under the ultimate control of the SEC. The AICPA ordered the Public Oversight Board (POB) to implement peer review, characteristic of almost all OECD countries. Not surprisingly, the POB would be one of the first victims of the Enron affair.

The aberrations of financial analysis

Enron's bankruptcy threw a harsh light on the practices of financial analysts. It is indeed striking that 16 out of the 17 analysts covering the corporation recommended the purchase of Enron shares up until October 2001. Once again, conflict of interest is behind such behaviour: these analysts most often work for investment banks offering advisory services to the corporations they analyse. Under these conditions, it can prove to be a costly move (both for the bank and the analyst's career) to issue a recommendation to sell. The mounting force of conflicts of interest may be properly appreciated when one realizes the ratio of buy recommendations versus sell recommendations, issued by all of the analysts in the United States: whereas in 1991 the ratio was 6 to 1, by 2000, it had risen to 100 to 1.[2]

Weaknesses in the Gatekeeper Thesis

All of the preceding arguments question the reliability of the chain of information. This brand of argument is the most common explanation for the Enron disaster and the subsequent financial scandals. The weaknesses of the rule-based approach to accounting, as well as the conflicts of interest in auditing and financial analysis, are mentioned regularly. In contrast, other gatekeepers have managed to minimize their role in these affairs. For ratings agencies, this favourable outcome is linked to the fact that on the whole they seemed to be more independent than securities analysts, and therefore less subject to conflicts of interest. That their lateness in downgrading Enron did not raise more questions is in the very least surprising.

The gatekeeper thesis still poses a problem. In fact, even if the United States was particularly affected by scandals related to the management of listed companies, European countries did not escape unscathed. Various affairs can be cited, though none having the magnitude of the US crisis: Vivendi and France Télécom in France, Ahold in the Netherlands, and Parmalat in Italy all contributed to varying degrees in undermining confidence in financial capitalism. Yet gatekeepers are, by their very nature, national. They consist of actors and procedures defined by national regulations. To explain the crisis in the United States by gatekeeper failure alone, attributing the failure to local factors (increasing conflicts of interest, more flexible jurisprudence on auditing, etc.), is either to ignore the difficulties outside the United States or to render the gatekeeper thesis so general as to dilute its message. Monitoring would thus be untrustworthy in every respect, everywhere. However, given such a level of gatekeeper incompetence, would it not be better (more logical) to turn attention to the intrinsic motivations of agents, to the conduct of firms themselves? To use a metaphor, the gatekeeper thesis would attribute violence in society to the incompetence of the forces of law and order without questioning the root cause of that violence.

BEYOND GATEKEEPER FAILURE: SHAREHOLDER SOVEREIGNTY AT THE ROOT OF THE CRISIS

On closer inspection, the repeated financial scandals on both sides of the Atlantic reveal a common rationale: the use of stock markets in a framework of aggressive acquisition policies with no obvious economic logic. This policy creates a strong dependence on financial markets for two reasons. On one hand, maintaining high stock market prices is a necessary condition for making acquisitions by exchange offers. Cash outflows, which would have increased indebtedness, are thereby limited. On the other hand, once the acquisitions have been made, a fall in stock market prices makes the balance sheet weak due to the depreciation of equity interests (the problem of goodwill). Again, Enron is a good example: the root of Enron's corruption was the systematization (radicalization) of an 'asset light' strategy that forced Enron constantly to acquire (mostly through capital markets) and resell assets, as discussed earlier. Accounting manipulations, most notably the use of offshore affiliates, were the means of camouflaging the inevitable failures of this strategy. The case of Parmalat, the largest food-processing corporation in Italy, came about for much the same reasons, earning it the nickname the 'European Enron' (see Box 8.2). Quoted on the Milan Stock Exchange, Parmalat was 51.3 per cent held by the family of the founder who was accused of having misappropriated more than one billion euros. The concentration of ownership did not in the least prevent an Enron-like scenario. The CFO/majority shareholder simply played the part of the managerial team in misappropriating assets.

BOX 8.2   PARMALAT: EUROPE'S ENRON

On 27 December 2003, the Parma tribunal declared Parmalat, employer of 36 350 people in nearly 30 countries, insolvent. The scandal would include most of the ingredients of the Enron affair. First, in the 1990s, the company launched an intensive policy of acquisition and diversification, accompanied by the raising of large amounts of cash on US and European stock and bond markets. Parmalat contracted 26 bond loans starting in 1996, for an estimated debt of seven billion euros by the time insolvency was declared. As with Enron, Parmalat had a multitude of offshore fronts designed to ease the balance sheet. These practices would particularly increase beginning in 1998. At the centre were the Bonlat Financing Corporation and the Epicurum funds, both registered in the Cayman Islands. The announcement by the Bank of America, on 19 December 2003, of a 'black hole' of 3.95 billion euros in Bonlat's accounts precipitated the company's downfall: these liquid assets, registered to the account of the offshore company with the Bank of America, only existed because of a false document. The revelations which followed increased the estimate of the black hole to between seven and 13 billion euros, close to 1 per cent of Italy's GDP. The hole was simply virtual assets compensating for real debt.

The misappropriation of funds by company executives taking advantage of the group's complex structure and the proliferation of monetary loops are yet more elements in common with Enron. In this regard, the CFO appears to bear heavy responsibility, although one might highlight the blindness, the complicity even, of Parmalat's auditors (Grant Thornton from 1990 to 1999, then Deloitte & Touche) as well as large Italian, US and German investment banks (Bank of America, Citigroup, Deutsche Bank), which supported Parmalat's fundraising on financial markets.

In the case of France Télécom, it is again the reliance on stock markets in order to implement a policy of accelerated development, which is the direct source of its difficulties (see Box 8.3). Nevertheless, this case differs from Parmalat and Enron in that fraudulent accounting practices were never uncovered.

BOX 8.3   FRANCE TÉLÉCOM'S ACQUISITION POLICY: FROM VALUE CREATION TO JOB DESTRUCTION

In 1995, the president who arrived to head up France Télécom (FT) was given the responsibility of preparing the state-owned operator for the opening up of its capital and for the liberalization of the telecommunications sector in Europe, scheduled for 1998. A policy of large-scale acquisitions was immediately embarked on, particularly well received in a period of rising stock markets. The policy was rewarded in FT's value creation classification: in June 1999, FT was placed first in France in the EVA/MVA ranking (see Chapter 1) made by the Parisian branch of the firm Stern, Stewart & Co. Vivendi was placed fourth. According to FT's president, each of the 500 sub-divisions of FT was in a position to calculate its EVA, marking a complete submission to the edicts of shareholder value.

The year 2000 saw no pause in this activity, in spite of the reversal in capital market trends. FT acquired 28.5 per cent of MobilCom's capital and bought Orange from Vodafone. The latter was bought at the astronomical price of 42 billion euros paid half in cash, half in new shares. This policy of international development, as well as the acquisition of UMTS licences, was expensive: in the year 2000 alone, FT's debt quadrupled to 60 billion euros. The debt-to-equity ratio reached 180 per cent. In March 2001, a bond issue for a record amount of 17.5 billion euros was launched in order to refinance the debt. The funds raised were not sufficient to reverse the trend: by the middle of the year, FT had debt of 65 billion euros. The company thus engaged in a policy of non-strategic asset disposal in the hopes of easing the pressure; debt financing for the year 2001 alone cost four billion euros. Balance sheet restructuring was impeded by continued depreciation of the company's stock market price, which lost 65 per cent of its value between January and September 2001. FT found itself trapped in a dynamic of debt appreciation/equity depreciation, which we identified at a theoretical level in the preceding chapter: stock market deterioration calls into question debt reduction by asset disposal, which reinforces the decline of stock market prices. Furthermore, goodwill depreciation worsened, forcing FT to make exceptional provisions of 10.2 billion euros. The results were immediate: the financial statements for the year 2001 showed a loss of 8.3 billion euros. In spite of this, FT continued to acquire, buying the Polish company TPSA in return for four billion euros more in debt. In June 2002, an off-balance-sheet liability of 457 billion euros was made public. This liability came from a financial transaction made on the disposal of its interests in Crown Castle International. That same month, the CEO of FT complained of the destabilizing behaviour of hedge funds. At the end of the month, the debt reached 70 billion euros, making FT the company with the highest debt in the world. In September, the CEO of France Télécom was replaced. His successor implemented a vigorous recovery plan. Using early retirement and hiring freezes, 13 000 jobs were eliminated (7500 in France) as part of a cost reduction programme.

In sum, the Enron, Parmalat and France Télécom cases bring to light a paradoxical affinity between managers' desire to expand and the defence of shareholder value. Rather than restraining managerial power, as conventional representations would have it, shareholder value enhances that power (Lordon, 2002). Constant reference to creating value for shareholders and stringent application of the commandments of the shareholder value doctrine (stock options, independent board of directors, EVA, etc.) are the only way to assure a continual rise in stock prices and, therefore, to guarantee the viability of a strategy of large-scale acquisitions. Conversely, shareholder sovereignty legitimizes this strategy by presenting takeovers as the ultimate expression of a true 'shareholder democracy'. The shareholder comeback was more to the advantage of company managers than to shareholders: the explosion of executive management remuneration (see Chapter 1) along with the mediocrity, even the detrimental effect, of takeovers in the creation of value (Coutinet and Sagot-Duvauroux, 2003) support this argument. It is also important to note that in addition to profiting managers, often indecently, the spread of pro-shareholder governance brings increasing instability. On one hand, shareholder value reinforces the instability of financial markets (identified in Chapters 6 and 7): it pushes managers to abuse financial markets' lack of objective indicators, and thus markets' credulity. On the other hand, applying shareholder value renders firms particularly vulnerable to capital market fluctuations: the more a firm opens its structures to financial logic (its balance sheet, its pay scales, its responsibility toward retirement financing, etc.), the larger the repercussions of the inherent instability of modern finance (the depreciation of goodwill, difficulty hiring and keeping a qualified workforce using stock options, the evaporation of pension fund assets, etc.).

As we have seen, gatekeepers seem largely incapable of keeping shareholder value on the right track. Nevertheless, recent years have seen all the other mechanisms associated with shareholder value explode – when they were not encouraging the aberrations. These mechanisms are threefold:

1. stock options, which are supposed to encourage managers to act in the best interest of shareholders;
2. institutional investors, which, as the biggest investors in the United States, are supposed to guarantee financial market discipline;
3. an independent board of directors, which is supposed to provide rigorous internal control.

Considering this, we cannot help but be surprised by the relative silence, at least in the United States, surrounding these three questions – so much silence that the legislative measures taken to contain the crisis do not even mention them, as we will see in the next section.

Stock options, symbolic of shareholder value, are much used in the United States; their use is becoming commonplace in Europe as well. They aim to align the interests of shareholders and of management, since options link the remuneration of the latter to stock market prices. The backbone of this method of remuneration is the hypothesis that managers, with a vested interest in the financial evaluation of their company, can have considerable influence on stock prices. Nonetheless, stock options have become the target of ever more numerous criticisms, both in principle and as a tool for incentivization. The majority of empirical studies underline, among other things, the determining role of interest rates in stock price formation. In these conditions, stock options look more like the means of personal enrichment, encouraging every manipulation that might give a favourable short-term financial market valuation, than the lever of a well-thought-out strategy. Enron's case is striking: in 2001, the year of bankruptcy, the CEO (replaced in February) made $9.6 million from stock options up until February; the CFO made $3 million.

We should describe two other problems connected with this method of remuneration, which the crisis in the United States brought out. On one hand, in contrast with wages, stock options are rarely registered as expenses. Thus they act as 'invisible' remuneration. From this point of view, the IASB's efforts to find a practical solution to registering stock options are commendable. On the other hand, as part of the liberalization of capital markets, Section 16(b) of the Securities Exchange Act was eliminated. This section obliged anyone given stock options to hold the underlying securities, acquired through exercise of the options, for at least six months. Now, executives exercise their options and immediately resell their shares (either back to the firm or on the secondary market) to collect the capital gains. It is less a question of ensuring a comfortable and durable position on the stock markets than contriving to benefit from favourable prices at the moment of sale, with no consideration for the long term. In summary, the regulation of stock options in the United States currently favours dissimulation of remuneration and short-termism.

The behaviour of institutional investors, engaged in fierce competition to capture household saving, is also problematic. Competition between investment funds affects firms, which must satisfy the profitability standards demanded of them. This constant pressure encourages managers to operate on a short-term basis; thus, risk-taking increases sharply. For institutional investors, however, the sources of profit matter much less than the profits themselves. Even when investors might have doubts about profit origin, or the solidity of the underlying business model, the logic of competition induces them to hold their tongue, as well as the stock. Indeed, it is preferable to avoid selling when other funds are keeping their stocks or looking to buy (Gordon, 2002). Selling a stock that will continue to grow in value sends investors a negative message about the quality of a fund's management. In this scenario, the idea that it is better to be wrong along with the others than to be right on one's own is quite applicable. Enron illustrates this better than any other case: in its last years, institutional investors held nearly 60 per cent of its stock. At no time, until the dramatic series of events of October 2001, did these funds voice the slightest criticism or the least doubt concerning the firm's strategy.

Finally, the crisis in the United States brought to light the dysfunctional aspects of the boards of directors. The board constitutes the main instrument of internal control in the shareholder vision of governance (see Chapter 2). The board's purpose, according to this doctrine, is to protect shareholders from managerial misconduct. This purely disciplinary vision of the board makes a cardinal virtue of the independence of its members. In other words, *exteriority* – one of shareholder sovereignty's obsessions – is introduced into the board. Yet, the board's justification lies in its *internal* character. Furthermore, shareholder value encourages the creation of special committees within the board: an audit committee to ensure the interface between management and the board of directors, on one hand, and the external auditor, on the other; a nomination committee to recruit the CEO; and a remuneration committee to supervise executives' salaries. Particular importance is accorded to the audit committee, which must consist entirely of independent directors. The Enron case is perplexing when considering the relevance of such a representation: Enron's board, composed of 12 'independent' directors out of a total of 14, saw nothing, and made themselves richer in the process. The audit committee, though properly legally constituted, endorsed all of Enron's financial manipulations. Finally, almost all the members of the board had stock options with the aim of bringing their interests in line with those of shareholders.

Coupled with gatekeeper failure, these various elements show that share-holder value is not up to the challenge. None of the safeguards put into place, from the independence of the board of directors to the audit firms, stood up to the frantic quest to create value for shareholders. As Cohen (2003) notes, it is paradoxical that the governance model in the United States, focused entirely on stacking up mechanisms of control, failed so spectacularly in controlling corporate actors. This paradox is so evident that political figures and specialists have focused all their attention on it instead of looking at a more important issue, the behaviour of firms. In fact, Berle and Means (1932) had already given us the keys to interpreting this phenomenon. Book II of *The Modern Corporation* focused on a study of jurisprudence in the United States. It concluded that legislation was struc-turally incapable of giving control to shareholders (see Chapter 2). The root of the problem was the necessarily external nature of the legislation; like small ('liquid') investors, it could not interfere with the managing of the company, which was the domain of the executive team. The capture of value is more likely to be achieved by way of operating transactions (or management), such as an acquisition policy, than by accounting fraud. If the latter is objectively detectable, and in this the behaviour of the auditors of Enron and Parmalat was reprehensible, courts do not, by definition, have the capacity to judge the merit of the transactions. In short, for Berle and Means, the loss of control is a congenital defect of shareholder sovereignty. The present crisis confirms the uselessness of a system of regulation that is exclusively disciplinary. The accumulation of accounting regulations in the United States, designed to anticipate every possible situation, did not prevent things from getting out of hand. If sufficiently motivated, actors always seem clever enough to find ways of circumventing even the most rigorous control mechanisms. The obsession with creating shareholder value constituted precisely such motivation, because both remuneration (via stock options) and the future of company management (via exchange offers and takeover bids) depended on it.

US AND EUROPEAN RESPONSES

At the heart of the political classes, the argument which attributed the Enron disaster to the bad behaviour of a few black sheep did not stand up to the multitude of scandals that followed in its wake: Qwest, Xerox, Global Crossing, Adelphia, ImClone, HealthSouth, Tyco, WorldCom, and so on. The magnitude of the phenomenon backed US regulators into a corner. On 30 July 2002, less than ten days after WorldCom's bankruptcy, the President of the United States signed into law a text voted by Congress on July 24, promulgating the Sarbanes-Oxley Act,[3] an explicit response to the loss of confidence in US security markets.

The Sarbanes-Oxley Act

Divided into ten chapters, the clauses of the Sarbanes-Oxley Act address three main issues: accounting, gatekeepers and corporate governance. The act is extra-territorial in nature and concerns all corporations listed on US markets, regardless of their nationality.

Concerning accounting, Section 108 of the law forced the SEC to launch a study on the possibility for the United States to switch to 'principle-based' accounting from an 'analytic' ('rule-based') approach. This study, released on 25 July 2003, recognizes the inadequacies of the US GAAP standards and their overly legalistic nature. It proposes a progressive move toward a principle-based approach. Most notably, this long-term process anticipates reducing the number of exceptions to each rule and abandoning overabundant references to threshold figures (such as the 3 per cent rule for SPEs). However, the congruence of rule-based accounting and US common law, which gives jurisprudence a decisive role, leaves little room for manoeuvre. The changes to come risk being relatively minor. Nevertheless, in a more anecdotal manner, the text does restrain the use of *pro forma* accounting, the abuse of which by numerous corporations, particularly in the telecommunications sector, has been underlined.

The most significant changes introduced by the Sarbanes-Oxley Act are at the level of gatekeeper regulations. However, only the audit profession is really affected. First, following the outright failure of peer review, the Public Oversight Board (POB) self-dissolved in March 2002. The POB had been in charge of implementing the peer review system. The Sarbanes-Oxley Act established a new supervisory body, the Public Company Accounting Oversight Board (PCAOB). It is composed of a minority of audit professionals (only two out of five members), and is under the direct supervision of the SEC. Second, to remedy the increasing number of conflicts of interest, from now on audit firms are forbidden from providing certain services to the firms they are auditing (appraisal or consulting services, creation and operation of financial data processing systems, etc.). In addition, the PCAOB has the authority to extend this list of forbidden activities in order to guarantee the stability of these new 'Chinese walls'. The extra-territorial nature of the law poses a problem, however. It obliges a non-US audit firm certifying the accounts of a company listed on US markets to respect the same obligations and bow to future injunctions of the PCAOB. The unilateral, hegemonic character of this clause has aroused indignation in Europe, but so far with no result.

What is more, even though the Sarbanes-Oxley Act endeavours to limit the benefits of lax or complacent auditing, the penalties for such behaviour have not been made any harsher. Furthermore, despite their ineffectiveness as gatekeepers from 1997 to 2001, securities analysts are the objects of fairly inconsequential clauses aimed principally at preventing conflicts of interest. The Act does not deal with the other gatekeepers: ratings agencies, law firms and investment banks.

Finally, as regards corporate governance, the Sarbanes-Oxley Act introduces three types of clauses. First, directors and managers must now personally certify the truthfulness of annual and quarterly accounts with the SEC.[4] Second, prison sentences and fines for managers are very clearly increased in the event of misdemeanour. Third, the audit committee, part of the board of directors, is given a greater role. The SEC is authorized to strike a company off the exchange if its audit committee, 'directly responsible for appointing, paying and supervising' the external auditor, is not entirely composed of independent members.[5] This last point marks a certain departure from US regulation in the sense that company law, which regulates the purely internal relations of a company, had been a matter solely for state law (see Chapter 3). This clause of the Sarbanes-Oxley Act implies an interference of federal law in the internal organization of companies, like in Germany (see Donald, 2003).

How should this law be assessed? First, it leads to a significant increase in the SEC's authority, the powers of which were already quite extensive. Reinforcing the position of federal law naturally means a considerable funding increase for the US stock market policeman (the SEC): from $438 million in 2002 to $670 million in 2003. However, the most important question is the scope of the Sarbanes-Oxley Act: does it extend as far as US regulatory bodies would have one believe? It is doubtful. This reform of US business law, taken as an emergency measure, is accompanied by muscular rhetoric aimed at preventing fraudulent behaviour. In reality, it brings few decisive changes. Considering the gravity of the crisis, one can in fact pass relatively severe judgement on this new law, a point which we will now develop.

As mentioned, the Sarbanes-Oxley Act focuses mainly on gatekeeper failures. For most commentators, the most notable move forward is the creation of a body responsible for audit supervision, the PCAOB. What is unique is the body's independence from the audit profession: only two out of five seats are held by professionals from the field of auditing. Nevertheless, the body's small size means the individual personalities of its members play a decisive role regarding its effectiveness as a mechanism of control.

Moreover, the pressure exerted by the audit industry in the United States could put a stop to any vague desire for change that the PCAOB may have (Cunningham, 2002). In addition, measures aimed at securities analysts are not very extensive, while ratings agencies slip through the net entirely.

In much the same way, the second element constituting the chain of information, accounting itself, is hardly touched by the Act. The problems anticipated in moving toward principle-based accounting, despite a general recognition of the flaws of a rule-based approach, have already been underlined. As for *pro forma* accounting, at the root of many accounting indiscretions, it has not been eliminated; the Act simply specifies that it should not be used to hide elements that result from using US GAAP, the same instructions as before, just formalized.

As limited as they are regarding the chain of information (gatekeepers and accounting standards), the Sarbanes-Oxley Act's clauses concerning corporate governance are even narrower in scope. Thus, and this despite increasingly virulent criticism, the subject of stock options is not even broached. This is doubtless the Act's most evident flaw. Looking more closely at the body of measures envisaged by the Act, Cunningham (2002), professor at Boston College Law School, irrevocably concludes, 'Virtually all [changes made by the Sarbanes-Oxley Act] were already in effect as a matter of custom or practice and/or due to requirements imposed by stock exchanges, regulators, state law, or other provisions of federal law' (p. 19).

Furthermore, and most importantly, the Sarbanes-Oxley Act does not call into question the source of the problem – a mode of governance focused exclusively on satisfying financial markets. Nothing is done to reduce the pressure placed on managers by the disclosure of quarterly results. On the contrary, the Act has been profoundly influenced by shareholder value. Concerning governance, the greatest structural reform is the strengthening of director independence through the new rules concerning the audit committee. In so doing, the text is following the commandments of the shareholder model as closely as possible, in which – and we have underlined this – independence is a cardinal virtue. Besides the fact that the independence of Enron's directors seems not to have prevented excess in the least, the insistence on the disciplinary function of the board of directors tends to remove it even further from the company's functioning and strategic issues. Independence becomes dangerous when established as the primary selection requirement: the central body of a corporation finds itself constituted of individuals so removed from it that they know nothing about its business or markets.

In short, the Sarbanes-Oxley Act can be summed up as follows: shareholder value is good, but its monitoring system failed. It is thus advisable to reinforce shareholders' means of control. The promulgation of the Act contributes to the strengthening of shareholder power by federal law, to the extent that this area of regulation, contrary to state law, has always been favourable to stockholders (see Chapter 3). Similarly, the clauses on accounting do not deal with the fundamental problem, an approach to accounting that is focused entirely on satisfying stock markets (see Chapter 5). To conclude, in its espousal of a minimalist thesis of gatekeeper failure (omitting ratings agencies and investment banks), the Sarbanes-Oxley Act, far from attacking the root of evil, fertilizes it.

European Reactions

While remaining more or less intact, European countries could not easily remain inactive faced with the violent upheaval in the United States. Confronted with the weakness, which the US market crisis revealed, of an oft-cited model of excellence, European regulatory authorities have most often been reactive rather than proactive. In France, the Financial Security Act of July 2003 is generally presented as the national, preventative response to the crisis. The law operates on three levels. First, taking the SEC as a model, it has increased the centralization of stock market authorities with the creation of the *Autorité des Marchés Financiers* (AMF), a fusion of the COB and the *Conseil des Marchés Financier* (CMF). Second, it has created the *Haut Conseil du Commissariat aux Comptes*, an independent organ of the profession responsible for auditing. Finally, the separation of auditing and consulting has been reinforced to avoid conflict of interest for the external auditors. Stock options and securities analysts have not been dealt with. This law, as interesting as it is, would not alone be able to prevent scandals like Enron from occurring in France. In that regard, it represents nothing more than a partial response to the loss of confidence in capital markets.

At the European level, the choice in favour of IFRS norms, with the adoption of regulation 1606/2002/EC in March 2002 (see Chapter 5), is willingly presented by the Commission as its principal preventative measure. Nevertheless, the Anglo-American orientation of the accounting system developed by the IASB, which favours shareholders, leaves us sceptical. Rather than consolidating elements particular to the European model, this choice brings Europe closer to US practices at the very moment these appear most fragile. For example, the fair value method – the warhorse of the IASB – is at the root of numerous accounting manipulations, the best illustration of which is the 'dark fibres' affair already mentioned. It is true that the IASB accounting system is principle-based and not analytic; but this is also the case for European accounting systems.

At the level of corporate governance itself, the misjudgements of European authorities are perhaps even more flagrant. Faced with an ever

increasing number of scandals across the Atlantic, in April 2002 the
European Commission decided to entrust the drafting of a report on desirable reforms in EU law to the hands of a 'high level group' of experts in
business law. Chaired by Jaap Winter, the group had been formed several
months earlier with the purpose of reflecting on how to respond to the
defeat of Directive XIII on takeover bids. A first report, called 'Winter I'
(2002a) (see Chapter 3, Box 3.3), was made on this issue in January 2002.
In November of the same year, the 'Winter II' report appeared (2002b),
proposing 'a modern regulatory framework for company law in Europe'.
The general orientation of the report, favourable to shareholder value, is
clearest in the following lines:

> In a proper system of corporate governance, shareholders should have effective
> means to actively exercise influence over the company. As we emphasised in our
> Consultative Document, shareholders are the residual claimholders (they only
> receive payment once all creditors have been satisfied) and they are entitled to
> reap the benefits if the company prospers and are the first to suffer if it does
> not. Shareholders need to be able to ensure that management pursues – and
> remains accountable to – their interests. Shareholders focus on wealth creation
> and are therefore, in the Group's view, very suited to act as 'watchdog' not only
> on their own behalf, but also, in normal circumstances, on behalf of other
> stakeholders. (p. 47)

Inspired in large part by the Sarbanes-Oxley Act, but having to take
European specificities into account, the report's conclusions are fairly
modest. The report proposes that the board of directors be made collectively responsible for the accuracy of the financial statements; moreover, the
report looks favourably on harsher punishment for fraud, most notably
banning a guilty party from working as a director anywhere in Europe.
The structure of *ad hoc* nomination, audit[6] and remuneration committees
within the board of directors poses its own particular problems. Conscious
of the US model of governance, the report insists on the advantages of
the autonomy of board members who head committees. The report immediately notes, however, that this arrangement would be difficult to adapt
to Europe. It would automatically exclude majority shareholders and
employee representatives, because their involvement in the firm would be
incompatible with the notion of independence. Majority shareholders are
present all over Europe, and board-level participation of employee representatives is characteristic of many member countries (see Chapter 3).
Independence, which can be criticized for the incompetence it entails, is also
incongruent with the European model of governance. Thus the report
adopts a moderate position, one of fairly limited scope: *ad hoc* committees
should constitute a majority (not a totality) of independent members. The

most daring clause in the report, which clearly differentiates itself from the Sarbanes-Oxley Act, is that it proposes stronger regulations on stock options. The group argues that shareholders should be better informed as to the use of stock options as a tool, as well as to the way they are recorded in accounting, without proposing any particular method.

To sum up, the 'Winter II' Report (2002b) illustrates the reaction of European regulatory authorities. They did not use the US crisis to reaffirm the specificities of the continental European model. Instead, they were content to copy measures taken in the United States, exploiting the relative quiet of the European landscape to justify less ambitious clauses.

CONCLUSION

Through an interpretation of the Enron affair, this chapter studied the reasons underlying the crisis financial capitalism is currently experiencing. Since the stock market downturn in March 2000, this crisis has manifested itself in an unprecedented series of bankruptcies and scandals. The choice of Enron as an example is justifiable for many reasons. Even though it was little known by the larger public, this corporation was considered as a model in its willingness to implement the whole gamut of managerial methods in vogue at the time (dematerialization of assets, project management, e-business, creation of value for shareholders, derivatives trading, etc.). Enron's bankruptcy, surpassed only by WorldCom's, is therefore of particular interest, especially considering that in its fall it took down the audit firm Arthur Andersen. Above all, it reveals, and at the same time is symbolic of, the tectonic drift of US and, to a lesser extent, European capitalism in the second half of the 1990s. In fact, the argument attributing the crisis to a few black sheep does not stand up to analysis. Since Enron, fraudulent activity has increased over the past several years. Given the choice between moral crisis (a mysterious decline in managerial ethics) and a structural crisis, we opt for the second interpretation. The standard argument, at least in the United States, is that the gatekeepers (in particular, the external auditors) seriously failed. It is this interpretation that presided over the drafting of the Sarbanes-Oxley Act, announced in July 2002, to contain the crisis. Consequently, the backbone of this law is the reinforcement of control mechanisms.

This interpretation of the crisis seems erroneous, however. Beyond the failure of the gatekeepers, the mode of governance itself is suspect. In other words, the manner in which companies are run in the United States, rather than their supervision, is the important issue. It is paradoxical that the crisis in the United States was perceived as a manifestation of the weakness of control mechanisms while these mechanisms have not ceased to grow in strength and importance over the last two decades. On the contrary, what the US experience teaches is that these *external* surveillance devices, however sophisticated they may be, have limits, a point already underlined by Berle and Means (1932). It is thus to the intrinsic motivations of actors, and finally, the aims of the firm, that we must turn.

The pressure exerted on governance under financial capitalism, centred on creating shareholder value even while shareholders are distanced from the firm, makes corporations sensitive to the fluctuations and exuberance of capital markets. The wild quest for maximum financial profitability in order to increase the market value of securities has been the true driver of financial drift in recent years. The scandals that have shaken confidence in US markets are a product of the spread of shareholder value rather than gatekeeper aberrations. That the interest of shareholders is central to a corporation is certain; that the interests of remote shareholders driven only by liquidity and profitability be the only objective is debatable.

It is thus troubling to observe that Europe, with its different vision of the firm (see Chapter 3), a vision explaining the smaller scale of its crises, did not take the opportunity afforded by the US crisis to affirm the originality of its model. In effect, regulatory bodies tended to align themselves with reforms in the United States, even while the opportunity arose to establish an alternative model, in which shareholders' interests were not the only ones recognized.

NOTES

1. The Powers Report (2002) remains the authoritative reference on this issue. The report was commissioned by Enron's board of directors in October 2001 and led by William Powers, Dean of the University of Texas Law School. The report is particularly eloquent on the subject of the accounting manipulations Enron's management carried out. The principal conclusions of the report were strongly contested by the board members. Another source is the US Senate Report (Permanent Subcommittee on Investigations of the Committee of the Governmental Affairs United States Senate, 2002). This document is based largely on the Powers Report, as well as a series of interviews with the principal members of Enron's board of directors. Our treatment of the Enron affair is largely based on these two sources.
2. Note that this ratio is always higher than 1: it makes sense that analysts issue more recommendations to buy, which interest all market investors, than recommendations to sell, which by definition concern only a small number of investors already holding the shares in question.
3. Named after the two main instigators, the Republican Michael Oxley, and the Democrat Paul Sarbanes.
4. Porsche's management cited this particular clause of the Sarbanes-Oxley Act when it announced in August 2002 that the company was abandoning plans for a listing on the New York Stock Exchange.

5. Note that even if the text does not specifically anticipate the obligation to put an audit committee into place, it does specify that in the absence of such a committee, all clauses dealing with this committee (notably the independence of its members) must be applied to the Board of Directors as a whole. The constrictive character of this clause leads one to conclude that the majority of listed companies will create an audit committee.
6. Concerning external audit, the Commission issued a recommendation on 16 May 2002, arguing for a clear separation between account certification and consulting activities.

9. In favour of economic democracy

Our analysis of contemporary, finance-dominated capitalism has four results.

The first concerns the firm. In its technical, financial, cognitive, and organizational aspects, the development of capitalism has reinforced its collective nature. The firm is a place of both cooperation, which underlies production, and conflicts of power; it is driven by interests that cannot be dissociated, but which are in part contradictory. In that respect, businesses are partnerships by their very nature. Therefore, the first concern of governance is not control, but the formation of a collective interest, a goal recognized and accepted by the company's stakeholders.

The second result concerns finance. The last 30 years have seen a major evolution from intermediary finance towards market finance. This evolution signifies a paradigm shift in risk assessment and management. The digital revolution allowed risk to be broken down into basic elements, arranged into tradable financial products and transferred to all financial institutions. The consequences of this revolution are far-reaching, yet ambivalent. This is not a linear evolution toward a utopia of perfect market systems. There are multiple possibilities for risk diversification, but risk transfer creates interdependencies that provoke destabilizing feedback when macroeconomic problems arise. Available funds increase, but the strong link between indebtedness and the valuation of equity capital leads to financial fragility. Reorganization of financial portfolios seems limitless thanks to market liquidity. Liquidity, however, depends on the inter-subjectivity between agents, which is affected by fluctuations in trust. The final result is a finance that is more unstable, that has a strong influence on the economic cycle and that is difficult to control through economic policy.

The third result concerns corporate governance specific to financial capitalism. Market finance's rise to power not only overturned the business environment, it also transformed firms' internal structures and objectives. The balance of power of the corporate hierarchy of the Fordist era was destroyed, while the figure of the shareholder was elevated to the pinnacle of the firm by the doctrine of shareholder sovereignty and the demands of profitability. Finance irrevocably introduced a contradiction into the system of governance. By promoting liquidity, finance separated shareholders from the firms they were supposed to control. The primacy of institutional investors exacerbated this trend. Controlling firms now means nothing more for shareholders than buying or selling shares, behaviour which is interfered with by collective fluctuations that either raise or lower markets. Thus a major dysfunction is introduced at the core of governance. In periods of stock market euphoria, collusion occurs between company managers with floating capital and shareholders hoping for unlimited enrichment. The collusion extends to financial professionals who benefit from the windfall. Stock price increases benefit everyone. When no internal opposition force exists, managers' hubris can lead to the headlong pursuit of risky, secret operations with strong leverage effect. Financial instability is invisible, because it is not in the interest of any of the financial agents in a position to pinpoint and denounce it to do so. When share prices fall, losses multiply and conflicts arise.

The fourth result is that the failure of shareholder sovereignty does not stay within the bounds of the relationship between managers and their shareholders. Because credit as a whole is directly dependent on the stock market (thanks to 'fair value' accounting and bank evaluation models of credit risk), the entire economy is subject to financial instability. The governance crisis is therefore irrevocably linked to the worrying drift of a financial capitalism which, far from putting finance at the disposal of investment with social progress in mind, instead makes stock market capital gains the alpha and omega of economic activity. Economic logic is turned completely upside-down. Firms seek primarily to protect shareholders from risk during periods of financial deflation. Risk is transferred to employees by aggressive restructuring and massive layoffs in order to reduce debt. It is also transferred to the nation as a whole by the continual drop in fiscal pressure on capital.

These results run counter to the dominant ideology, which brandishes morality but is little interested in the reasons behind the phenomena. This ideology regrets the drift of corporate governance. It is filled with indignation over the gross misappropriation of funds by powerful corporate executives. It points the finger at the complicity of certain links in the financial chain: auditors, but also financial analysts, accused by shareholder associations which view themselves, justly, wronged. This ideology, however, completely ignores investment banks, consulting firms and ratings agencies, whose role in the most striking fraudulent bankruptcies is nothing but evident.

In short, whether coming from the media, the academic community, financial supervisory boards or political authorities, the recommended treatment is often the same: shareholder control of firms must be upheld primarily by threat of hostile takeover. The doctrine of shareholder sovereignty is not only the best way, but also the only way compatible with the supremacy of market finance, attributed with every virtue. Financial capitalism will constitute the ultimate form of capitalism, blending the end of the nineteenth century's respect of private property with the effectiveness of the concentration of productive capital specific to managerial capitalism. It is thus advisable to tighten regulations on control and to make punishments for deviancy harsher.

THE NECESSARY INTERWEAVING OF ECONOMICS AND POLITICS

How do partisans of the doctrine of shareholder value view the role of politics? As mentioned, the doctrine is based on two hypotheses. On one hand, corporations are property held by shareholders, who are thus the only legitimate candidates for controlling them. On the other hand, the stock market is the institution which best reallocates this ownership on the condition that it remains transparent. Nevertheless, and according to the most enlightened authors of the liberal spectrum, the 'invisible hand' of the market cannot move without the help of the state, which must provide the proper institutional base. However a contradiction that menaces financial capitalism introduces itself at this level (Rajan and Zingales, 2003), because if governments are indispensable, they do not automatically act in the general interest. Influential private interests can turn government action toward market repression or corruption. Reforms must therefore be found which allow governments to support markets without interfering in their workings. If that is done, governance can move towards what is considered to be the best possible model: control by stock markets, which has no equal in creating wealth and the opportunity to innovate. In this regard, the Sarbanes-Oxley Act is moving in the right direction. Other reforms should follow to hinder private interests from paralysing the disciplinary role of markets or from turning markets to their advantage: anti-trust laws to crack down on abusive concentrations of power; a security net for victims of competition; unrestricted access to foreign capital; an all-out ideological offensive exhorting public opinion to ignore the siren-song of anti-globalization incantations.

In this apologetic conception of financial markets, politics follows the markets' lead. The search for the general interest consists in working for a pure and perfect market. This normative approach is based on a homogenizing ideological construction. It claims, in effect, that it is possible to make the economy evolve towards a non-contradictory state. If markets are perfect, there is no more separation between private and social interests. In equilibrium, there remain no contradictions among private interests: every individual plan is realized. This is why the ideal of perfect markets equals the ideal of perfect planning, as shown by the theoretical debates of the

1930s. When one is not content with imagining these ideals as part of an impossible reality, but instead tries to force them on real societies, the result is a totalitarian nightmare. It is the common destiny of ultra-liberalism and communism. Both claim to move beyond politics to a state where each individual is in harmony with society.

One does not create satisfactory social order by claiming to move towards utopia. Stalinist socialism was not a move towards communism. Nevertheless, people believe, or say they believe, that liberal reform is a move towards perfect markets. That is why the International Monetary Fund (IMF) gave its blessing to, and even encouraged, scandalous acts in the name of liberalism: the organized theft of public property under Yeltsin; the selling off of the public domain to foreign interests under Menem. In both cases, the destruction of national sovereignty led to social chaos.

These extreme phenomena are not aberrations. They are found at the end of the ideological path that denies the inextricable character of social contradictions. In secular societies, where sovereignty emanates from the people, democracy is the only political process that can avert the drift toward totalitarianism. The market, in contrast, accommodates itself to any political regime that affirms and supports the primacy of private enrichment. In other words, the market and democracy are two profoundly different forms of social relationships.

The Austrian school, most notably Hayek (1960), does not make the mistake of thinking of the economy as a system of perfect, entirely self-governing markets. Markets are institutions that evolve along with other social institutions. Institutions and behaviour adapt to one another by respecting tradition, which at the same time transmits and transforms a culture from one generation to the next. Tradition engenders the acceptance and respect of institutions, because no one created them with a specific goal in mind. They are outside individual interests. These traditional institutions inspire confidence, because no one thinks that anyone else can change them to his or her personal advantage.

Hayek is also very hostile to political 'constructivism', understood as a process which institutes and guards the rules of social life, and which imposes them on the members of society. Following the Austrian legacy, Hayek holds that civic order is distinct from political order. It is organic. In his conception, human freedom is not a presupposition of a pure economy, which considers economics as completely separate from the other social sciences. There is no 'natural' sovereignty for either consumer or shareholder; but the market is the institution by which human freedom, still following tradition, emerges little by little from the criss-crossing of allegiances, alliances and gifts that are given to each person and that constitute his or her social being. When the market derives from a long evolution that protects it from arbitrary powers, it is the institution that reveals the fair price. In contrast, the state is perceived as a force which annihilates freedom; it is a subjugating machine.

Contrary to this, we think that the freedom of one translates into the oppression of others, if that freedom is not reined in by an institutional framework elaborated through political processes. As we showed through a study of asset and debt evaluations in Chapter 6, the market stages a logic of opinion. This logic aims at condensing unanimity in prices. We showed that this unanimity is fleeting, constantly called into question by clashes between contradictory economic interests. That is why markets are inherently unstable. The social bond it produces – namely, liquidity – polarizes these conflicts. Because it accords a certain protection to those who can acquire it, liquidity sets rich against poor, lenders against debtors, capitalists against employees, long-term production for others (the many) against the immediateness of private wealth for the few.

Democracy proceeds from a logic of deliberation whose goal is the formation of a collective interest. In deliberation, parties' private interests are transformed: collective interest is neither the aggregation nor the confrontation of private interests. The political process forms progressive compromises between vested interests. Compromises are the result of democracy overcoming conflict. Thus collective interest does not predate the process that elaborates it. Such is the significance of majority rule, which sanctions this process. Unanimity is not found in the outcome of deliberation, but in the adherence to democratic sovereignty. This adherence means accepting from the beginning that private interests will be transformed through deliberation in order to conform to compromise.

The intimate interweaving of economics and politics in the social sphere is not without consequence for economic science. It means that no 'pure economy' exists. In effect, the pure economy approach presupposes the possibility of elaborating a science of the effectiveness of means to achieve pre-existing ends, expressed in separate, individual utility. This hypothesis is consubstantial with equilibrium, being the absence of contradiction. However, in human societies, ends and means are reciprocal. They are two aspects of contradictory interests put into motion by the formation of compromises, which in turn provoke new contradictions, and so on. In no way is this development a convergence toward an equilibrium.

It follows that politics is not separate from society. Politics is present in any human group where the idea of collective interest or common good exists, regardless of the group's size or activity. Firms, as human groupings involved in production for others, cannot escape politics. Therefore, the current governance crisis is symptomatic of a much deeper problem. In the 30 years following the Second World War, the interweaving of economics and politics created a mixed economy capable of promoting social progress. The financial liberalization that has developed since the 1970s broke this rationale, or at least made it incoherent. It did not provide a model of the firm capable of taking up the threads of social progress. The consequences are dramatic: recurring crises; greater inequality; the corrosion of social cohesion because of long-term unemployment; the disappearance of any hope of progress for large social categories of citizens. The daunting question behind the corporate governance crisis is thus the following: what kind of political economy is needed to put financial capitalism back on the road to social progress?

THE FAILURE OF SHAREHOLDER SOVEREIGNTY

Politics springs up in a corporation when private ownership dissociates itself from the power of coordinating the human resources involved in production. This separation is inherent to the development of capitalism: owners search for an adequate form of protection through liquidity. Financial markets constitute the right social organizations to realize these ends. With market liquidity, the corporation ceases to be an object of ownership; it requires the elaboration of a collective interest.

As early as 1932, Berle and Means showed the extent of dissociation in the United States between ownership focused on liquidity and the firm; between the beginning of the twentieth century and the 1930s, firms developed an operating structure that was complex and hierarchical as they increased in size (concentration of capital) and scope (business diversification). The decades that followed would see an ever greater divide between a theoretical representation of capitalism, which denied that the separation of ownership and control made social contradictions greater, and the reality of an economy in which large managerial firms, distanced from their shareholders, were gaining ground.

On the theoretical side, legal and liberal conceptions of private property, like pure market economic theory, refused to take account of the transformation of private property as stock market liquidity progressed (see Chapter 2). In the United States at least, jurisprudence used the doctrine of shareholder sovereignty to affirm shareholders as the only legitimate agents of control in large firms. This affirmation presupposed a double semantic slide:

> Ownership of capital equity
> ⇔ Ownership of corporations
> ⇔ Ownership of firms.

From these equivalences, the firm is considered as an object of property rights that legal subjects (shareholders) are authorized to control. These equivalences, however, are sophisms. A listed company (firm) is not an individual corporation with multiple owners. Shareholders have the right to dividend payments as owners of equity capital. Therefore, they have a private interest, among other private interests, in the distribution of the added value produced by the firm. This sharing-out nevertheless follows from the collective interest elaborated within the firm.

While legal and economic theories were espousing shareholder sovereignty, internally controlled managerial firms blossomed in both Europe and the United States within a growth regime that fostered the development of collective bargaining and social rights. In correlation, financial markets were put under strict public surveillance after being discredited by the excessive speculation of the 1920s.

It is interesting to observe the manner in which economics and politics interweaved in managerial firms at the height of the Fordist growth regime (Aglietta, 1997). While stock markets were reduced to insignificance, the development of the industrial firm led to the expansion of wage-earning labour, organized into socio-professional strata in the technostructure of firms. The recognition of common interests among employees led to a dual union organization (sector and profession), the importance of which in any given country was influenced by the existence or non-existence of powerful socialist parties. Union activism in return provoked professional employer associations to use pressure tactics from product markets to labour markets. Political negotiation of social compromises resulted in collective agreements and legislation. A huge domain of social rights was instituted (from working conditions to health insurance), the extent of which varied from country to country. These rights nevertheless had a large enough common base in all Western countries that it was justifiable to speak of the advent of the 'labour society' (Aglietta and Brender, 1984).

The labour society reinforced managerial power while strictly limiting its arbitrariness. The rules of increasing income with seniority, of promotion, of worker recruitment from various social categories, all became part of the hierarchical structure of firms. This was so much the case that managers were controlled by the technostructure that produced these counter-powers. Managers were free in their productive and strategic choices to maximize the growth of the firm, but within negotiated limits incorporated into the organization of the firm. These limits, which restricted managerial power at the microeconomic level, were at the heart of a virtuous macroeconomic circle. The increase in worker income, the spread of mass consumption and the progress of productivity strengthened each other. Thanks to the advance of democracy into labour law (social rights), the dynamism of capitalism was the vehicle of social progress for several decades.

The Perverse Return of the Shareholder

In the 1980s, a change occurred. Shareholder value began to receive support from two sources: the growing power of institutional investors and the development of agency theory. In the United States, the law, particularly federal, followed this movement. Control mechanisms, such as financial transparency requirements, the SEC's power, the regulation of the auditing profession, and so on, did not cease to grow during the 1980s and 1990s. More than ever, at the theoretical level, corporate governance was thought of in terms of control, in a strictly disciplinary fashion.

In this regard, the crisis that has been shaking up the US business world since 2001, with a series of bankruptcies and financial scandals, is quite instructive. None of the control mechanisms worked, highlighting the fragility of the governance system in the United States (see Chapter 8). An even more paradoxical process comes to light behind this crisis. Never have managers been as powerful, or at least as well remunerated, as they have been since the return in force of the shareholder.

The liberalization of financial markets and the rise to power of the savings collected by institutional investors did not transfer power from managers to shareholders. Rather, that power was displaced from entrenched managers to a managerial elite supported by investment banks. This elite, which passes from firm to firm through the processes of mergers and acquisitions, no longer seems to have as its objective the growth of the firm as it did during the Fordist era. Rather, the aim is to get a maximum cash flow from the firm into its own pockets by taking advantage of stock market liquidity. Since investment banks are interested in encouraging a maximum exchange of stocks, it is not surprising that mergers and acquisitions explode during periods of stock market euphoria, nor is it surprising that the economic effectiveness of many of these mergers and acquisitions is debatable. Their purpose is often the redistribution of power within a privileged social category, during which exorbitant incomes are made (Lordon, 2002).

Whereas entrenched managers were controlled by the technostructure of their firms, today's managers, at least those in firms that largely depend on stock markets, do not have this safeguard. Structural changes – from pyramidal to a decentralized network – crushed the intermediate strata of the technostructure. The financial constraints of states, the weakening of employees' collective interests, the appearance of professionals exercising their power of individual negotiation and the pressure for large financial returns have collectively contributed to reducing social rights in continental

Europe, and to dismantling them completely in the UK and the United States. The dissolution of internal checks and balances in firms has left managers with a great deal of power.

Drawing support from the financialization of firms, the managerial elite is a network of managers, investment bankers, law firm partners and management consultants. These agents occupy overlapping positions on boards of directors and nomination and remuneration committees. When a nomination takes place, the committee determines the conditions of the contracts based on the most recent situations of the firms to which the committee members belong. As manager rotation among firms has become more and more rapid, there is greater opportunity for higher remuneration at each changeover, creating an increasing spiral effect that is running out of control.

By freeing itself from social constraints and the worry of keeping the hierarchical structure of firms stable, the managerial elite, especially within the 'new economy', can drain firms' value added to increase its personal gain. The interest of today's managers lies in manipulating stock market prices in the short term, even by fraudulent means, in order to realize as quickly as possible gains on their own stock options, all to the detriment of shareholders. The consequences lead to either the dilution of capital or the massive outflow of cash in order to buy back shares. The result is that in 2001, CEO remuneration in stock options rose 43.6 per cent in value on the S&P 500 index, while total returns from equity capital fell by 12 per cent. When the stock market is not buoyant, CEOs resort to expedient 'golden parachutes' to inflate their incomes. These comprise enormous severance packages, going so far as to give lifetime benefits to CEOs who leave the company, and to their families.

The reinforcement of this elite's power figures in the income explosion of the largest firms' top managers. In 1980, the average income of the CEOs of these firms in the United States was 40 times the average salary of a worker. In 1990, it was 85 times greater, and in 2003, it jumped to 400 times greater. While in recent years average worker salaries have stagnated, profits fallen and stock markets plunged, the growth of managers' incomes has accelerated. At work is a veritable re-concentration of wealth that is sending the United States back to the 'gilded age' of social inequality, the first third of the twentieth century (Krugman, 2002). Note that as services gain increasing importance in Western economies, productivity and wealth creation assessment become more problematic (see Chapter 1). This hides, in part, the income transfers that lead to the re-concentration of wealth in the hands of the richest. Consequently, this re-concentration is made easier.

Even though media reports of the excesses of the former CEOs of Vivendi, General Electric, or the New York Stock Exchange enraged public opinion, the underlying transformations that permitted and validated these excesses, which are infecting capitalism, are far from being understood.

Resolving a Paradox

In their 1932 work, Berle and Means offer an interesting key to interpreting the current paradox, where the number of reforms in defence of the shareholder is multiplying while the managerial elite is increasingly abusing value. The two authors had already pointed out the law's powerlessness to contain the excesses of managers. The abuses of value are partly linked to the management of firms itself. It is in their choices of investment or acquisition strategies that managers most often increase their personal wealth to the detriment of shareholders and/or workers. It is thus always possible to justify these choices in the name of industrial or financial strategy, and it is difficult for courts to contest. Courts, by definition, do not have the capacity to judge for themselves the merit of managers' decisions. They are exterior to the firm as much as the shareholders concerned with preserving the liquidity of their shares. In the end, objectively perceptible cases that involve outright abuse (for example, insider trading or the misuse of corporate funds) are fairly rare. In the same manner, gatekeepers (auditors, financial analysts, ratings agencies) that are supposed to guarantee the transparency of capital markets have little to say in managerial decisions. Outside the firms, they can only monitor a firm's behaviour *ex post*, the limits of which are now evident. This is no doubt the crucial point: shareholder sovereignty is fundamentally unstable, because it cannot be realized. The main principle of this doctrine is to combine liquidity and control. Liquidity, however, implies maintaining a distance and is synonymous with exteriority. Berle (1963) expresses this idea most clearly:

> To accomplish this liquidity, it is necessary that the property [...] have no relation whatever to its owner except that relation arising from the owner's capacity to transfer it. Nothing can be liquid if any value assigned to it depends upon the capacity or effort or will of the owner. Marble would stop being readily salable if its value depended on having the sculptor transferred along with it. (p. 25)

Based on a philosophy of dispossession (see Chapter 2), the doctrine of shareholder value intends to construct an institutional architecture aimed at annihilating the autonomous nature of firms, which results from financial market liquidity. It is a worthy endeavour: the more the interests of shareholders are privileged, the more the firm must be managed in the name of an exterior party (financial markets). This contributes to making managerial power less responsible. Shareholder value reinforces the discretionary power of managers rather than limiting it.

Berle and Means's critique of the doctrine of shareholder value is thus two-fold. On one hand, they claim that this doctrine is mistaken. It refuses to take note of the ways private ownership is changing with the development of market liquidity. Shareholders cannot claim control, because they have traded it for liquidity. On the other hand, Berle and Means see shareholder value as a dead end: it is useless to try to give shareholders control through positive laws. It must be noted that this double critique comes from an analysis that is more legal than economic. In other words, Berle and Means reject the doctrine of shareholder value without studying other processes of value creation in firms (microeconomic analysis) or how financial markets function (macroeconomic analysis). Taking these two dimensions (microeconomic and macroeconomic) into account, however, tends to reinforce their arguments against shareholder value.

Chapter 2 showed how wealth in a firm is created by bringing together human, financial, tangible and intangible capital specific to firms. This creation process reveals the fundamentally collective nature of the firm. The radical uncertainty weighing on the temporal progression of this combination of resources (contractual incompleteness, in the language of the theory of contracts), as well as the difficulty of putting collective action into motion, argues for an exercise of power that favours the involvement of the various stakeholders. In contrast, by sending a signal to all the stakeholders that the resolution of unforeseen problems will be handled in the sole interest of the shareholders, shareholder primacy runs the risk of deteriorating the quality of these commitments, and thus the competitiveness of the firm.

Capital market instability upholds Berle and Means's conclusion as well. On one hand, market excesses favour the hijacking of value, or fraudulent behaviour, on the part of managers. Markets are even easier to manipulate when they are buoyant (when there is a market bubble). Evidence is found in the manner in which the executives of Worldcom, Enron, and so on, took advantage of blind confidence in markets despite the safeguards set up to prevent such abuse. This predatory behaviour, disguising the misappropriation of wealth as the creation of value for shareholders, tends to increase market instability. On the other hand, the more sensitive firms are to shareholder interests (or the more they are penetrated by financial logic), the more affected they are by market instability. One need only look at the increasing threat of goodwill to firms. The presence of blockholdings is one way of limiting capital market instability. Protecting these blocks, which are part of a continental European model of governance (see Chapter 3), is desirable. This can be done most notably through preserving the legal mechanisms that support these blockholdings (shares with multiple voting rights, limited voting rights, etc.).

In fact, shareholder value is no more tenable from an economic point of view than it is from a legal one. Remember that the economic justification for shareholder primacy is that the shareholders are the only ones assuming the residual risks of the firm. Observation over the last two decades shows the contrary: shareholders have not ceased to transfer risk to workers through the gradual dismantling of the social rights acquired during the expansion of the labour society.

In the historic phase of managerial control up until the end of the 1970s, workers were insured against risk through collective agreements and employment stability. Banks suffered losses only in the case of default, because the value of debt did not depend on market assessment. Shareholders took upon themselves the largest part of the risk. The significant stock market losses of the 1970s led to the renewal of the doctrine of shareholder primacy. Today, there is a completely new power game being played. Even though they do not control firms, shareholders manage to use financial market pressure on firms to redistribute risk to workers through wage and employment adjustments. Productivity gains are reflected in profitability without improving actual wages. The share of dividends on profits increases, especially when markets drop. The macroeconomic relationships that constituted the virtuous circle in the labour society have been turned completely upside down.

As we showed in studying financial logic, banks no longer play their role in risk transformation either. They largely redistribute it to households by way of transfers to institutional investors. In addition, the growing weight of defined-contribution pension funds and the increasingly procedural definition of the fiduciary duties of financial industry actors (Montagne, 2003) tend to substitute an obligation of results with an obligation of means in the management of collective savings. This contributes to the transfer of risk to workers.

In spite of individual episodes where managers extorted exorbitant incomes by profiting from shareholders' inability to control them, these two categories of agents both benefit from the pressure financial markets place on firms. This leads to ineffective risk distribution. More and more risk is taken on by those agents least able to diversify it – employees as producers and as savers. This perverse evolution of contemporary capitalism can only be challenged by a deepening of democracy in the economic order.

ECONOMIC DEMOCRACY BEYOND SHAREHOLDER SOVEREIGNTY

Let us begin with the following statement: the firm is not the property of the shareholders. Shareholders are the owners of nothing but their capital investment in equities for which the company, as a legal entity, has fiduciary duties. Moreover, the greater the liquidity of financial markets, the more external shareholders are to the company, and the more the running of the company becomes entirely dependent on a managerial elite.

The concentration of power at the top of a company is the price paid in exchange for capital market liquidity. This concentration of power, it must be noted, is also an efficiency factor, guaranteeing a specialization in business management. Must we then accept it without further discussion? Berle and Means's answer is no (see Chapter 2). To the contrary, it is necessary to harness this power so that it will be exercised not in the interests of the ones wielding it (managers), but in the interest of the ones it affects: shareholders, certainly, but also workers and, even further, the communities in which these companies thrive. In other words, power must be given a purpose distinct from the interests of those who hold it. The notion of ownership supposes precisely the opposite: a moral person possesses 'subjective' power over his or her object of ownership, in the sense that this moral person can do as he or she pleases with it (see Robé, 1999).

The tradability of securities and the liquidity of markets allow firms to escape the sphere of ownership: neither shareholders nor managers can claim to have subjective power over the firm. A parallel can be drawn with the state. The distinctive feature of a democratic state is that the concentration of power within its apparatus, necessary to its effectiveness, is only possible if this power is given a final end different from the interest of the apparatus itself. The exercise of power is subject to the will of the people, the national community, according to democratic procedures. Thus the idea defended by Berle and Means is that capital market liquidity necessitates a rethinking of the nature of power in large corporations. Power must be exercised in the name of the community that constitutes the corporation. The separation of ownership and control renders the firm autonomous of the shareholders. It would be advisable to make managers answerable to all the company's stakeholders, not just shareholders. The firm is not an object of ownership, but an institution, and must be governed as such. This analysis is surprisingly pertinent to the present day. Faced with the drift of shareholder value, an alternative mode of corporate governance is proposed here. Managers' responsibilities to the company, as a collective entity, are the source of their legitimacy. Note that this mode of governance is upheld by the current economic theory of the firm that says the scope of directors' and executives' responsibilities must be enlarged in order to favour the involvement of the various stakeholders. Managers' power therefore consists in coordinating assets specific to the company, the first of those being employee skills; this kind of coordination sets a productive power into motion. Thus governance must be thought of as the search for ways to make managerial power more accountable in order to implement the collective interest of the firm.

This truth should gain ground because of its very obviousness. There are firms that employ hundreds of thousands of people, whose added value surpasses the GDP of the world's poorest countries, and whose strategies directly affect the lives of millions of people. How can one still claim that such entities are objects of ownership? Civil law, the basis of legal theory, conceives of social relationships only in terms of subject and object of ownership. The dominant economic theory postulates that the economy is a system of autonomous contractual relationships in society, regulated solely by market mechanisms. This crucible of academic representations leads to a conception of the firm as either an object of ownership or a nexus of contracts. Both negate the necessity of establishing a collective interest to orientate company management. This denial has a high price: the eruption of social contradictions for which no adequate regulatory mediation can be found.

In the 1920s, as in the 1990s, the effervescence of unrestricted financial markets led to major crises. If the macroeconomic effects have been different, it is only due to the political action taken concerning monetary and fiscal policy, as shown in Chapter 7. As we have already stated, the response to the corporate governance crisis of the period between the First and Second World Wars was structural: internally controlled managerial firms incorporating compromises from the labour society.

There is no doubt that if there is not a profound change in governance, financial disturbances will continue to erupt, misappropriation of funds prosper, social inequalities increase, democracy decline. The poor control of collective risks and the disengagement of citizens are two evils undermining democracy; the only way to lessen their impact is to further implicate democracy in the collective entity at the heart of contemporary societies: the firm. Nevertheless, one must not commit the error of thinking that it suffices to return to the first sort of labour society. In the last 30 years, capitalism has produced irreversible changes, rendering the old system of governance by internal control obsolete. The hierarchical techno-structure has been increasingly replaced by the network firm integrating decentralized units through the flow of information and money. Financial markets, which experienced a decline after the 1930s Depression, will continue to play an essential role, for reasons brought to the fore in the study of financial logics (Chapter 6). More and more, innovative technologies require collective action: increasing returns to scale, network effects with externalities of demand, environmental and ethical implications. The productive choices of firms have large-scale social implications. They are political.

It follows that the social compromises of the Fordist era are no longer effective. There can no longer be a question of shared responsibilities, where company managers had exclusive control of the organization of production and where economic democracy progressed through the development of social rights. Democracy must now take hold of the entirety of company goals; it must elaborate the collective interest, which in turn, lends legitimacy to corporations' activities.

We showed as early as Chapter 2 that the firm is by nature a partnership. It associates stakeholders who must participate in the definition and the control of a firm's objectives, because their involvement in the company constitutes risks that cannot be contractualized. Employees who bring specific skills to a firm share in its risks much more than the widely dispersed shareholders whose stake in the company has the advantage of being liquid. What is more, employee competencies gain value by their complementarity. Employees with specific skills are not only concerned with their individual incomes, but with the evolution of the firm over time, whose value depends on the value given to human capital. Economic Democracy is the deliberative process by which the interests of human capital define the interests of the firm.

Employee Representation on the Board of Directors

The board of directors must play a crucial role in this governance.[1] As a firm's central organ, it must be in charge of the procedural definition of company interest and of the control (*ex post*) of the taking into account of this interest in the running of the company. The implications of this principle on the composition of the board of directors are immediate. To begin with, let us briefly review the recommendations of the doctrine of shareholder sovereignty. According to this doctrine, the board of directors cannot be a deliberative body, to the extent that this doctrine stipulates that the purpose of a firm is to maximize financial returns for shareholders. The interests that the board must take into account in its strategic decisions are defined *ex ante*, apart from any deliberation or compromise. In these circumstances, the purpose of the board of directors is control. The contradiction at the base of shareholder value – the desire to combine exteriority (liquidity) and control – is found here: in order to prevent collusion between the controllers (board members) and the controlled (managers), the autonomy of the former becomes a cardinal virtue. There is no longer one code of 'good governance' that does not favour the autonomy of a certain number of directors or that does not strive to offer an operational definition of what 'autonomy' could be. In the end, this autonomy can be expressed by one word: exteriority. It is the rationale of shareholder value: how can an internal power be controlled from the outside? As much as possible, board members should have no links to management. In concentrated sectors, this most often means having no links with either the sector or the profession. The assessment of the board of directors offered by the doctrine of shareholder value is paradoxical in that it advocates an increasing *exteriority* for this *internal* mode of control. This exteriority obviously has a price: incompetence.

When the board of directors is conceived of as a deliberative body, in charge of defining the general interest and controlling its implementation, there is no longer any reason to insist on board member exteriority. Instead, individuals are needed who, without complying with management's demands, must still possess the knowledge needed to clearly elaborate the compromises necessary to the firm's development. Here is not the place to advocate a particular model for the organization or composition of boards of directors. Rather than outline an optimal model in the manner of contract theory, it is necessary to underline the fact that the definition of general interest is political in nature. It depends on culturally legitimate representations, meaning representations that are recognized as fair and that favour involvement and cooperation. In the same way that a democratic state does not specify an ideal form of the organization of power, corporate governance must be capable of functioning within diverse forms of capitalism which remain quite real, contrary to the 'end of history' argument (see Chapter 3).

This vision of the board of directors gives new appeal to German and Swedish governance models that are often considered obsolete. They present an original configuration: opening supervisory boards (Germany) or boards of directors (Sweden) to employee representatives with rights equal to shareholder representatives. When a vested interest participates on the board of directors, it is more certain that their interests will be taken into account in the company's development strategy. Worker information/consultation rights are insufficient. The elected worker representatives must have a deliberative voice in corporate decision making (Olivier and Sainsaulieu, 2001). As the weight of financial considerations in the decision-making process tends to increase, opening the board of directors to employees, representative of a firm's collective competencies, would allow for the formation of adequate checks and balances of power. The presence of employee representatives would result in a board of directors that is both strategic, in defining the general interest, and disciplinary, in scrutinizing the value of management's decisions. In effect, these representatives have an ambivalent or dual status that combines autonomy and competence: autonomy, because their intentions would not be the same as those of management; competence, because they have a status internal to the firm, contrary to the typical 'ideal' board member defended by shareholder sovereignty.

Among other things, our analysis argues for a rejection of mechanisms that aim at short-circuiting the board of directors or the supervisory board during hostile takeovers, on the grounds that shareholders are the only ones who have the right to decide on the fate of the company (as a moral person or legal entity). This 'principle of neutrality', at the heart of European Directive XIII on takeover bids (see Chapter 3), enters into profound conflict with the democratic implementation of a collective interest in the firm.

If there is no direct participation of workers on the board of directors or the supervisory board, then works councils constitute employees' main vehicle of involvement in the decision-making process. A first step is granting employees the right to information and consultation, accompanied by an obligation on the part of managers to take information from workers into consideration when making decisions. This form of involvement, weaker than democratic governance through the board of directors, is characteristic of continental European countries. It allows for the creation of an interface with management (Wheeler, 1997). Nevertheless, this involvement must be concrete so that employees do not find that strategic decisions for mergers or relocation are announced as finalities, as has too often been the case these last years. Endowing works councils with real rights of co-determination is something that must be given consideration. An example would be to accord a veto right to worker representatives on certain subjects of primary importance (Le Crom, 2003) like the *Betriebstrat* has in Germany.

ECONOMIC DEMOCRACY AND SOCIAL OWNERSHIP OF CAPITAL

The development of network technologies is increasingly distancing intra-periodical exchanges from the fiction of a perfect market (Curien and Muet, 2004). Demographic shifts lead to intergenerational exchanges which render the fiction of the private ownership of firms, already called into question by liquidity, more and more untenable.

The first epoch of the labour society was the socialization of income according to a principle of horizontal solidarity. According to the quality of the democratic demand for social cohesion, this solidarity took either the form of contribution (Germany, France) or redistribution (Northern Europe). Vertical solidarity is the socialization of capital, which marks the new epoch of the labour society. The non-recognition of this evolution – the privatization of intergenerational social rights – has already provoked human tragedy in Japan, the UK, and the United States. As demographic changes move forward, political conflicts provoked by financial losses of private, non-guaranteed pension funds will intensify. Intergenerational contradictions will give birth to political mediation allowing compromises that guarantee rights to deferred income. These compromises will affect the social ownership of capital and thus will have a strong effect on corporate governance.

The point is to find the best possible way of managing collective employee savings: worker savings plans and worker pension plans. It is a political action that raises the problem of corporate responsibility concerning these savings, because they are, in effect, deferred wages. The earnings from these savings are not personal income resulting from the individual choice of deferred consumption. They are primary income, the result of participation in production.

Worker savings plans are financed in part by salary contributions and in part by deductions from the company's gross profit. Worker representatives must therefore be involved in creating these plans and in controlling the manner in which they are invested. Worker pension plans are compensation for a social debt. In effect, they are rights acquired in return for services rendered during a working life. Inscribed in the liability of pension funds and life insurance companies, these rights are the obligation of society as a whole. They are inalienable and must be politically recognized as such. The ability to honour them must be a commitment on the part of the entire nation, because it is the condition of citizen participation.

It follows that funds raised by these two types of collective savings must not be managed like private financial institutions. In compensation for the social debt registered in their liability, the property held in their asset must be considered as social property. In the same way that banks are subject to specific regulation because they manage to their liability a collective (public) good (money), collective savings funds must also be managed under the control of society, whether they be public, corporate or associative. That is what is at stake in a renewal of democracy in the labour society. Politics must dominate finance, not be led by it.

Such an approach is indispensable in guaranteeing a proper retirement to all citizens. It goes against financial logics that led to excessive speculation in the 1990s, to huge losses on the part of insurance companies and to gaping holes in the capitalization of private pension funds that followed the collapse of the stock market.

Collective savings can and must influence the financial industry in its entirety, if the recognition of the social responsibilities they imply leads to management principles that do not transfer risk to savers. The diversification of investments is necessary in order to limit this risk. These worker savings or pension funds must not have any particular attachment, as shareholders, to their companies of origin. More globally, collective savings funds can help reduce financial instability if more rigorously supervised on the prudential level and controlled by the representatives of the subscribing savers according to criteria that take the implementation of democratic mechanisms in the firm into consideration.

In studying the behaviour of the financial industry, we showed that it presents two characteristics totally opposed to the logic of truly social ownership of capital. First, savers have no control over the investment of their savings that have been placed in collective investment funds or in private pension funds. Second, management of mutual funds is transferring more and more of the risk onto savers because of pressure from financial lobby groups and managers of large corporations. This transfer of risks operates mostly through mutual funds, which only have short-term obligations, and pension funds, which are moving more and more towards defined contributions. In addition, the delegation of funds results in high commissions. Savers' return on investment is thus burdened by scandalously onerous management and administration fees. In fact, thousands of people offering the same service, constituting an enormously over-capacitated industry, must be paid by these collective funds. These non-guaranteed funds proliferated because the financial industry benefited from tax breaks that channelled investments to their advantage. Thus the entire financial chain of analysts, brokers, investment bankers and ratings agencies must also be paid – for financial returns that fluctuate with stock markets.

Reaffirming democratic control of this industry would significantly lower costs and socialize (de-individualize) risks. Putting savings in the hands of the financial industry is a drift that must be reversed; to do so, a debate oriented along social-democratic lines must be engaged in European countries where it has not already begun. This debate must promote public (state) funds and statutory company funds, making it possible to capitalize on worker savings and pension funds while respecting strict criteria of social utility.

In order to benefit from tax incentives, funds that claim to manage collective investments should respect terms and conditions incorporating the following criteria:

- Formal contributor representation in the proceedings on the orientation and the control of investment fund policies;
- Introduction of social responsibilities in the form of redistribution of benefits to contributors with the lowest incomes;

- Enlargement of performance indicators for the assets in which the funds are invested, in order to take into account a company's goals and its ability to achieve them (research and development; quality of working conditions, particularly in developing countries; investment in environmentally friendly practices);
- Return objectives on a three-to-five-year period, rather than a three-to-six-month period, in order to avoid overbidding by managers looking to beat their competitors in the short term; this competition leads to mimetic behaviour that amplifies market ebbs and flows;
- Direct management of the allocation of funds among the large categories of financial assets, and strict control of delegated management inside these categories with the constraint of a minimum return, possibly indexed using macroeconomic indicators and having goals compatible with those of the funds themselves.

Two types of regulatory organizations must be created to reinforce the process of the socialization of savings. Governments should favour the creation of ratings agencies financed by taxes levied on financial institutions. These agencies would take into account broader performance criteria, differentiating themselves from existing mercantile agencies. Independent public agencies must also be created to supervise funds' compliance to the terms and conditions.

There is no doubt that such a political initiative would have a considerable stabilizing influence on market finance. Along with Chapter 7's propositions for the prudential regulation of financial intermediaries and for monetary policy, the aforementioned initiative would constitute a suitable institutional framework for financial globalization, if pursued in the largest capitalist countries. It is useless to say that the behaviour of finance, as it exists today, does not allow for these reforms. The problem must be approached from another angle. It is a matter of having the political and institutional means necessary to make finance take the criteria of social returns into account.

A Public Savings Fund

An appropriate response must also be found to the threat the future deterioration of demographic balance poses to contributory pension schemes, while preserving the solidarity inherent to this principle. Whatever the legal form of retirement rights, it is first necessary to note that, from a macroeconomic point of view, the benefits of a given period are taken from the production of that same period. On the other hand, the return from contributory pensions is based on the economic growth rate while the return from capitalized pensions is based on the actual interest rate. The risks associated with these two regimes are just as different. The public contributory system is subject to the risk of intergenerational political conflict if the active population is not happy with the elevated fiscal pressure of maintaining the system, or if public debt eats up an ever greater portion of GDP. Capitalization systems, when they are private and non-guaranteed, are vulnerable to risks associated with financial instability.

Faced with these contradictions, the accumulation of obligatory contributions in a public (state) fund would have the following advantages.

- The first and most evident advantage, far from negligible, is *operational*. The operational costs of an obligatory public fund per unit of invested savings are lower than private collective investment funds, because overcapacities are eliminated and exaggerated fund management income is avoided.
- The second advantage is *political*, and decisive. Being invested in permanent public capital, the rights held by the accumulated savings of citizens have institutional guarantees that are much more solid than the transfer rights included in the annual budget.
- The third advantage is *financial*. As capital invested in production, public funds reduce the burden of public debt on future generations, on the condition that the return is superior to the interest rate on the public debt.
- This leads to the fourth advantage, which is *economic*. An investment fund gives public power the means of raising potential growth if it allows public–private collaboration in infrastructure, education, and technological innovation.

Countries who saw ahead were those where public debate led to a political accord, authorizing a marginal and regular rate of annual contributions and a capitalization of the funds thus raised. Such is the path of Canadian reform, which is taking advantage of this period in which the demographic structure remains favourable to the active population.

Of course, the effectiveness of a public (state) fund depends on the manner in which it is invested. It must respect the general criteria outlined above. In countries where such funds have recently been established, they should be placed under Parliamentary control and be managed by an independent public authority. The most important condition to fulfil is that at absolutely no moment, and on absolutely no pretext, can the Treasury have access to these resources. These conditions can assure public confidence in the continuity of this public capital.

CONCLUSION: IN FAVOUR OF A EUROPEAN MODEL OF GOVERNANCE

Throughout this book, we have noted the opposition between continental European governance practices and the US model that today is in crisis. Financial globalization certainly contaminated a number of firms. Furthermore, some aberrations can be observed in the European system of majority blockholdings. The worst occurred in Italy: the Parmalat scandal is the largest to date in the European Union. In France, France Télécom's enormous debt also revealed an upset in governance that the shareholder state did not curb. Nevertheless, the deceptive liberalism reigning in Europe, which is busy undermining state authority and dismantling the public domain, is much more of a threat to democracy than the risk of being submerged by the US model. The 1990s showed very clearly that the socialist and social-democratic parties in power were completely paralysed, stunned even, by the rising wave of stock market speculation. Without batting an eyelash, they endorsed the abandonment of sovereignty that came with the creation of the euro, without trying to construct so much as the embryo of a European economic policy (Fitoussi, 2002).

One recurring theme of the political campaign following the ratification of the Maastricht treaty was that the formation of a European economic area unified by a common currency would give back the autonomy that was being threatened by financial globalization. Europe, however, has never been so much in the tow of the United States as since the creation of the euro. The euro in and of itself is not the problem, but the renouncing of an active economic policy. Held in the shackles of EU regulations, stripped of monetary tools by a central bank mired in an outmoded doctrine, paralysed before the prospect of federalism but incapable of the slightest cooperation, governments are completely powerless in the face of the instability of the world economy. Is it so surprising that democracy in Europe is on the retreat, when political leaders present the financial logic as inevitable?

The principal lesson of this book is that capitalism cannot promote social progress if the market is not subject to democratic control. In the current phase of the labour society, the stakes should lead to the mobilization of a large political interest in favour of a double reform: *on one hand, to introduce democracy into the heart of the firm in order to elaborate a collective interest and to control its implementation; on the other hand, to develop the means of regulating finance by supervising all financial institutions and by reforming the criteria for the investment of collective savings.* It is not possible to regain the means of public action against global risks and against the ripping apart of social cohesion, under attack from growing inequality and intolerable injustices, without engaging in these structural reforms. They counter the defeatist attitude that is running about Europe under the pretence of economic liberalism.

What are the social forces that could support this system of governance? There are some managers of European multinational companies who understand just how much their legitimacy is threatened by this financial game. The recent possibility of conferring a European status to companies operating in several EU member states gives a legal basis for negotiating governance principles that give controlling bodies in corporations the capacity to elaborate a collective interest. Such initiatives would speed up collaboration between the labour unions of several countries in order to defend democratic principles of governance that go beyond national borders.

But that is not enough. A category of shareholders must be introduced into finance whose interest lies in promoting performance criteria that hold to democratic principles of governance. These shareholders must become preponderant in the allocation of capital. This category of shareholder exists, but it is mute, dispersed, without influence and manipulated by the financial industry. It is the large mass of saving workers for which current forms of financial investment are unable to guarantee an acceptable retirement.

It falls to the governments of European countries to promote collective savings funds with defined benefits, vested by the law and monitored by independent public agencies. A government initiative to harmonize the requirements of public (state) funds would also open the door to a European fund. This would especially guarantee the transfer of worker rights under the conditions of job mobility while at the same time respecting the fundamental obligation of defined benefits.

At this moment, the European Union is a sundry collection of countries suffocated by paralysing EU regulations, undermined by conflicts of interest and endowed with inadequate common institutions. It is foolish to believe that reform can come from such an assembly. Whether we call them 'reinforced cooperation', the 'hard core' or 'variable geometry', initiatives able to lead the way out of stagnation can only come from a constellation of countries around France and Germany, or they will not come at all.

It would be vain to hope that a transformation of capitalism in Europe could restore its economic power of the past. Over the next 50 years, economic power will irrevocably shift toward Asia. Europe, however, can still propose a model of economic democracy to help new and growing labour societies find the lost path of social progress.

NOTE

1. Boards of directors are part of 'mono-partite' internal governance systems, while supervisory boards are part of 'bi-partite' systems (see Chapter 3). The difference between the two is of secondary importance. It is simply a question of organization, which does not relate to the responsibility or the goal of a firm. Shareholder value can be implemented in both mono-partite and bi-partite systems. In that case, either boards of directors or supervisory boards should be composed exclusively of shareholder representatives. To the contrary, co-determination does not presuppose a German type of bi-partite system, as is too often thought. In Sweden, for example, co-determination is associated with a mono-partite system with employee representatives sitting directly on the boards of directors. Thus we think that the mono-partite vs. bi-partite debate is a false one. It turns attention away from the fundamental question of corporate responsibility. As a result, the commentary that follows on boards of directors is equally applicable to supervisory boards.

Bibliography

Admati, A. and P. Pfeiderer (1997), 'Does it all add up? Benchmarks and the compensation of active portfolio managers', *Journal of Business*, **70** (3), 323–50.

Aglietta, M. (1997), *Régulation et crises du capitalisme*, Paris: Odile Jacob.

Aglietta, M. (2003), 'Les dérivés de crédit stimulent les transferts de risque bancaire', *Banque Magazine*, **652**, November, 38–42.

Aglietta, M. and A. Brender (1984), *Les métamorphoses de la société salariale*, Paris: Calmann Lévy.

Aglietta, M. and A. Orléan (2002), 'Les crises contemporaines de la finance libéralisée', in *La monnaie entre violence et confiance*, Paris: Odile Jacob, pp. 242–82.

Aglietta, M., L. Scialom and T. Sessin (2000), 'Pour une politique prudentielle en Europe', *Revue d'Economie Financière*, **60** (5).

Albert, M. (1991), *Capitalisme contre capitalisme*, Paris: Le Seuil.

Alchian, A. (1969), 'Corporate management and property rights', in H. Manne (ed.), *Economic Policy and the Regulation of Corporate Securities*, Washington, DC: American Enterprise Institute, pp. 337–69; reprinted in E. Furubotn and S. Pejovic (eds) (1974), *The Economics of Property Rights*, Cambridge: Ballinger Publishing Company, pp. 133–50.

Allen, F. and D. Gale (2000), 'Bubbles and crisis', *The Economic Journal*, **110**, January, 236–55.

Amann, B. (1999), 'La théorie des droits de propriété', in G. Koenig (ed.), *De nouvelles théories pour gérer l'entreprise du XXIème siècle*, Paris: Economica, pp. 13–60.

American Law Institute (1993), *The Corporate Governance Principles*, Philadelphia: ALI.

Andrade, G., M. Mitchell and E. Stafford (2001), 'New evidence and perspectives on mergers', *Journal of Economic Perspectives*, **15**.

Anthony, R. (1987), 'We don't have the accounting concepts we need', *Harvard Business Review*, January–February, 75–83.

Armour, J., S. Deakin and S. Konzelmann (2003), 'Shareholder primacy and the trajectory of UK corporate governance', University of Cambridge, ESRC Centre for Business Research, Working Paper 266.

Artus, P. (1995), *Anomalies sur les marchés financiers*, Paris: coll. Économie Poche, Economica.

Artus, P. (2002), *La nouvelle économie*, Paris: La découverte, coll. Repères.

Askenazy, P. (2000), 'The consequences of new workplaces practices in the United States: the Neo-Stakhanovism', mimeo, Cepremap.

Baker, M. (1998), 'Fund managers' attitudes to risk and time horizons: the effect of performance benchmarking', *European Journal of Finance*, **4**, 257–78.

Banerjee, A. (1992), 'A simple model of herd behaviour', *Quarterly Journal of Economics*, **107** (3), August, 797–818.

Barca, F. and M. Becht (eds) (2002), *The Control of Corporate Europe*, Oxford: Oxford University Press.

Barker, D. and D. Holdsworth (1993), 'The causes of bank failures in the 1980s', *Federal Reserve Bank of New York Research Papers*, 9325, August.

Basel Committee on Banking Supervision (2001), 'The new Basel capital accord', Committee document, January.

Batsch, L. (1999), *Finance et stratégie*, Paris: Economica.

Batsch, L. (2003a), 'Gouvernance: la faillite d'une approche?', Communication presented at the *Neuvièmes journées d'histoire de la comptabilité et du management*, 'Le gouvernement d'entreprise: perspectives historiques', Université Paris IX – Dauphine, 20–21 March.

Batsch, L. (2003b), *Le capitalisme financier*, Paris: La découverte, coll. Repères.

Baudchon, H. and O. Brossard (2001), 'Croissance et technologies de l'information en France et aux Etats-Unis', *Revue de l'OFCE*, **76**, 53–115.

Baudchon, H. and O. Brossard (2003), 'Definitions and measures of ICT impact on growth: what is really at stake', Communication presented at the *Conférence de l'Association de Comptabilité Nationale*, 'La mesure de la Nouvelle Économie', Paris, November 2002.

Baudru, D., S. Lavigne and F. Morin (2001), 'Les investisseurs institutionnels internationaux. Une analyse du comportement des investisseurs américains', *Revue d'Économie Financière*, **1** (61).

Becht, M. and R. Ailsa (1999), 'Blockholding in Europe: an international comparison', *European Economic Review*, **43**, 1049–56.

Becht, M. and C. Mayer (2002), 'Introduction', in F. Barca and M. Becht (eds), *The Control of Corporate Europe*, Oxford: Oxford University Press, pp. 1–45.

Beffa, J.-L., L. Langenlach and J.-P. Touffut (2003), 'How to interpret the takeover bid directive?', *Prisme*, **1**, The Saint-Gobain Centre for Economic Studies, September.

Bellon, B., A. Ben Youssef and R. Rallet (2003), 'Le retour de la Nouvelle Économie', in B. Bellon, A. Ben Youssef and A. Rallet (eds), *La Nouvelle Économie en perspective*, Paris: Economica, pp. 7–16.

Benghozi, P.-J. and P. Cohendet (1999), 'L'organisation de la production et de la décision face aux TIC', in E. Brousseau and A. Rallet (eds), *Technologies de l'information, organisation et performances économiques*, Paris: Commissariat général du Plan, pp. 161–232.

Bensoussan, A., M. Crouhy and D. Galai (1994), 'Stochastic equity volatility related to the leverage effect. I. Equity volatility behaviour', *Applied Mathematical Finance*, **I**, 63–85.

Bentson, G. and A. Hartgraves (2002), 'Enron: what happened and what we can learn from it', *Journal of Accounting and Public Policy*, **21**, 105–27.

Bentson, G. and G. Kaufman (1997), 'FDICIA after five years', *Journal of Economic Perspective*, **11** (3), 139–58.

Berle, A. (1963), *The American Economic Republic*, New York: Harcourt, Brace and World.

Berle, A. and G. Means (1932), *The Modern Corporation and Private Property*, New York: Harcourt, Brace and World.

Bernanke, B.S. (2002), 'Deflation: making sure it doesn't happen here', speech before the National Economists Club, Washington, DC, 21 November.

Bernanke, B.S. *et al.* (1999), *Inflation Targeting: Lessons from the International Experience*, Princeton, NJ: Princeton University Press.

Bernstein, P. (1953), 'Profit theory – where do we go from here?', *Quarterly Journal of Economics*, **67**, 401–22, reprinted in S. Blumner (ed.) (1969), *Readings in Microeconomics*, Scranton: International Textbook Company, pp. 239–52.

Bhide, A. (1993), 'The hidden cost of stock market liquidity', *Journal of Financial Economics*, **34**, 31–51.

Bignon, V., Y. Biondi and X. Ragot (2004), 'An economic analysis of fair value: the evolution of accounting principles in European legislation', *Prisme*, **4**, The Saint-Gobain Centre for Economic Studies, March.

Biondi, Y. (2003), *La nature économique de l'entreprise au croisement des théories économiques et de la comptabilité*, PhD dissertation in Economics, Université Lumière Lyon II.

Black, B. (2001), 'The legal and institutional preconditions for strong securities markets', *UCLA Law Review*, **48**, 881–955.

Black, F. (1995), 'Internet rates as options', *Journal of Finance*, **50**, 1371–6.

Blair, M. (1993), 'Financial restructuring and the debate about corporate governance', in M. Blair (ed.), *The Deal Decade: What Takeovers and Leveraged Buyouts Mean for Corporate Governance*, Washington, DC: Brookings Institution.

Blair, M. (1995), *Ownership and Control: Rethinking Corporate Governance for the Twenty-first Century*, Washington, DC: Brookings Institution.

Blair, M. and L. Stout (1999), 'A team production theory of corporate law', *Virginia Law Review*, **85**, 247–328.

Bois, M. (2001), 'Juste valeur et risque de modèle', in J.-F. Casta and B. Colasse (eds), *Juste valeur: enjeux techniques et politiques*, Paris: Economica, pp. 167–77.

Boltanski, L. and E. Chiapello (1999), *Le nouvel esprit du capitalisme*, Paris: Gallimard.

Boot, A. (2000), 'Relationship banking: what do we know?', *Journal of Financial Intermediation*, **9** (1), 7–25.

Bordo, M. and O. Jeanne (2002), 'Boom – bust in asset prices, economic stability and monetary policy', NBER Working Paper, 8966, May.

Bordo, M., B. Eichengreen, D. Klingebiel and M. Martinez-Peria (2001), 'Financial crises: lessons from the last 120 years', *Economic Policy*, April.

Bordogna, L. and F. Guarriello (eds) (2003), *Aver voce in capitolo. Societa europea e participazione dei lavoro nell'impressa*, Roma: Edizioni Lavoro.

Borio, C., W. English and A. Filardo (2003), 'A tale of two perspectives: old or new challenges for monetary policy?', BIS Working Paper, 217, February.

Borio, C., C. Furfine and P. Lowe (2001), 'Procyclicality of the financial system and financial stability: issues and policy options', in *Marrying the Macro and Micro- Prudential Dimensions of Financial Stability*, BIS Papers, **1**, 1–57.

Bossaert, T. (2003), 'Lessons for and from asymmetric asset allocation', in European Asset Management Association, *Boom and Bust*, October, London: EAMA, pp. 103–9.

Boutillier, M., A. Labye, C. Lagoutte, N. Lévy and V. Oheix (2002), 'Financement et gouvernement des entreprises: exceptions et convergences européennes', *Revue d'économie politique*, **112**, 499–544.

Bouton, D. (2002), *Pour un meilleur gouvernement des entreprises cotées*, Rapport du comité conjoint MEDEF et AFEP/Agref.

Boyer, R. (2004), *The Future of Economic Growth: As New Becomes Old*, Cheltenham, UK and Northampton, MA, USA: Edward Elgar.

Boyer, R. and Y. Saillard (1995), *Théorie de la Régulation: l'état des savoirs*, Paris: La Découverte.

Bratton, W. (2002), 'Enron and the dark side of shareholder value', *Tulane Law Review*, **76**, 1275–362.

Brender, A. and F. Pisani (2001), *Les marchés et la croissance*, Paris: Economica.

Brender, A. and F. Pisani (2003), 'Risque de déflation par la dette en Europe et aux Etats-Unis', *Revue de l'OFCE*, **86**, July, 31–41.

Bresnahan, T., E. Brynjolfsson and L. Hitt (2002), 'Information technology, workplace organization, and the demand for skilled labour: firm-level evidence', *Quarterly Journal of Economics*, **117** (10), 339–76.

Bruck, C. (1988), *The Predators' Ball: The Junk Bond Raiders and the Man Who Staked Them*, New York: Simon and Schuster.

Burkart, O. (1999), 'Comparaisons internationales des structures de financement', *Revue d'Économie Financière*, **54**, 13–38.

Cadbury, A. (1992a), 'The financial aspects of corporate governance', *The Code of Best Practice*, Work Group Report, London: Gee.

Cadbury, A. (1992b), Cadbury Report, *Report of the Committee on the Financial Aspects of Corporate Governance*, London: Gee.

Campbell, J. and R. Shiller (1988), 'Stock prices, earnings and expected dividends', *Journal of Finance*, **43** (3), July, 661–77.

Cartelier, J. (2004) 'Sur les rapports entre comptabilité et pensée économique: quelques observations exploratoires', miméo, presented at the seminar *Économie des Institutions*, 22 February 2004, FORUM, Université Paris X – Nanterre.

Casta, J.-F. and B. Colasse (eds) (2001), *Juste valeur: enjeux techniques et politiques*, Paris: Economica.

Catala, N. (1980), 'L'entreprise', in G. Camerlynck (ed.), *Droit du travail*, vol. 4, Paris: Dalloz.

Chabanas, N. and E. Vergeau (1996), 'Nationalisations et privatisations depuis cinquante ans', *INSEE Première*, **440**, April.

Challe, E. (2002), *Prophéties auto-réalisatrices et volatilité des cours boursiers*, PhD dissertation in Economics, Université Paris X – Nanterre.

Chandler, A. Jr (1962), *Strategy and Structure: Chapters in the History of American Business Enterprises*, Cambridge, MA: MIT Press.

Charreaux, G. (1999), 'La théorie positive de l'agence: lecture et relectures . . .', in G. Koenig (ed.), *De nouvelles théories pour gérer l'entreprise du XXIème siècle*, Paris: Economica, pp. 61–141.

Charreaux, G. (2000), 'Le conseil d'administration dans les théories de la gouvernance', *Revue du Financier*, 4th quarter, 6–17.

Charreaux, G. and P. Desbrières (1998), 'Gouvernance des entreprises: valeur partenariale contre valeur actionnariale', *Finance, contrôle, Stratégie*, **1**, 57–88.

Chatterjee, S. (2003), 'Enron's incremental descent into bankruptcy: a strategic and organisational analysis', *Long Range Planning*, **36**, 133–49.

Cioffi, J. (2005), 'Expensive retrenchment: the regulatory politics of corporate governance reform and the foundation of finance capitalism in the United States and Germany', in J. Levy (ed.), *The State after Statism: New State Activities in the Age of Globalization and Liberalization*, Cambridge, MA, USA: Harvard University Press, forthcoming.

Cioffi, J. and S. Cohen (2000), 'The state, law and corporate governance: the advantage of forwardness', in S. Cohen and B. Gavin (eds),

Corporate Governance and Globalization. Long Range Planning Issues, Cheltenham, UK and Northampton, MA, USA: Edward Elgar, pp. 307–49.

Clark, R. (1985), 'Agency costs *versus* fiduciary duties', in W. Pratt and R. Zeckhauser (eds), *Principals and Agents: the Structure of Business*, Cambridge, MA: Harvard Business School Press, pp. 55–79.

Coase, R. (1960), 'The problem of social cost', *Journal of Law and Economics*, **3**, 1–44.

Coffee, J. (1991), 'Liquidity versus control: the institutional investors as corporate monitors', *Columbia Law Review*, **91** (6), 1277–368.

Coffee, J. (2001), 'The rise of dispersed ownership: the role of the law in the separation of ownership and control', The Center for Law and Economic Studies, Columbia Law School, Working Paper 182.

Coffee, J. (2002), 'Understanding Enron: it's about the gatekeepers, stupid', Columbia Law School Working Paper 207, July.

Cohen, D. and M. Debonneuil (1998), 'L'économie de la nouvelle économie', in D. Cohen and M. Debonneuil (eds), *Nouvelle économie*, Report of the Conseil d'Analyse Economique, Paris: La documentation française, pp. 9–50.

Cohen, E. (2000), 'Analyse financière et comptabilité', in B. Colasse (ed.), *Encyclopédie de comptabilité, contrôle de gestion et audit*, Paris: Economica, pp. 17–28.

Cohen, E. (2003), 'Défaillance de la chaîne informationnelle ou crise des modes de contrôle des entreprises', *Rapport moral sur l'argent dans le monde en 2002*, Paris, pp. 75–82.

Colasse, B. (2000), 'Cadres comptables conceptuels', in B. Colasse (ed.), *Encyclopédie de comptabilité, contrôle de gestion et audit*, Paris: Economica, pp. 93–104.

Colasse, B. (2001), *L'analyse financière de l'entreprise*, Paris: La découverte, coll. Repères.

Colette, C. and J. Richard (2000), *Comptabilité générale. Les systèmes français et anglo-saxons*, Paris: Dunod.

Committee on the Global Financial System (2002), *Credit Risk Transfer*, October, Bâle: BRI.

Committee on the Global Financial System (2003), *Incentive Structures in Institutional Asset Management and their Implications for Financial Markets*, BIS Report 21, March, Bâle: BIS.

Commons, J. (1934), *Institutional Economics. Its Place in Political Economy*, New York: Macmillan Company.

Conyon, M. and K. Murphy (2000), 'The prince and the pauper. CEO pay in the United States and the United Kingdom', *Economic Journal*, **110**, 640–71.

Corbett, J. and T. Jenkinson (1996), 'The financing of industry, 1970–89: an international comparison', *Journal of Japanese and International Economies*, **10**, 71–96.

Cossin, D. (2001), 'Credit risk: the new frontier of risk management', in Z. Mikdashi (ed.), *Financial Intermediation in the 21st Century*, New York: Palgrave, pp. 198–208.

Coutinet, N. and D. Sagot-Duvauroux (2003), *Économie des fusions et acquisitions*, Paris: La découverte, coll. Repères.

Coutrot, T. (1998), *L'entreprise Néo-libérale: Une Nouvelle Utopie Capitaliste?*, Paris: La Découverte.

Cozian, M., A. Viandier and F. Deboissy (1999), *Droit des sociétés*, Paris: Litee.

Crédit Suisse Financial Products (1997), *Credit Risk+: A Credit Risk Management Framework*, London: Crédit Suisse.

Crouhy, M., D. Galai and R. Mark (2000), 'A comparative analysis of current credit risk models', *Journal of Banking & Finance*, **24**, 59–117.

Crouzet, P. and N. Véron (2002), 'La mondialisation en partie double. La bataille des normes comptables', *En temps réel*, Les Cahiers, 3.

Cunningham, L. (2002), 'The Sarbanes-Oxley yawn: heavy rhetoric, light reform (and it might just work)', Research Paper No. 01, Boston College Law School.

Curien, N. and P.A. Muet (2004), *La société de l'information*, Rapport du Conseil d'Analyse Économique, 47.

Danielsson, J. and H.S. Shin (2003), 'Endogenous risk', in *Modern Risk Management: A History*, London: Risk Books.

Danielsson, J., P. Embrecht, C. Goodhart, C. Keathag, P. Muennich, O. Renault and H.S. Shin (2001), 'An academic response to Basel II'. FMG Special Paper, 150, LSE.

Davis, E. and B. Steil (2001), *Institutional Investors*, Cambridge, MA: MIT Press.

Deakin, S. and G. Slinger (1997), 'Hostile takeover, corporate law, and the theory of the firm', *Journal of Law and Society*, **24**, 124–51.

Demsetz, H. (1967), 'Toward a theory of property rights', *American Economic Review*, **57**, 347–59, reprinted in E. Furubotn and S. Pejovic (eds) (1974), *The Economics of Property Rights*, Cambridge: Ballinger Publishing Company, pp. 31–42.

Diamond, D. (1984), 'Financial intermediation and delegated monitoring', *Review of Economic Studies*, **51**.

Diamond, D. (1997), 'Liquidity, banks and markets', *Journal of Political Economy*, **105** (5), 928–56.

Dietsch, M. and D. Garabiol (2003), 'Bâle II et la stabilité fiananciére', *Banque Magazine*, No. 651, October, 56–60.

Donald, D. (2003), 'Some observations on the use of structural and reme- dial measures in American and German law after Sarbanes-Oxley', *German Law Journal*, **4** (2), February.

Durand, P. (1947), *Traité de droit du travail*, Paris: Dalloz.

Easterbrook, F. and D. Fischel (1993), *The Economic Structure of Corporate Law*, Cambridge, MA, USA, and London: Harvard University Press.

Eymard-Duvernay, F. (2001), 'L'Économie des conventions a-t-elle une théorie politique?', in P. Batifoulier (ed.), *Théorie des conventions*, Paris: Economica, coll. forum, pp. 279.

Faccio, M. and L. Lang (2000), 'The separation of ownership from control; an analysis of ultimate ownership in Western European corporations', mimeo, Università Cattolica del Sacro Cuore, Milan.

Fama, E. (1980), 'Agency problems and the theory of the firm', *Journal of Political Economy*, **88**, 288–307.

Fama, E. and M. Jensen (1983), 'Agency problems and residual claims', *Journal of Law and Economics*, **26**, 327–49.

Fanto, J. (1998), 'The role of corporate law in French corporate gover- nance', *Cornell International Law Journal*, **31**, 31–91.

Favereau, O. (1994), 'Règles, organisation et apprentissage collectif: un par- adigme non standard pour trois théories hétérodoxes', in A. Orléan (ed.), *Analyse économique des conventions*, Paris: PUF, pp. 113–37.

Favereau, O. (1997), 'L'incomplétude n'est pas le problème, c'est la solu- tion', in B. Reynaud (ed.), *Les limites de la rationalité. Tome 2: les figures du collectif*, Paris: La Découverte, pp. 219–304.

Fisher, I. (1932), *Booms and Depressions*, New York: Adelphi Company.

Fisher, I. (1933), 'The debt-deflation theory of great depressions', *Econometrica*, October.

Fitoussi, J.P. (2002), *La règle et le choix*, La République des Idées, Paris: Le Seuil, September.

Frison-Roche, M.-A. (2002), 'Le droit français des sociétés entre corporate governance et culture de marché', in D. Plihon and J.-P. Ponssard (eds), *La montée en puissance des fonds d'investissement; quels enjeux pour les entreprises?*, Paris: Les études de la documentation Française, pp. 77–91.

Furubotn, E. and S. Pejovic (1972), 'Property rights and economic theory: a survey of recent literature', *Journal of Economic Literature*, **10**, 1137–62.

Galbraith, J.K. (1967), *The New Industrial State*, Boston: Houghton Mifflin.

Garabiol, D., V. McCarrol and M. Bézard (2002), 'Les biais concurrentiels de la réforme de Bâle', *Banque Magazine*, No. 642, 42–3.

Gaughan, P. (1996), *Mergers, Acquisitions and Corporate Restructurings*, New York: J. Wiley & Sons.

Gehrke, I. (2002), 'Valeur actionnariale: le rattrapage de l'Allemagne', in D. Plihon and J.-P. Ponssard (eds), *La montée en puissance des fonds d'investissement; quels enjeux pour les entreprises?*, Paris: Les études de la documentation Française, pp. 147–62.

Gennotte, G. and H. Leland (1990), 'Market liquidity, hedging and crashes', *American Economic Review*, **80** (5), December, 999–1021.

Gierke, O. (1874), *Die Grundbegriffe des Staatsrechts und die neuesten Staatsrechtstheorien*, 2nd edn, Tübingen: Mohr, 1915.

Gilson, R. and R. Kraakman (1991), *Reinventing the Outside Director: An Agenda for Institutional Investors*, report prepared within the framework of the John M. Olin Program in Law and Economics.

Goetschy, J. (2002), 'EU social policy and developments in worker involvement arrangements: from multi-level governance to company level worker participation', in M. Gold (ed.), *Industrial Democracy in Europe*, Cheltenham, UK and Northampton, MA, USA: Edward Elgar.

Goldstein, A. (1996), 'Privatizations and corporate governance in France', *Quarterly Review of the Banca Nazionale del Lavoro*, **199**, December, 455–88.

Gompers, P.A. and A. Metrick (2001), 'Institutional investors and asset prices', *Quarterly Journal of Economics*, **116** (1), 229–59.

Goodhart, C. (2002), 'Basel and pro-cyclicality', in *Bumps on the Road to Basel*, London: Centre for the Study of Financial Innovation.

Gordon, J. (2002), 'What Enron means for the management and control of the modern business corporation: some initial reflections', *University of Chicago Law Review*, **69**, Summer.

Gordon, R. (2001), 'La technologie et les succès de l'économie américaine', in Centre Saint-Gobain pour la Recherche en Économie, *Institutions et croissance*, Paris: Albin Michel économie.

Gorton, G. and A. Winton (2002), 'Financial intermediation', NBER Working Papers 8928.

Greenan, N. and J. Mairesse (1996), 'Computers and productivity in France: some evidence', NBER Working Papers 5836.

Griliches, Z. (1994), 'Productivity, R&D, and the data constraint', *American Economic Review*, **84**, 1–23.

Grossman, S. and O. Hart (1986), 'The costs and benefits of ownership: a theory of vertical and lateral integration', *Journal of Political Economy*, **94**, 691–719.

Grossman, S. and J. Stiglitz (1980), 'On the impossibility of informationally efficient markets', *American Economic Review*, **70**, 393–417.

Grumbach, T. (1995), 'Citoyenneté, entreprise et contrat social', *Droit ouvrier*, June, 235–57.

Haas, F. (2003), 'Vers un continuum de marchés? Modèles structurels et interactions entre marchés de crédit et d'actions', *Revue de la Stabilité Financière*, Banque de France, June, 80–98.

Hansmann, H. and R. Kraakman (2001), 'The end of history for corporate law', *Georgetown Law Journal*, **89**, 439–68.

Hart, O. (1995), 'Corporate governance: some theory and implications', *The Economic Journal*, **105**, 678–89.

Hauriou, M. (1910), 'La théorie de l'institution et de la fondation', *Cahiers de la nouvelle journée*, **4**.

Hayek, F.A. (1960), *The Constitution of Liberty*, Chicago: University of Chicago Press.

Hempell, T. (2002), 'What's spurious, what's real? Measuring the productivity impacts of ICT at the firm-level', ZEW Discussion Paper 02–42.

Henry, D. and D. Dalton (2003), 'Information technology producing industries – hopeful signs in 2003', *Digital Economy 2003*, Economic and Statistics Administration, 9–48.

Hirschey, M. (2001), 'Cisco and the kids', *Financial Analysts Journal*, July–August, 48–58.

Holmström, B. and S. Kaplan (2001), 'Corporate governance and merger activity in the US: making sense of the 1980s and 1990s', National Bureau of Economic Research, Working Paper 8220.

Honoré, A.M. (1961), 'Ownership', in A.G. Guest (ed.), *Oxford Essays in Jurisprudence*, London: Oxford University Press, pp. 107–47.

IASC (1998), *Normes comptables internationales (IAS)*, Paris: Expert Comptable Media.

Jackson, G. (2001), 'The origins of non-liberal corporate governance in Germany and Japan', in W. Streeck and K. Yamamura (eds), *The Origins of Non-liberal Capitalism: Germany and Japan*, Ithaca, NY: Cornell University Press.

Jeffers, E. and D. Plihon (2002), 'Importance et diversité des investisseurs institutionnels', in D. Plihon and J.-P. Ponssard (eds), *La montée en puissance des fonds d'investissement; quels enjeux pour les entreprises?*, Paris: Les études de la documentation Française, pp. 17–27.

Jensen, M. (1983), 'Organization theory and methodology', *Accounting Review*, **58**, 319–39.

Jensen, M. (1986), 'Agency costs of free cash flow, corporate finance, and takeovers', *American Economic Review*, **76**, 323–29.

Jensen, M. (1989), 'Eclipse of the public corporation', *Harvard Business Review*, **67**, 61–74.

Jobert, A. (2000), *Les espaces de la négociation collective, branches et territoires*, Toulouse: Octares.

Jorgenson, D. and K. Stiroh (2000), 'U.S. economic growth in the new millennium', *Brookings Papers on Economic Activity*, **1**, 125–211.

Journal officiel des communautés européennes (2001), *Directive 2001/86/CE du Conseil*, L 294, 10 October, pp. 22–32.

Jürgens, J. and J. Rupp (2001), *The German System of Corporate Governance: Characteristics and Changes*, Berlin: CGEP, January.

Kaplan, N. (2003), 'Valuation and new economy firms', in W. Hunter, G. Kaufman and M. Pomerleano (eds), *Asset Price Bubbles*, Cambridge, MA: MIT Press, pp. 391–402.

Kay, J. and A. Silberston (1995), 'Corporate governance', *National Institute Economic Review*, **3** (95), 84–97.

Khallouf, J. (2003), 'Stabilité financière: l'impact contrastée de Bâle II et des normes IAS', *Banque magazine*, **649**, July–August, 34–40.

Kindleberger C.P. (1996), *Manias, Panics and Crashes, a History of Financial Crises*, 3rd edn, New York: Macmillan.

Klee, L. (2000), 'Normes comptables internationales', in B. Colasse (ed.), *Encyclopédie de comptabilité, contrôle de gestion et audit*, Paris: Economica, pp. 919–30.

Koo, R. (2003), *Balance Sheet Recession: Japan's Struggle with Uncharted Economics and Its Global Implications*, Indianapolis, IN: J. Wiley & Sons.

Krugman, P. (2002), 'For richer', *New York Times*, 20 October.

La Porta, R., F. Lopez-de-Silanes and A. Shleifer (1999), 'Corporate ownership around the world', *The Journal of Finance*, **54**, 471–517.

La Porta, R., F. Lopez-de-Silanes, A. Shleifer and R. Vishny (1998), 'Law and finance', *Journal of Political Economy*, **106**, 1113–55.

Lazonick, W. and M. O'Sullivan (1997), 'The finance of industrial development: the United States and the United Kingdom', *Financial History Review*, **1** (4).

Lazonick, W. and M. O'Sullivan (1999), 'In search of "shareholder value": the historical transformation of corporate control and strategy in the United States', Communication at the *Conference on the Political Economy of Shareholder Value*, Royal Holloway Management School, University of London, 16–17 April.

Lazonick, W. and M. O'Sullivan (2000a), 'Maximising shareholder value: a new ideology of corporate governance', *Economy and Society*, **29** (1), 13–35.

Lazonick, W. and M. O'Sullivan (2000b), 'Perspectives on corporate governance, innovation and economic performance', *Economy and Society*, **1** (29).

Le Crom, J.-P. (2003), *L'introuvable démocratie salariale*, Paris: Éditions Syllepse.

Leland, D. (1994), 'Corporate debt value, bond covenants and optimal capital structure', *Journal of Finance*, **XLIX** (4), September, 1213–52.

Levine, R. (2000), 'Bank-based or market-based financial systems: which is better?', mimeo.

Liebowitz, S. (2002), *Rethinking the Network Economy*, New York: AMACOM.

Lintner, J. (1965), 'The valuation of risk assets and the selection of risky investments in stock portfolios and capital budgets', *Review of Economics and Statistics*, **47**, 13–37.

Lordon, F. (2000), 'La création de valeur comme rhétorique et comme pratique. Généalogie et sociologie de la valeur actionnariale', in *L'Année de la régulation*, vol. 4, Paris: La Découverte, pp. 117–67.

Lordon, F. (2002), *La politique du capital*, Paris: Odile Jacob.

Loughran, T. and J. Ritter (2002), 'Why don't issuers get upset about leaving money on the table in IPOs?', *Review of Financial Studies*, **15** (2), 413–43.

Lubochinsky, C. (2002), 'Quel crédit accorder aux spreads de crédit?', *Revue de la Stabilité Financière*, Banque de France, November, 85–102.

Lyon-Caen, G. (1955), *Manuel de droit du travail et de la sécurité sociale*, Paris: Dalloz.

Magnier, V. (2002), 'L'évolution du gouvernement d'entreprise en France', in D. Plihon and J.-P. Ponssard (eds), *La montée en puissance des fonds d'investissement; quels enjeux pour les entreprises?*, Paris: Les études de la documentation Française, pp. 67–75.

Manne, H. (1965), 'Mergers and the market for corporate control', *Journal of Political Economy*, **73**, 110–20.

Marris, R. (1964), *The Economic Theory of Managerial Capitalism*, Glencoe, UK: Free Press.

Mathérat, S. (2003), 'Normalisation comptable internationale et stabilisation financière', *Revue de la Stabilité Financière*, Banque de France, **2**, June, 139–61.

Mayer, C. (1988), 'New issues in corporate finance', *European Economic Review*, **32**, 1167–88.

Mayer, C. (1996), 'Corporate governance, competition, and performance', OECD Economics Department WP 164.

Mayer, C. (2001), 'Structure de financement et organisation des entreprises, in J.-P. Touffut, *Institutions et croissance*, Saint-Gobain Centre for Economic Studies, Paris: Albin Michel, pp. 143–74.

Merton, R. (1974), 'On the pricing of corporate debt: the risk structure of interest rates, *Journal of Finance*, **28**, 449–70.

Minsky, H. (1982), 'The financial instability hypothesis: capitalist processes and the behaviour of the economy', in C.P. Kindleberger and

J.P. Laffargue (eds), *Financial Crises*, Cambridge, MA: Cambridge University Press, pp. 13–47.

Mishkin, F. (2000), 'What should central banks do?', *FRB St. Louis Review*, **82** (6), November/December.

Mistral, J. (2003), 'Rendre compte fidèlement de la réalité de l'entreprise. Remarques sur la réforme comptable et la qualité de l'information financière', in *Les normes comptables et le monde post-Enron*, Report for the Conseil d'Analyse Économique, Paris: La documentation française, pp. 7–55.

Montagne, S. (2003), *Les métamorphose du trust: les fonds de pension américains entre protection et spéculation*, PhD dissertation in Economics, Université Paris X – Nanterre.

Moreau, M. (2001), 'L'implication des travailleurs dans la société européenne', *Droit social*, November, 967–76.

Morgan, J.P. & Co. (1997), *An introduction to Creditmetrics*, www.fin.bwl. uni-mainz.de/creditmetrics. html, April.

Morin, F. (1998), 'Le modèle français de détention et de gestion du capital. Analyse, prospective et comparaisons internationales', *Rapport pour le Conseil d'Analyse Économique*, Paris: Les Éditions de Bercy, coll. Études.

Morin, F. (2000), 'The transformation of the French model of Shareholding and Management, *Economy and Society*, February.

Morris, S. and H.S. Shin (1998), 'Unique equilibrium in a model of self-fulfilling currency attacks', *American Economic Review*, **88** (3), 587–97.

Morris, S. and H.S. Shin (1999), 'Risk management with interdependent choice', *Financial Stability Review*, Bank of England, November, 140–5.

Morris, S. and H.S. Shin (2000), 'Global games: theory and applications' Cowles Foundation Discussion Papers 1275, Cowles Foundation, Yale University.

Müller-Jentsch, W. (1995), 'Germany: from collective voice to co-management', in J. Rogers and W. Streeck (eds), *Works Councils: Consultation, Representation, and Cooperation in Industrial Relations*, Chicago: The University of Chicago Press, pp. 53–78.

Mullineux, A. (1996), 'The fundings of non-financial corporations in the EU (1971–1993): Evidence of Convergence?', mimeo.

Myners, P. (2001), *Institutional Investment in the United Kingdom*, March, London: HM Treasury.

OECD (1998), *Tendances des marchés de capitaux*, **69**, February, Paris: OECD.

OECD (1999), *Principles of Corporate Governance*, Paris: OECD.

OECD (2001), *Institutional Investors, Financial Market Trends*, vol. 80, Paris: OECD, pp. 43–130.

OECD (2004), *Principles of Corporate Governance*, Paris: OECD.

Oliner, S. and D. Sichel (2000), 'The resurgence of growth in the late 1990s: is information technology the story', *Journal of Economic Perspectives*, **14**, 3–22.

Olivier, B. and R. Sainsaulieu (2001), *L'entreprise en débat*, Paris: Presses de Sciences Po.

Orléan, A. (1989), 'Comportements mimétiques et diversités des opinions sur les marchés financiers', in P. Artus and H. Bourguinat (eds), *Théorie économique et crises des marchés financiers*, Paris: Economica, pp. 45–65.

Orléan, A. (1999), *Le pouvoir de la finance*, Paris: O. Jacob.

O'Sullivan, M. (2000), *Contests for Corporate Control; Corporate Governance and Economic Performance in the United States and Germany*, Oxford: Oxford University Press.

O'Sullivan, M. (2001), *A Revolution in European Corporate Governance? The Implications of Recent Developments in the Role of the Stock Market in Five European Economies*, Summary Report of the research project *Corporate Governance, Innovation, and Economic Performance in the European Union*, INSEAD, August.

Paillusseau, J. (1984), 'Les fondements du droit moderne des sociétés', JCPE.

Paillusseau, J. (1999), 'Entreprise, société, actionnaires, salariés, quels rapports?', in *Chronique*, Paris: Recueil Dalloz, pp. 157–66.

Permanent Subcommittee on Investigations of the Committee of the Governmental Affairs United States Senate (2002), *The Role of the Board of Directors in Enron's Collapse*, Report 107–70, July, Washington, DC.

Petit, H. (2003), 'Les déterminants de la mise en œuvre d'un mode de gestion de l'emploi', *Économie et statistique*, **361**, 53–70.

Petit, P. (1998), 'Formes structurelles et régimes de croissance de l'après-fordisme', in *L'Année de la Régulation*, vol. 2, Paris: La Découverte, pp. 169–96.

Petit, P. (2003a), 'Les temps de la Nouvelle Économie', in B. Bellon, A. Ben Youssef and A. Rallet (eds), *La Nouvelle Économie en perspective*, Paris: Economica, pp. 25–40.

Petit, P. (2003b), 'Large network services and the organisation of contemporary capitalism', Communication presented at the workshop *Globalization and Diversity of Capitalism / New Concepts for a Post-NeoLiberal Era*, London School of Economics, 23–24 June.

Piluso, N. (2003), 'Taux de salaire et chômage d'équilibre: influence de la création de valeur actionnariale', Presented at the seminar MINI-FORUM, Université Paris X – Nanterre.

Plihon, D. (ed.) (2002), *Rentabilité et risque dans le nouveau régime de croissance*, Report for the Commissariat général du Plan, Paris: La documentation française.

Plihon, D. (2003), *Le nouveau capitalisme*, Paris: La découverte, coll. Repères.

Powers, W. (ed.) (2002), *Report of Investigation by the Special Investigate Committee of the Board of Directors of Enron Corp*, February.

Prowse, S. (1994), *Corporate Governance in an Institutional Perspective: A Survey of Control Mechanisms among Large Firms*, Bâle: BIS.

Rajan, R. and L. Zingales (1998), 'Financial dependence and growth', *American Economic Review*, **88**, 559–86.

Rajan, R. and L. Zingales (2003), *Saving Capitalism from the Capitalists*, New York: Random House.

Rebérioux, A. (2002), 'European style of corporate governance at the crossroads: the role of worker involvement', *Journal of Common Market Studies*, **40**, 111–34.

Rebérioux, A. (2003a), 'Les marchés financiers et la participation des salariés aux décisions', *Travail et emploi*, **93**, January, 23–41.

Rebérioux, A. (2003b), 'Gouvernance d'entreprise et théorie de la firme: quelle(s) alternative(s) à la valeur actionnariale?', *Revue d'économie industrielle*, **103**, 4th quarter, 85–110.

Reifschneider, D. and J.C. Williams (2000), 'Three lessons for monetary policy in a low-inflation era', *Journal of Money, Credit, and Banking*, **32** (4), November, 936–66.

Reuschlein, H. and W. Gregory (1979), *Agency and Partnership*, Saint Paul: West Publishing.

Revue d'économie financière (2003), 'Juste valeur et évaluation des actifs', **71**.

Richard, J. (1996), *Comptabilité et pratiques comptables*, Paris: Dalloz, coll. Connaissance du droit.

Richard, J. (2002), 'Comment la comptabilité traditionnelle allemande protège les créanciers et les managers: une étude historique et sociologique', *Document de travail du CEREG*, 2002/01, Université de Paris Dauphine.

Riley, B. (2003), 'Tracking errors', in European Asset Management Association, *Boom and Bust*, October, London: EAMA, p. 103.

Ripert, G. (1951), *Aspect juridique du capitalisme moderne*, Paris: LGDJ.

Robé, J.-P. (1999), *L'entreprise et le droit*, Paris: PUF.

Roe, M. (1994), *Strong Managers, Weak Owners: The Political Roots of American Corporate Finance*, Princeton, NJ: Princeton University Press.

Romano, R. (1996), 'Corporate law and corporate governance', *Industrial and Corporate Change*, **5**, 277–339.

Rule, D. (2001a), 'Risk transfer between banks, insurance companies and capital markets', *Financial Stability Review*, Bank of England, December, 137–59.

Rule, D. (2001b), 'The credit derivatives market: its development and possible implications for financial stability', *Financial Stability Review*, Bank of England, June, 117–40.

Sapir, J. (2000), 'Les débats refoulés des années trente', in *Les trous noirs de la science économique: Essai sur l'impossibilité de penser le temps et l'argent*, Paris: Albin Michel, pp. 99–136.

Sapir, J. (2002), 'Démocratie et économie', in *Les économistes contre la démocratie: Pouvoir, mondialisation et démocratie*, Paris: Albin Michel, pp. 185–211.

Saunders, A. (2000), 'Low inflation: the behaviour of financial markets and inflation', *Journal of Money, Credit and Banking*, **32** (4), part 2, 1058–87.

Schmalenbach, E. (1961), *Le bilan dynamique*, Paris: Dunod; 1st edition 1926.

Segrestin, D. (1992), *Sociologie de l'entreprise*, Paris: Armand Colin.

Shapiro, C. and H. Varian (1999), *Information Rules: A Strategic Guide to the Network Economy*, Cambridge, MA: Harvard Business School Press.

Sharpe, W. (1964), 'Capital asset prices: a theory of market equilibrium under conditions of risk', *Journal of Finance*, **19**, 425–42.

Shiller, R. (1981), 'Do stock prices move too much to be justified by subsequent changes in dividends?', *American Economic Review*, **71**, June, 421–36.

Shiller, R. (1991), *Market Volatility*, Cambridge, MA: MIT Press.

Shiller, R. (2000), *Irrational Exuberance*, Princeton, NJ: Princeton University Press.

Shleifer, A. and R. Vishny (1997a), 'A survey of corporate governance', *Journal of Finance*, **52**, 737–83.

Shleifer, A. and R. Vishny (1997b), 'The limits of arbitrage', *Journal of Finance*, **52** (1), 35–55.

Shukla, E. and C. Trzcinka (1992), 'Performance measurement of managed portfolios', *Financial Markets, Institutions and Investments*, **1** (4), 1–58.

Söderström, H.T. (ed.) (2003), *Corporate Governance and Structural Change: European Challenges*, SNS Economic Policy Group Report.

Solow, R. (1957), 'Technological change and the aggregate production function', *Review of Economics and Statistics*, **39**, 65–94.

Solow, R. (1987), 'We'd better watch out', *New York Review of Books*, 12 July, p. 36.

Stiglitz, J. and A. Weiss (1981), 'Credit rationing in markets with imperfect information', *American Economic Review*, June.

Stiroh, K. (2002), 'Reassessing the impact of IT in the production function: a meta-analysis', mimeo.

Streeck, W. (2001), 'The transformation of corporate organization in Europe: an overview', in J.-P. Touffut (ed.), *Institutions, Innovation and Growth:*

Selected Economic Papers, The Saint-Gobain Centre for Economic Studies, Cheltenham, UK and Northampton, MA, USA: Edward Elgar, pp. 4–44.

Svensson, L. (1999), 'Monetary policy issues for the eurosystem', Seminar Papers 667, Stockholm University, Institute for International Economic Studies.

Thoraval, P.-Y. and A. Duchateau (2003), 'Stabilité financière et nouvel accord de Bâle', *Revue de la Stabilité Financière*, **3**, 53–67.

Turner, L. (1993), 'Prospects for worker participation in management in the single market', in L. Ulman, B. Eichengreen and W. Dickens (eds), *Labor in an Integrated Europe*, Washington, DC: The Brookings Institution.

Van der Elst, C. (2000), 'The equity markets, ownership structures and control: towards an international harmonization?', Ghent University, Financial Law Institute, Working Paper.

Van Osnabrugge, M. and R. Robinson (2000), *Angel Investing*, San Francisco: Jossey-Bass.

Véron, N. (2002), 'Après Enron et WorldCom: information financière et capitalisme', *Commentaire*, **99**, 600–18.

Viénot, M. (1995), *Le conseil d'administration des sociétés cotées*, Rapport du comité conjoint, Paris: CNPF-AFEP.

Viénot, M. (1999), *Rapport du comité sur le gouvernement d'entreprise*, Comité conjoint, Paris: CNPF-AFEP.

Walter, C. (2003), 'Excessive volatility or uncertain real economy? The impact of probabilist theories on the assessment of market volatility', in European Asset Management Association, *Boom and Bust*, October, London: EAMA, pp. 15–29.

Walton, P. (2001), *La comptabilité anglo-saxonne*, Paris: La Découverte, coll. Repères.

Wermers, R. (1999), 'Mutual fund herding and the impact on stock prices, *Journal of Finance*, **54** (2), 581–622.

Wheeler, S. (1997), 'Works councils: towards stakeholding?', *Journal of Law and Society*, **24**, 44–64.

Williamson, O. (1964), *The Economics of Discretionary Behavior: Managerial Objectives in a Theory of the Firm*, New Jersey: Prentice Hall.

Williamson, O. (1975), *Markets and Hierarchies: Analysis and Antitrust Implications*, New York: Free Press.

Williamson, O. (1985), *The Economic Institutions of Capitalism*, New York: Free Press.

Williamson, O. and J. Bercovitz (1996), 'The modern corporation as an efficiency instrument: the comparative contracting perspective', in C. Kaysen (ed.), *The American Corporation Today*, New York and Oxford: Oxford University Press, pp. 327–55.

Winter, J. (ed.) (2002a), *Report of the High Level Group of Company Law Experts on Issues Related to Takeover Bids in the European Union*, Brussels, January.

Winter, J. (ed.) (2002b), *A Modern Regulatory Framework for Company Law in Europe: A Consultative Document of the High Level Group of Company Law Experts*, Brussels, November.

Zajdenweber, D. (2003), 'Is price volatility irrational?', in European Asset Management Association, *Boom and Bust*, October, London: EAMA, pp. 30–9.

Zingales, L. (1998), 'Corporate governance', in P. Newman (ed.), *The New Palgrave Dictionary of Economics and the Law*, London: Stockton Press, pp. 497–502.

Zingales, L. (2000), 'In search of new foundations', *Journal of Finance*, **55**, 1623–53.

Index